The Economics of
Energy Policy

The Economics of Energy Policy

THOMAS G. WEYMAN-JONES

Loughborough University of Technology

Gower

© Thomas G. Weyman-Jones, 1986

333.79
W54e

Published by
Gower Publishing Company Limited,
Gower House,
Croft Road,
Aldershot,
Hants GU11 3HR
England

Gower Publishing Company,
Old Post Road
Brookfield
Vermont 05036
U.S.A.

British Library Cataloguing in Publication Data

Weyman-Jones, Thomas G.
    The economics of energy policy.
    1. Power resources—Great Britain
    I. Title
    333.79'0941   HD9502.G72

ISBN: 0 566 00919 6
        0 566 05084 6 (pbk)

5/

Typeset by Guildford Graphics Limited, Petworth, West Sussex
Printed by Blackmore Press, Shaftesbury, Dorset.

Contents

Preface

There has been an explosion of interest in energy economics in recent years, and this book draws together much of this work on pricing policy, investment policy and demand studies, particularly in the context of UK energy supplies. It is written for students specialising in energy economics or public sector economics, and for professional economists in the energy sector. The first half of the book concentrates on the demand studies and the applied welfare economics of pricing and investment policy, while the second half consists of a series of case studies on different areas of importance in the energy field. Among the issues examined are oil, nuclear power, coal supply, conservation, privatisation, security of supply and fuel prices.

The UK is fortunate in having a long and celebrated history of contributors to energy and public sector economics, and the impact of the writings of such economists as Michael Crew, Robert Millward, David Pearce, Ray Rees, Ralph Turvey and Michael Webb has been both enormous and much admired. This book tries to follow in this demanding tradition.

More immediately my academic interest in this area was stimulated by Professor Roy Webb but, in addition, I had the great benefit of working as an economist in the UK Gas Council and the State Treasury of Victoria (Australia). Consequently, I am particularly grateful to Geoff Moore and Peter Wade for what I have learned about energy economics and economic policy 'at the coal face'. None of these individuals or organisations is, of course, in any way responsible for any errors of omission or commission contained in what follows.

Peter Maunder and Dennis Swann originally encouraged me to write this book, and Su Spencer has been a model of efficiency and patience in turning a scrappy manuscript into the finished article. In addition, several generations of students at Lough-borough have sharpened my understanding of the issues discussed in the book. To all, I am extremely grateful.

Finally, I must express thanks to my wife, Carol, and the boys for patiently tolerating the intrusion of this book into family life.

Thomas Weyman-Jones

1

The energy balance

Introduction

This book is about the problem of allocating resources efficiently in the supply of fuels to firms and households in the UK. It therefore takes the form of applied welfare economics, as well as considering the empirical evidence on market behaviour in fuel demand and supply.

Of the four chief fuels in use—coal, oil, gas and electricity—three are produced in the public sector by nationalised industries, while privately-produced oil is central to energy policy in particular and macroeconomic policy in general, both because its world-determined price is often taken as the marginal cost of energy, and because the advent of indigenous oil production has significantly altered the nature of the UK's production structure.

The precise topics to be considered are explained in more detail later in this introductory chapter, but can briefly be mentioned here. Of fundamental importance is the demand for energy, or rather the demands for individual fuels, and Chapter 2 will provide a survey of the wide body of research work done on this topic in recent years. The overwhelming evidence of a statistically significant price elasticity of energy demand means that pricing policy is of critical importance. Chapters 3 and 4, therefore, together tackle the theory and practice of marginal cost pricing for efficient resource allocation. From that point onwards the discussion focuses on important policy case studies. Although these have all proved to be topical in recent years, they are chosen because they illustrate important economic questions and principles. In turn, the topics examined are nuclear power investment (Chapter 5), gas and electricity prices (Chapter 6), North Sea oil (Chapter 7), and, finally, a collection of policy issues: energy conservation, privatisation of the nationalised energy industries, security of supply, and the role of coal in UK energy policy decisions (Chapter 8).

Specific problems of theory—second-best constraints, uncertainty, discounting for time, and so on—are incorporated into the case studies where their importance is particularly relevant.

To begin with, however, it is essential to have an overview of the economist's approach to energy policy problems, and this is best described by looking at an energy balance table.

The UK energy balance

Table 1:1 sets out the energy flows in the UK economy from initial inputs to final consumption for the year 1983. The unit of measurement is heat supplied in billions (i.e. 10^9) therms. Initial inputs of energy to the economy are the primary fuels: coal, natural gas, crude oil and primary electricity. (The last comprises nuclear-generated electricity and hydroelectricity.)

The North Sea dominates the production of primary fuels for the UK, (Table 1.1, row 1) with the supply of crude oil and natural gas having replaced coal as the chief indigenously-produced primary fuel. The amount of primary fuel input available to be converted is determined by the sum of home production and trade in primary fuels.

Row 2 shows imported inputs added to indigenous production. Of these, there is a negligible level of coal imports which are subject to informal quotas in the UK, and a large amount of crude oil imports (17.3 billion therms) in the form of heavier crudes to combine for refinery purposes with the light crude found in the North Sea. In addition there are natural gas imports from the Norwegian sector of the North Sea.

Row 3 shows exports of primary fuels, chiefly in the form of light crude oil, much of which has gone into the European Community, along with some coal for continental power stations. Row 4 contains some statistical tidying-up of the large totals involved in rows 1–3, along with bunkers (i.e. tanker shipping, and so on) and stocks.

4

Table 1.1: Summary UK energy balance, 1983

Source	Heat supplied: units: billion (10^9) therms Primary fuel availability				
	coal	oil	natural gas	primary electricity	Total
1. Production	28.9	49.8[a]	14.4[a]	4.7[b]	97.8
2. Arrivals	1.5	17.3	4.3	—	23.0
3. Shipments	− 1.9	− 36.0	—	—	− 37.9
4. Bunkers, stock changes, and statistical difference	− 1.3	− 0.6	—	—	− 1.8
5. Available supply of primary fuels before conversion	27.3	30.5	18.7	4.7	81.1
6. Fuel use and losses in conversion					26.9

	Energy consumption by final user				
	coal products	petroleum products	gas	all electricity	Total
7. Iron & steel	1.8	0.4	0.4	0.3	2.9
8. Other industry	2.1	4.3	5.4	2.2	14.0
9. Transport	—	14.2	—	0.1	14.3
10. Domestic	2.9	0.9	8.9	2.8	15.5
11. Other consumers[c]	0.6	2.5	2.3	2.0	7.4
12. Final energy consumption	7.4	22.4	16.9	7.5	54.2

Notes:
a. From British sector of the North Sea.
b. Nuclear: 4.2; hydro: 0.5.
c. Public administration (schools, hospitals, etc.), commerce and agriculture.
Source: Department of Energy, *Digest of United Kingdom Energy Statistics,* (London, HMSO), 1984.

Row 5 contains the primary fuel input to the UK economy, i.e. the available supply for direct consumption, or more usually for transformation in petroleum refineries and electricity power stations into the secondary fuels which can be used by the fuel equipment and appliances of industrial and domestic consumers. The refineries and power stations themselves consume fuel and, at the same time, give rise to losses in conversion, (e.g. the waste heat discharged through power station chimneys and cooling towers), as shown in row 6.

The essential balance in the table is: row 12 = row 5 − row 6, and in turn: row 5 is the sum of rows 1–4, while row 12 is the sum of rows 7–11. In this way, row 12 shows the consumption of energy by final users after the conversion processes, and this is disaggregated over rows 7–11 into different market sectors. Note that the fuels in this second half of the table are in the secondary form of petroleum products, coal products and total electricity supplied.

Conventionally, five final markets are distinguished in the UK energy statistics, though the dominant sectors are industry, domestic and transport. Industry is usually subdivided into iron and steel which has a concentration of coal products in its consumption, and other industry, where all four fuels are of importance. The transport sector is clearly dominated by the demand for motor spirit and aviation gasoline. The domestic sector contains the household demand for central heating (dominated in 1983 by gas), appliance use and low-temperature water heating. Over the early 1980s, the domestic sector gradually overtook other industry as the largest fuel market in terms of total consumption.

Finally, the commercial office, public buildings and agricultural consumption is aggregated as other consumers, where, although the heat requirements may be smaller than for the contracting other industry sector, the numbers of consumers are likely to grow if the structure of the economy shifts from industry to services.

Economists conventionally model behaviour patterns in terms of markets, and the energy balance table, as shown in Table 1.1, is a useful starting point for economic analysis. In the primary fuel half of the table, three of the columns are solely the province of nationalised industries, and hence government policy towards those industries is critical both in microeconomic and macroeconomic terms for the evolution of primary fuel supplies. Similarly, only the transport sector is able to avoid the direct impact of public sector pricing policy in its final fuel consumption. It is no surprise, therefore, that pricing for efficient resource allocation is the fundamental consideration of energy policy-making.

It must be noted, however, that not all commentators on energy policy start from an energy balance table like this one. An alternative decomposition of energy consumption is to examine the end-use

6

of energy purchases. For example, this approach will distinguish between fuel use for low-temperature process heating, high-temperature furnaces, space heating, water heating, feedstocks and lubrication. These end-use categories embrace different markets simultaneously, and require a completely different, though not necessarily incompatible, modelling approach from that of the economist. Among the best examples of the end-use approach is the study by Leach (1977), and this ought to complement any concentration on the economist's views of energy economics analysis. Nevertheless, this book concentrates exclusively on the economic approach of modelling the behaviour of consumers and private and public sector firms operating in separate fuel markets.

The use of the word 'fuels' needs emphasis, since the economist takes for granted the physical laws relating to the idea of energy; the energy economist is solely concerned with fuels as commodities which are conceptually no different from guns and butter, or water and diamonds. Talk of an 'energy crisis', or whatever, only makes sense to the economist as an imbalance between the supply and demand of some particular fuels, a situation which will result in some form of rationing or allocation, most usually by price changes.

Plan of the book

The demand for energy is critical, and Chapter 2 presents an introduction to and review of some of the chief studies of aggregate energy demand and individual fuel consumption done in recent years. The period before 1973–74 was characterised by very little variability in real energy prices, and although economists felt that pricing policy was important, it was difficult to measure elasticities of demand with any degree of accuracy. The post-1973 fuel price rises changed all this, and the importance of allowing for price responses in energy demand became very clear.

Pricing policy is therefore of central importance to energy policy, and since substantially more than half of both primary fuel input and final energy consumption is supplied through the nationalised industries in the public sector, the focus of attention must be concentrated on these industries. Chapter 3 therefore sets out the conflicting arguments on the appropriate policies for efficient resource allocation in these parts of the economy with a large public sector representation, in particular the domestic fuel market. Marginal cost pricing has received most emphasis, but the qualifications which must be applied to take account of financial constraints in the public sector and of the redistributive implications of marginal cost pricing have greatly complicated the analytical results of economists working in this area.

Whether or not the principle of marginal cost pricing is adopted, the practical calculation of marginal cost and its relation to investment and scrapping policy requires detailed treatment in Chapter 4. The House of Commons select committee on energy (SCE 1984) is only the most recent in a long line of such official bodies to become embroiled in the use of long-run marginal cost (LRMC) in setting energy prices, and SCE (1984) indicates that the committee, if anything, retired defeated by the UK Treasury's view of the subject. Chapter 4 indicates, via the economist's concentration on short-run marginal cost pricing and appropriate cost-benefit analysis, the most useful approach to LRMC calculation in fuel supply.

Chapter 5 takes up the first of the detailed case studies in the book. It considers the case put forward in 1979–80 by the Central Electricity Generating Board (CEGB) for embarking on a new nuclear power programme in preference to the use of coal-fired generators. Following trenchant criticism by the Monopolies and Mergers Commission, the Board subsequently reviewed the presentation of its case for the Sizewell 'B' Public Inquiry. The 1979–80 debate, however, makes a useful case study for opening up the economic issues involved. Among those considered in Chapter 5 are questions of supply reliability and uncertainty, along with the basic economics of electricity load scheduling.

The case study in Chapter 6 examines the practical design of tariffs for gas and electricity consumers in all markets. The theoretical principles of Chapter 4 undergo substantial transformation when the CEGB, area electricity boards, and the British Gas Corporation have to decide on real tariff structures. In this context, the empirical evidence on consumer responses to 'time of use' (tou) prices is also examined.

Chapter 7 turns to a different theme: the macroeconomic impact of North Sea oil on the UK's economic structure. This is preceded by an analysis of whether the market-determined depletion rates of private sector oil companies can in any sense be regarded as providing the socially desired outcome. The chief problem of North

Sea oil has been its so-called deindustrialisation effect, and this is analysed in conjunction with the issue of how best to use the gift of additional real GNP that North Sea oil represents.

In Chapter 8, four case studies of other important issues are examined. The first is the role of energy conservation and in what sense, if any, this can be regarded as equivalent to another source of fuel supply. The second issue is that of the privatisation of parts of the nationalised fuel industries. The debate on this has been stimulated both by government policy over the 1979–84 period, and by the movement towards deregulation in the United States. The particular problems of deregulating the fuel industries are explored here.

A third issue examined in the final chapter is that of security of supply as an energy policy objective. It might be expected that market forces can accommodate some of the risks involved in dependence on a variable source of supply, but economic policy may be needed if there are external effects which market behaviour cannot handle.

Finally, consideration is given to development of government statements on the topic of energy policy itself. In practice, such official policy documents as the 1978 Green Paper (Cmnd. 7101) have paid particular attention to the role of the National Coal Board. This final section therefore considers the economics of pit closures when coal imports can undercut indigenous production, and the appropriate policies to take account of the social costs involved.

Economic science and political economy

The limits on the attention that should be paid to economics are debateable, and it is essential that the economist's discussion of policy matters makes his or her value judgements as explicit as possible. In similar vein to the vast majority of studies in applied welfare economics, the discussions in this book do not stop at the consideration of a Pareto-optimal outcome alone. This, according to Robbins (1935, 1980), however, is the limit on economics as a science. Since many policies are analysed that involve reallocating resources from a non-optimal position to an efficient outcome irrespective of whether there are some losers in the process, it is clear that the work lies more properly in the realm of political economy. In this, it is in the company of virtually every discussion of applied economic policy in the energy economics field, and of almost all cost-benefit analysis.

2

The demand for energy

Introduction

The introductory chapter on the framework of energy statistics has considered the overall relationship between primary energy consumption and national income, with the conclusion that attention had to be directed to disaggregated studies including the effect of energy prices.

In this chapter, the wealth of case studies on energy demand carried out over recent years is examined for the underlying themes of price and income response and the importance of lags in their effects. As always the centre of the economic approach is the concept of a market, as distinguished from the end-use approach to describing energy demand that concentrates on the need for such items as low-temperature space heating. This is because economic theory is formulated in terms of an individual's behavioural response to market signals in the form of prices. His or her responses are constrained by the income and wealth that he or she disposes of, and these may also be the result of market forces. A market, then, consists of the aggregate of individual purchasing power for a particular commodity matched against the aggregate of the supply behaviour of the individual firms producing the commodity.

The next section describes a method classifying such market commodities in the field of energy, and sets out the problems that energy demand studies have tried to resolve. Following this, several case studies are examined, and finally, an attempt is made to draw together the principal results on elasticities of demand and the length of lags in economic behaviour.

11

Energy in particular markets

The energy balance table provided a two-way classification of final energy consumption:

1. consumption of energy (i.e. all fuel types) in three sectors of the economy: residential, industrial and transport; and
2. consumption of individual fuels (electricity, gas, coal and oil), which again could be examined in residential, industrial and transport sectors.

Consider first the distinction between energy and particular fuels. The two ideas can be separated by the assumption of two-stage budgeting, illustrated in Figure 2.1. This figure describes two-stage budgeting for a single consumer, but it could easily be adapted to the case of a firm purchasing inputs like capital, labour and raw materials as well as energy.

Starting from the left-hand side of the figure, the consumer must decide how to allocate his total consumption expenditure, y, between certain broad groups of commodities such as energy and food. He therefore first decides on an energy budget, y_e, as a proportion of his total expenditure y. At stage 2, further right in the figure, he must decide how to allocate y_e between the different fuels (e.g. electricity and gas) which make up the basic commodities he purchases.

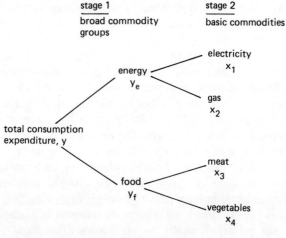

Figure 2.1

The advantage of thinking about purchases in this way is that it may greatly reduce the number of factors that have to be considered when explaining the demand for energy and fuels. In Figure 2.2, the consumer's stage 2 decisions on purchases of the two commodities, gas and electricity, are made by his reaching the highest indifference curve tangent to the budget restraint, which is fixed in position by $\frac{y_e}{p_1}$ and $\frac{y_e}{p_2}$. The amounts he consumes are x_1^* and x_2^* of gas and electricity. From Figure 2.2 they depend only on three factors:

    (i)   the price of gas, p_1,

    (ii) the price of electricity, p_2, and

    (iii) the energy budget, y_e,

so that the gas demand function would be written as:

$$x_1^* = f^1(p_1, p_2, y_e) \tag{2.1}$$

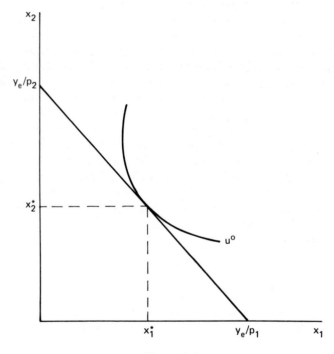

Figure 2.2

and the electricity demand function as:

$$x_2^* = f^2(p_1, p_2, y_e) \tag{2.2}$$

which means many other apparently necessary variables affecting consumption of food and so on can effectively be ignored.

However, the cost of being able to think only in terms of a small number of variables at stage 2 is that very narrow assumptions must be made about the nature of consumer tastes. For example, one set of conditions that permits the economist to think of gas demand as depending only on fuel prices and the energy budget is that the marginal rate of substitution between gas and electricity— i.e. the slope of the indifference curves in Figure 2.2—is not affected by his consumption of any other commodity.

Now consider stage 1. The economist would like now to think of the demand curve for energy itself, x_e, as dependent on the prices of the broad commodity groups, and total expenditures:

energy: $x_e = \varphi^1(p_e, p_f, y)$ (2.3)

food: $x_f = \varphi^2(p_e, p_f, y)$ (2.4)

In order to make stage 2 consistent with, but separate from, stage 1, severely restrictive assumptions again are needed, e.g. that in constructing a 'price of energy', the prices of individual fuels do not alter relative to each other, so that the quantity of energy can be measured by energy expenditure at constant prices.

Within this framework, then, the economist can model the demand for particular fuels or for a broad commodity such as energy. Both models have been widely studied, and in both approaches single-equation demand studies (e.g. looking at an equation like (2.1) in isolation) and demand system studies (e.g. looking at equations (2.3) and (2.4) together) have been carried out. Before looking at some of these case studies, consider the factors that the economist will look for.

Consumer choice models

Most studies of demand are concerned with explanation rather than forecasting—indeed, there are arguments for not looking at behavioural models at all when forecasting is needed. When it comes to the theory of consumer (or producer) choice, economics has very precise explanations of behaviour, and usually these are framed in terms of elasticities of response.

Consider the general case of Figure 2.3 where there are two commodities, x_1 and x_2, two prices which are assumed to be outside the consumer's control, p_1 and p_2, and an already committed value for total expenditure, y. In the top part of the figure is illustrated the consumer's equilibrium point as he tries to maximise the utility from consuming x_1 and x_2 as represented by the indifference curves

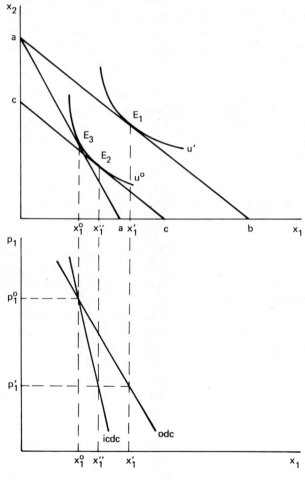

Figure 2.3

15

u^0 and u^1, while not exceeding his total expenditure, y, represented by budget lines aa, ab, and cc. Suppose he starts at equilibrium E_2, on u^0 with budget line cc. Should his income constraint move out to ab (staying parallel to cc since prices have not changed), he may consume more of both x_1 and x_2 (but he will consume less of any of the commodities that is 'inferior'). One set of parameters to be measured consists, therefore, of the income elasticity of demand for each commodity consumed, ε_{1y} and ε_{2y} in this case, i.e. the percentage rise in the amount of the commodity consumed relative to the percentage rise in total expenditure.

Suppose now the consumer starts at E_3 on budget line aa. Should price, p_1, of commodity x_1 fall, the budget line pivots through a to ab, and the consumer may raise his consumption of x_1 from x_1^0 to x_1' in moving to point E_1. The bottom half of the figure graphs this rise in consumption against the drop in price from p_1^0 to p_1' to produce the ordinary demand curve (odc). For this ordinary demand curve, interest centres on the own price elasticity of demand, ε_{11}, the percentage change in x_1 consumption relative to the percentage change in price. Note that p_2 was held constant during the operation, thereby helping to fix the position of odc. Were p_2 to change as well, then a new set of equilibrium positions would be worked out resulting in the odc curve shifting position. This gives rise to the measure of cross-price elasticity of demand, ε_{12}.

However, the effect of a change in price can be decomposed into income and substitution effects as shown in the top half of Figure 2.3. Starting from E_3 again, budget line cc reflects the new set of relative prices (lower p_1; unchanged p_2) associated with ab, but has been positioned so that the consumer remains on his initial indifference curve. The resulting rise in x_1 consumption, $(x_1'' - x_1^0)$ reflects substitution of now cheaper x_1 for x_2, while cancelling out the effect of lower p_1 in permitting the consumer to buy more of all commodities. Graphing this substitution effect alone against the price change yields the demand curve labelled icdc in the bottom half of the figure. By excluding the income effect of the price change on x_1 consumption, $(x_1' - x_1'')$ this icdc demand curve reflects income-compensated price responses, and is known as the income-compensated demand curve or Hicksian demand curve. It too has elasticity parameters associated with it: η_{11} the compensated own price elasticity of demand and η_{12} the compensated cross-price elasti-

16

city of demand which measures how icdc would shift if p_2 changed.

Clearly, the ordinary and income-compensated demand curves are related, since the odc is obtained by adding an income effect to the icdc, and this relationship can be measured by the elasticities. Consider the effect of a drop in price on x_1 when x_1 has a very small share in the allocation of the consumer's expenditure, y. The income effect on purchasing power arising from lower p_1 only carries small weight in affecting overall price responses compared with the case when x_1 takes a very large share of the consumer's budget. Writing w_1 for the share of x_1 in the overall expenditure, y, it can be shown that the ordinary and compensated elasticities are related as follows:

$$\varepsilon_{11} = \eta_{11} - w_1 \varepsilon_{1y} \qquad (2.5)$$

(and the negative sign reflects the fact that η_{11} will be negative, while ε_{1y} will be positive for normal goods). This Hicks–Slutsky equation (2.5) permits measurement of compensated elasticities from knowledge of ordinary price and income elasticities.

With this theoretical background, the economist may take a fuel demand system such as equations (2.1) and (2.2) and seek to measure the elasticities econometrically. However, it is first necessary to write (2.1) and (2.2) in a particular functional form suitable for regression analysis. This is not quite as straightforward as it sounds, since the economist may choose an easy-to-measure functional form that turns out to be inconsistent with the general ideas discussed in the diagrammatic analysis.

Consider one much-used starting point. Suppose the economist is prepared to assume that the elasticities involved in the slope and position of odc and icdc are constants. The system (2.1) and (2.2) can therefore treat elasticities as parameters. In that case, there will always be numerically constant relationships between the proportional changes in the x's and the proportional changes in the p's and y, permitting the economist to write (2.1) and (2.2) as the constant elasticity of demand system:

$$\log x_1 = \alpha_1 + \varepsilon_{11} \log p_1 + \varepsilon_{12} \log p_2 + \varepsilon_{1y} \log y \qquad (2.6)$$

$$\log x_2 = \alpha_2 + \varepsilon_{21} \log p_1 + \varepsilon_{22} \log p_2 + \varepsilon_{2y} \log y \qquad (2.7)$$

With equations (2.6) and (2.7), therefore the ε's become parameters to be measured statistically, while the logarithmic terms are the variables whose values need to be observed as actual data.

But the economist cannot apply (2.6) and (2.7) blindly. Suppose he did so, and measured the elasticities with the following result:

$$\varepsilon_{11} + \varepsilon_{12} + \varepsilon_{1y} > 0 \qquad (2.8)$$

There is no statistical reason why this should not happen, but it cannot make economic sense. Suppose all prices (p_1 and p_2) and total expenditure available, y, each rose by 10 per cent. In effect the consumer is no better off, and unless he suffers from money illusion, should not alter his purchases. But the result in (2.8) predicts that he will incease his net purchase of x_1 after a 10 per cent rise in income and all prices, so that he clearly does suffer from money illusion. As a result the economist has to restrict his estimation of (2.6) and (2.7) to avoid results like (2.8) which are inconsistent with the theoretical predictions of consumer analysis.

To ensure absence of money illusion impose ($\varepsilon_{11} + \varepsilon_{12} + \varepsilon_{1y} = 0$) on equation (2.6):

$$\log x_1 = \alpha_1 + \varepsilon_{11} (\log p_1 - \log p_2) + \varepsilon_{1y} (\log y - \log p_2) \quad (2.6a)$$

This is a popular model for econometric analysis, since the economist may argue that attention can be restricted to only two commodities in the economy: x_1, in which he is interested, and x_2, which represents all others. The variable p_2 then becomes an index for all other prices in the economy and the independent variables are $\log (p_1/p_2)$, the log of the price of x_1 relative to all other prices, and $\log (y/p_2)$ the log of *real* income.

But despite the critical importance of elasticity information, there is no presumption in modelling that such elasticities have to be constant, and many other parameterisations are important and indeed preferable from a theoretical point of view. Among the most useful are those that parameterise the fundamental economising behaviour of consumers. As an example, the Stone–Geary utility function may be adopted:

$$U = \beta_1 \log(x_1 - \gamma_1) + \beta_2 \log (x_2 - \gamma_2) \qquad (2.9)$$

where γ_1 and γ_2 are said to be the subsistence levels of the two (or more generally, n) commodities, e.g. energy x_1 and other goods, x_2). By parameterising, i.e. holding constant the β_i and γ_i, the economist is modelling the fundamental marginal rate of substitution (MRS) between the commodities:

$$MRS = -\frac{\beta_1/(x_1 - \gamma_1)}{\beta_2/(x_2 - \gamma_2)}$$

and this is a particularly useful starting point since it can be used to ensure the convex to the origin indifference curves of neoclassical demand theory. By equating this MRS with the market price ratio, $-(p_1/p_2)$, a set of demand functions can be derived, which under simple conditions, $(\beta_1 + \beta_2 = 1, x_i > \gamma_i)$, yield the well-known linear expenditure system (LES):

$$x_i = \gamma_i + (\beta_i/p_i)(y - \Sigma p_j\gamma_j); \ i = 1,2$$

so that demand depends on all prices, but when all prices are constant, the Engel curve for each commodity is linear above the subsistence levels of consumption and income.

Once again ordinary and compensated price elasticities can be derived, but these are no longer constants. The essential lesson of modelling like this is that the economist can design his model or parameterisation to yield the information he wants in a manner free from internal contradictions, as long as he is prepared to pay the price of accepting the restrictions that are consequences of his particular parameterisation.

Production models

Exactly the same methodology can be applied to modelling industrial demand for energy and fuels. Once again a two-stage process can be used. This time the interest centres on input demand functions. In Figure 2.4 an isoquant map is shown for the inputs capital, K, and energy, E. A cost-minimising firm will try to minimise the cost of achieving its output target, x. Consequently it uses inputs K and E in combinations determined by their relative prices, p_K and p_E, measured by the slope of the isocost line tangent to the output target isoquant x°. Two possible isocost lines giving two possible K/E ratios are shown.

Again, input demand functions can be derived depending on the autonomous or exogenous variables, this time p_K, p_E and x, the prices and the output target:

$$K = f^1(p_K, p_E, x) \tag{2.10}$$

$$E = f^2(p_K, p_E, x) \tag{2.11}$$

19

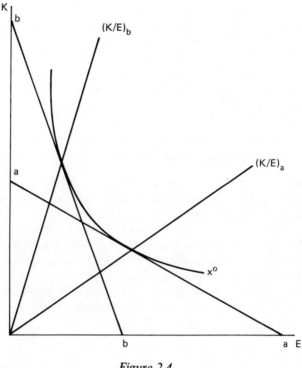

Figure 2.4

Once again elasticities can be measured by adopting a suitable functional form or parameterisation for (2.10) and (2.11). Note there is no output effect here unlike the consumer case. By separately measuring the effect of x on E in (2.11), any price effects are with respect to the isoquant x°, and hence simply reflect substitution of one input for another without permitting the firm to move, for example, to a higher isoquant when p_E falls.

The substitutability of one input for another is of crucial importance in energy demand; for example, did higher oil prices cause a shift towards other fuels in production, or towards other inputs rather than energy? The elasticity of substitution, σ, is used to measure this effect. In Figure 2.4, suppose the initial price ratio (p_E/p_K) is given by the isocost line aa, and a subsequent one by bb. Clearly, there has been a relative rise in energy prices, and a shift towards a less energy-intensive and more capital-intensive

20

production process. The strength of response depends on the curvature of the isoquant measured by σ. Let the symbol ^ represent the percentage change in a variable, then:

$$\text{elasticity of substitution, } \sigma = (\hat{K} - \hat{E})/(\hat{p}_E - \hat{p}_K) \qquad (2.12)$$

so that if p_E changes 10 per cent more than p_K, and as a result K changes 5 per cent more than E, the elasticity of substitution is $(5/10) = 0.5$.

There is a precise relationship between input demand elasticities for a change in energy prices and the elasticity of substitution:

$$\varepsilon_{EE} = -S_K\sigma \qquad (2.13)$$

$$\varepsilon_{KE} = S_E\sigma \qquad (2.14)$$

where S_K and S_E are the shares of capital and energy in total input expenditures. (2.13) says that as energy prices rise, the percentage fall in energy demand is higher, the higher is substitutability and the more of the budget is spent on capital.

Figure 2.4 emphasised that ε_{EE} and ε_{KE} are measured for a constant level of output—i.e. they are analogous to the substitution effect elasticities of consumer theory. But output might indeed change. Look again at Figure 2.4, and represent the rise in energy prices by pivoting the budget line down through the point a on the vertical axis. There should now be a tangency with a lower isoquant and a further effect on E. Why? The reason is that the higher price of energy should have raised the firm's unit cost curve and, in a competitive market, raised market price, thus causing a final demand contraction for the firm's product, x, represented by the new lower output. In this event the total input demand elasticity ε_{EE} will be higher in absolute value than (2.13) suggests. The additional terms that allow for changing final demand levels when an input price changes depend on the own price elasticity of demand for the final product, ε_{XX}:

$$\varepsilon_{EE} = -(S_K\sigma - S_E\varepsilon_{XX}) \qquad (2.15)$$

$$\varepsilon_{KE} = S_E(\sigma + \varepsilon_{XX}) \qquad (2.16)$$

Suppose now (2.15) and (2.16) are applied to the aggregate economy, and Figure 2.4 is used to represent the production of GNP using national capital and energy stocks. A rise in energy prices, as happened in the 1970s, will clearly lower energy consumption even if GNP is constant, but may also lower GNP by shifting the economy's aggregate supply curve (the sum of all the firms' supply curves) to the left. The net effect is given by (2.15). But this need not mean unemployment for other factors, as (2.16) shows. Whether or not other inputs, represented here by K, also contract depends on the net effect of σ and ε_{XX}. If the substitution towards K overcomes the depressing effect on GNP, then other inputs may actually experience a rise in demand when energy prices rise.

If an economist wanted to measure this additional output effect, he might begin with a model of competitive profit-maximisation, in which the firm's objective is:

$$\text{maximise } \pi = px - p_K K - p_E E$$

where p is the price at which it sells its output x, so that px is total revenue. Output itself is still the outcome of production processes given by the production function reflecting current technology:

$$x = F(K,E)$$

and hence the firm's input decisions depend now on the variables p_K, p_E and p, the level of x being now part of the outcome of its decision-making process:

$$K = f^1(p_K, p_E, p) \tag{2.10a}$$

$$E = f^2(p_K, p_E, p) \tag{2.11a}$$
$$x = f^3(p_K, p_E, p)$$

The input demand functions do now incorporate an output effect, since as p_E changes, for example, x, output, will also change, thereby necessitating a further change in energy input over and above the substitution with capital, K.

Both forms of input demand function: those corresponding to cost-minimisation (2.10) and (2.11), and those corresponding to profit-maximisation (2.10a) and (2.11a) have been used by energy economists.

In reality, of course, firms will use more than two inputs, and the elasticity of substitution idea needs a little generalisation to allow for this. Suppose the price of energy rises, and as a result firms use less energy-intensive equipment so that K rises relative to E. The firms may also respond by an even greater substitution towards labour, L, so that there is a net fall in the use of equipment, even though that equipment is now less energy-intensive. The appropriate measure for this is the Allen partial elasticity of substitution, σ_{KE}, which would show in this case that K and E were complements rather than substitutes. In other words σ_{KE} is a measure of substitution between these two inputs when all input prices, but not all other *inputs* are held constant.

The discussion so far has been entirely in terms of responses of energy and fuel consumption to price and output or expenditure changes. But such changes will not occur instantaneously since both firms and consumers face costs of adjustment when seeking to change their relative use of fuels and other commodities. The cost of adjusting shows up as lags and delays in responsiveness so that it is important to distinguish between short-run (s) and long-run (l) elasticities. As an example we could have:

$$\varepsilon_{EE}^{s}/\varepsilon_{EE}^{l} = \lambda \qquad (2.17)$$

where λ, the ratio of the short-run to the long-run elasticity, may be called the coefficient of partial adjustment, i.e. the proportion of planned changes in consumption of E that can be accomplished within a specified time-period, following a change in p_E.

A convenient and easy-to-use assumption which characterises many models is that all these short-run to long-run ratios are identical and constant:

$$\varepsilon_{EE}^{s}/\varepsilon_{EE}^{l} = \varepsilon_{KE}^{s}/\varepsilon_{KE}^{l} = \ldots \lambda \text{ (constant)}$$

but this should only be regarded as the most naive model possible. As we shall see below, some economists have been prepared to assume λ itself is an endogenous variable determined by choice-making behaviour in response to market signals.

The discussion of the last few pages has attempted to bring out in very simple terms a few characteristics of the energy demand case studies about to be considered. Briefly these are:

1. The economist usually has some precise parameters he wishes to measure: e.g. price elasticities, the elasticity of substitution, or the speed of response.

2. He must devise a convenient functional form (or parameterisation) for the model, that allows the characteristics to be measured either as constants or as easily solved variables.

3. The parameterisation used should not be inconsistent with the underlying theory (which does not itself require any convenient functional form).

In the case studies which follow, the individual models differ greatly, but they all have the above characteristics in common.

Case studies of energy demand

This section looks at some important case studies of the demand for energy as a broad commodity. It is necessarily more technical than the rather simple discussion of general principles above, since it describes the models used in the different studies. In every case, however, the primary concern is with elasticity measurement. Naturally, in view of the enormous number of energy demand studies, this review of case studies can only be incomplete; it offers a flavour of the work done in this field.

A model which had an important impact on energy demand studies is that of Nordhaus (1977). It was international in context, and developed for a period before the world was reacting to high price rises in crude oil. The data set used covered the United States and six European countries including the UK, for the period 1955–72. The dependent variable was useful energy consumed per capita in each of three sectors: domestic, transport and industrial demand; the efficiency data for converting to useful energy were similar to those used by the UK Department of Energy (1978).

Starting from a general equilibrium framework of producers and consumers, and applying the assumption of constant elasticities, and the absence of money illusion, Nordhaus is able to arrive at an energy demand equation for each sector of the economy that is analogous to equation (2.6a) above:

$$\log e_i^* = \alpha_i + \beta_i \log(p_e/p) + \gamma_i \log(y/p) \qquad (2.18)$$

where e_i^* is desired per capita useful energy consumption in sector i (domestic, industrial or transport), p_e is the price of energy, p is the gross national product (GNP) deflator or price index for converting money income to real income, and y is per capita GNP. Applying the partial adjustment hypothesis that only a constant proportion, λ, of any disequilibrium between desired energy e_i^* and actual energy consumption e_i is made up in one year, provides the final equation that allows for lags in response:

$$\log e_{it} = \lambda\alpha_i + \lambda\beta_i \log (p_e/p)_t + \lambda\gamma_i \log(y/p)_t + (1-\lambda) \log e_{it-1}$$
$$(2.19)$$

The parameters $(\lambda\beta_i)$, and $(\lambda\gamma_i)$ are the constant short-run elasticities of demand and their long-run counterparts are β_i and γ_i.

Table 2.1 gathers the Nordhaus estimates for the UK for the domestic and industrial sector price elasticities, the transport sector having negligible values. Two implications stand out: first, elasticities are relatively low, but with the industry sector apparently much more responsive than the domestic sector; secondly, the delayed response is very short, the implied partial adjustment coefficients suggesting that the time lapse before 90 per cent of a price effect has occurred is 0.8 years for the domestic sector and 1.01 years for the industrial sector.

Table 2.1: Nordhaus's useful energy price elasticities for UK, (ε_{EE})

	short-run	long-run
domestic	−0.36	−0.38
industrial	−0.79	−0.88

A very different form of model has been applied to a similar data base in a variety of US studies, and Pindyck (1979) can be taken as typical. Pindyck's study is much more ambitious, since he modelled both stages of the two-stage budgeting process. Here, the focus is on his overall energy studies.

Pindyck's model is typical of many studies which sought to model the underlying taste structure of the domestic sector, and the underlying cost structure of firms. Taking the industrial sector first, the two questions of interest are the size of energy price elasticities and whether energy is a complement or substitute for capital in production processes. It might be the case that a firm's initial attempts to economise on energy following an energy price rise involve it in scrapping machinery so that both capital and energy are decreased, but that in the long run firms are able to build up a less energy-intensive capital stock so that capital and energy are long-run substitutes.

To investigate the production structure two equally useful routes are possible: the production function and the cost function. Referring to Figure 2.4 it can be seen that as a firm expands its output and hence hires more inputs, it moves to tangencies with higher and higher isocost lines. The information about the production structure that is needed may therefore be discovered in the way costs depend on output levels and input prices. Thus a general long-run total cost function can be written:

$$C = C(x, p_L, p_K, p_E) \tag{2.20}$$

where x is the level of output, and p_L, p_K and p_E are the respective prices of labour, capital and energy. Pindyck parameterises this function with a quadratic approximation in the logarithms of the variables, i.e. he writes

$$
\begin{aligned}
\log C = {} & \alpha_0 + \alpha_x \log x + \alpha_L \log p_L + \alpha_K \log p_K + \alpha_E \log p_E \\
& + \tfrac{1}{2}\gamma_{xx}(\log x)^2 + \tfrac{1}{2}(\gamma_{LL}(\log p_L)^2 + \gamma_{LK} \log p_L \log p_K + \\
& \ldots + \gamma_{EK} \log p_E \log p_K + \gamma_{EE}(\log p_E)^2) + \gamma_{xL} \log p_L \\
& \log x + \\
& \ldots + \gamma_{xE} \log p_E \log x
\end{aligned}
\tag{2.21}
$$

This *translog* cost function is powerful because it is a very general approximation to (2.20) above, allowing the economist to impose many of the interesting properties of production functions on the equation. Generally, it is not estimated in this form because of the likelihood of being unable to distinguish statistically amongst the many different variables. Instead, Pindyck and others using this methodology employ the fact that the proportional rise in costs, C, relative to the proportionate rise in an input price must be identical to that input's share of total costs, s_i. In other words, if the price of energy rises by 10 per cent and expenditure on energy accounts for half of all costs, then costs will rise by 5 per cent. Hence the share of each input in cost, s_i, can be equated with the proportionate rise in C from an input price rise predicted by the approximation equation (2.21) above. Thus:

$$
s_E = \frac{\delta \log C}{\delta \log p_E} = \alpha_E + \gamma_{EL} \log p_L + \gamma_{EK} \log p_K + \\
\gamma_{EE} \log p_E + \gamma_{Ex} \log x
\tag{2.22}
$$

and similar equations can be derived for s_L and s_K (though one, of course, will be redundant). Equations like (2.22), when fitted, leave some parameters of (2.21) unknown, but nevertheless provide sufficient information to measure not only price elasticities but also the Allen elasticities of substitution (AES), discussed earlier.

Pindyck's sample pools time series (annual) data for 1959–74 over Canada, the US and eight European countries, including the UK. Regional dummy variables were added to allow the intercept terms in the above equation (2.22) to vary across countries. Concentrating on the measures of price elasticity of energy demand and the Allen partial elasticities of substitution, Table 2.2 presents Pindyck's estimates for the UK.

Table 2.2: Pindyck (1979) estimates for UK own price elasticity of industrial energy demand (ε_{EE}) and partial elasticities of substitution between capital and energy (σ_{KE}) and labour and energy (σ_{LE}), based on 10 countries' pooled sample

ε_{EE}	σ_{KE}	σ_{LE}
−0.84	0.66	0.97

The own price elasticity figure for industrial energy demand is comparable to Nordhaus's long-run estimate, and both σ_{KE} and σ_{LE} indicate that capital and labour are long-run substitutes for energy.

The positive estimate (indicating substitutability rather than complementarity) for σ_{KE} differs from some earlier studies. Generally, it seems to be the case that studies based on annual time series samples show K and E to be complements, while those based on cross-section or pooled time series and cross-section samples, such as Pindyck's, show K and E to be substitutes. Pindyck is prepared to argue that time series samples reveal only short-run effects, while cross-section data may reveal long-run effects. Arguments like this, which often arise in demand studies, are based on the following reasoning.

If Y_{it} is a variable that can vary over time, t, and over countries (or households or some other cross-section unit), i, then by looking only at time series data, the economist can measure variation over time of the mean within countries, i.e. a short-run effect. However, by looking at cross-section data, he can measure variation over countries of the mean over time, i.e. a long-run effect. Although Pindyck does not break down his pooled sample into separate constituents in this way, it is clearly on these lines that he claims to have measured long-run effects. Certainly, it is true that his

27

results show greater price responses in energy demand than had been conventionally assumed in the 1950s and 1960s.

Pindyck also carries out an energy demand study for the residential sector of the US, European and Japanese economies. The basic philosophy is analogous to that of the industrial model. The underlying taste structure of residential consumers is represented by the indirect utility function, i.e.

$$U = v(p_E, p_F, p_C, p_D, p_T, p_O, y) \qquad (2.23)$$

where the prices are those for the broad commodities: energy (E), food (F), clothing (C), durables (D), transportation and communications (T) and other goods (O). This is then approximated by an analogous translog function, and share equations derived for measuring the parameters. The results again showed relatively high long-run elasticities, the residential energy own price elasticity for the UK being $\varepsilon_{EE} = -1.09$ (in 1973).

All of these studies incorporate the UK into an international sample. The Department of Energy (1983) has produced aggregate energy studies for both the UK domestic and industrial sectors. The underlying model is analogous to that of Nordhaus, except that instead of assuming a fixed adjustment parameter between actual and desired consumption, the models assume that it is one or more of the explanatory variables that give rise to a delayed response. In both sectors desired energy consumption depends on income, price and temperature; in the industrial sector past values of energy prices have a delayed impact on energy consumption, while in the domestic sector, past values of both price and income have a delayed effect. In both cases the impact declines exponentially as time passes, and in the domestic sector the rate of exponential decline of past prices and income effects is identical for both. The long-run price elasticities of useful energy consumption are found to be: industry: -0.224; domestic: -0.43. These are certainly lower than many other researchers have found.

The overall conclusion of these broad aggregate studies of energy demand is that price elasticities though small in the short run are nevertheless significant, and are found to be much larger when delayed responses are allowed. The strength of these conclusions is heavily reinforced when studies of the demand for individual fuels are considered.

28

Case studies of fuel use

Most econometric work has been directed towards sectoral consumption of individual fuels, e.g. residential electricity usage or industrial gas consumption, rather than the broad energy aggregate.

There are several modelling problems specific to these studies which need to be analysed, as pointed out by Taylor (1975). First, there is the difficulty of measuring price. Many electricity tariffs have contained quarterly standing charges (A), and block discounts, so that the price of the last unit of electricity falls as higher and higher consumption levels are taken on: e.g. p_1^a for the first units, p_1^b for the rest.

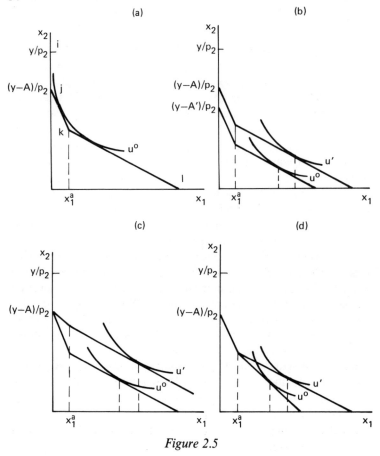

Figure 2.5

Figure (2.5a) shows by the segmented line ijkl the effect such a tariff has on the budget constraint between electricity, x_1, and another commodity, x_2. It may, for example, lead to more than one equilibrium for the consumer. It is particularly important to note that if either the fixed charge, A, rises (Figure 2.5b) or the price of the first block of consumption, p_1^a, rises (Figure 2.5c) there is simply an income effect. The usual substitution and income effects of a price change only arise with a change in the marginal price of electricity, p_1^b (Figure 2.5d).

However, many empirical studies adopt as *the* price of electricity, the average price, ap, i.e. total bill ÷ consumption:

$$ap = \frac{1}{x_1} [A + p_1^a x_1^a + p_1^b (x_1 - x_1^a)]$$

This results in a problem of bias in the elasticities and difficulties in identifying the demand function, as illustrated in Figure 2.6.

In Figure 2.6(a), the economist has used the final marginal energy charge. As p_1^b changes, he correctly identifies two points (p_1', x_1') and (p_1'', x_1''), on the demand curve. In Figure 2.6(b), the economist has used ap obtaining the downward sloping supply curve SS. A shift in the demand curve generates two observations (x_1, ap^1) and $x_1', ap)$ which could be mistaken for an elastic demand response to price.

A second difficulty arises when there are separate day and night consumption prices. In the latter case there are two demand functions to be estimated separately, and average electricity consumption is only a hybrid commodity.

A third important point concerns the fact that fuel consumption is used in conjunction with a stock of fuel-using equipment. For example, if K is the rated capacity of electricity-using appliances (in kW), while x_1 is annual consumption (kWh), then:

$$x_1 = hK \tag{2.24}$$

where h is the utilisation rate of appliances. Short-run effects then reflect the influence of, for example, the price of electricity, on the utilisation rate of a given stock:

$$\left(\frac{\delta x_1}{\delta p_1} \right)^s = \frac{\delta h}{\delta p_1} \cdot K \tag{2.25}$$

while long-run effects reflect the impact of price on the stock of appliances at some *desired* utilisation rate, h^*:

$$\left(\frac{\delta x_1}{\delta p_1}\right)^1 = h^* \cdot \frac{\delta K}{\delta p_1} \tag{2.26}$$

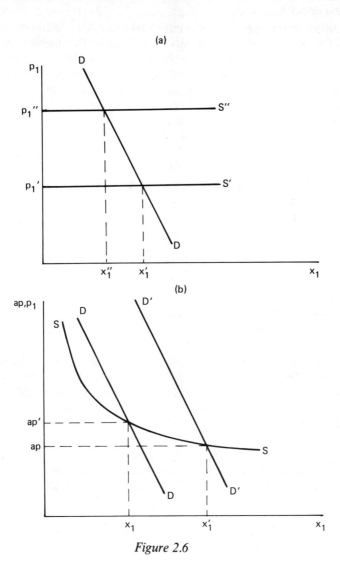

Figure 2.6

Taylor argued that fuel studies need to take account of these factors by (i) using marginal prices and separating out income effects, (ii) separately estimating demand curves for peak and off-peak usage if prices differ, and (iii) using the stock of appliances as an explanatory variable to determine the relationship between long- and short-run elasticities.

It is nevertheless true that many studies do not meet these standards. However, there is one UK study (Ruffell 1977) which clearly does meet the Taylor standards. Ruffell examined the UK quarterly household demand for electricity from 1955 to 1968 over all the area boards in a pooled sample. He took the stock of appliances as given, and examined the effects of such variables as the electricity, gas and coal prices, consumption expenditures and weather variables on consumer utilisation rates. Ruffell points out that the utilisation effects are difficult to disentangle. If it is assumed that h and K are independent in (2.24) then (2.25) follows for the short-run utilisation effect. However, h and K may not be independent in which case:

$$\left(\frac{\delta x_1}{\delta p_1}\right)^s = K \cdot \left(\frac{\delta h}{\delta p_1} + \frac{h}{K}\frac{\delta K}{\delta p_1}\right) \qquad (2.27)$$

In other words, the short-term price effect is the sum of utilisation (h) and cross-appliance–utilisation (K–h) effects, which may differ in sign. Not much can be done about this without explicitly modelling (2.26), for which information about h* is needed.

Concentrating on (2.25) Ruffell includes (1/K) amongst the variables explaining h in order to eliminate the mean cross- (K–h) effect. He was conscious of the difficulty of measuring the marginal price of electricity and used both the final marginal price in the declining block rates and a tariff function that determined marginal price as a function of amounts consumed. Price elasticities with the first version are significantly negative, those with the second version significantly positive, though this may arise because of the incorporation of both h and K–h effects in (2.25). Ruffell's overall conclusion is that there are variations in household electricity demand which are not simply related to appliance ownership, but which can be explained by ordinary demand theory.

Important models of natural gas demand such as those of Balestra

(1967) have also emphasised the importance of the stock of appliances and equipment. Balestra distinguishes between *new* gas demand at time t, and *committed* demand derived from utilisation of the stock of appliances inherited from a previous period, and dependent on the depreciation rate on gas equipment. New gas demand then depends on economic factors including gas prices, income and new total energy demand, with the latter similarly being determined by prices, income and household formation. In this way, changes in gas demand are determined by price and income effects and the depreciation rates of the fuel-using appliances. Using average price data, Balestra found statistically significant long-run gas price elasticities in the region of -0.7 for the US.

Two models which have considered the interaction of all fuel types together are those of Pindyck (1979) and Peterson (1979). Pindyck's study uses the stage 2 budgeting analysis corresponding to his stage 1 energy analysis described earlier. In this sense, expenditure on durable goods for the residential sector, and expenditure on capital equipment for the industrial sector, are assumed to have no effect on individual fuel demands, having simply helped to determine the overall allocation to energy.

Using components of national consumer price indices to measure prices (and therefore probably picking up average price effects), Pindyck is able to calculate 'total' price elasticities for both the residential and industrial sectors. These elasticities assume that fuel price changes do have a feedback effect on the total amount of energy consumed. His results for the UK are reported in Table 2.3.

Peterson (1979) has carried out a similar analysis for 17 different sectors of the UK economy, including industrial and residential consumers. His approach is to apply an approximation to the long-run energy cost function of each sector, i.e.:

$$C_E = C_E (x_E, p_1 \ldots p_6) \tag{2.28}$$

where x_E is the sector's use of energy, and $p_1 \ldots p_6$ are six fuel prices, assuming that economic agents in each sector try to produce their energy usage from the cheapest combination of fuels. His model differs from Pindyck's in the choice of approximating function used in place of (2.28) (he uses the generalised Leontieff instead of translog). Aggregating across all sectors, Peterson finds two positive price elasticities for fuels which do not figure largely in energy consumption (gas oil and coke), and the negative own price elastici-

33

ties for the four major fuels, as shown in Table 2.3. None of these results includes the feedback of higher fuel prices on total energy sales.

Table 2.3: Individual fuel price elasticities of demand based on energy cost-minimisation

	solid	liquid	gas	electricity		
(a) Pindyck (1979), including output effects:	−1.35	−0.37	−1.44	−0.56		

	coal	coke	gas oil	fuel oil	gas	electricity
(b) Peterson (1979), excluding output effects:	−0.02	0.14	0.63	−0.58	−0.93	−0.03

Apart from Ruffell's work, all the models described in this and the preceding section have examined only the average fuel or energy usage over the year without paying any attention to the timing of consumption. However, with a growing international interest in peak-load pricing, there has been a recent trend to studying the time-of-use (tou) pattern of electricity and gas consumption, and this analysis too has produced some very interesting elasticity estimates. Because of its relevance to the important problem of determining tou energy prices, this type of demand study is treated separately in Chapter 6 below.

All of the studies so far have used fairly conventional demand equations, but recent work at the UK Department of Energy has developed along slightly different lines, though the overall importance of price effects in the models is still emphasised. Some of the Department of Energy (1983) models are based on the multinomial logit approach to deriving demand equations.

Consider first the basic choice of buying energy. Suppose P (0 ⩽ P ⩽ 1) is the probability of any one consumer purchasing energy, and further suppose that this probability rises with some index of the propensity to buy, Z, as illustrated in Figure 2.7's cumulative frequency distribution, $P = F(Z)$. As the attributes of the commodity, energy, cause the propensity to buy, Z, to rise, it becomes more and more certain that the consumer will purchase energy. If we assume that this response at first grows slowly, then accelerates

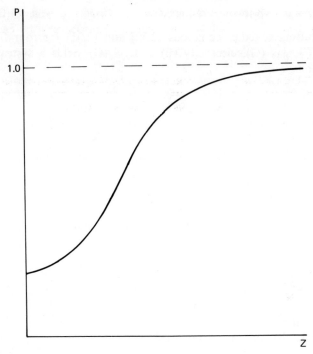

Figure 2.7

and then tails off, then a convenient model is the logistic function producing:

$$\log (P/1 - P) = Z \tag{2.29}$$

When more than one commodity choice is possible, we can model the odds of buying fuel type i rather than fuel type j in an analogous manner:

$$\log (P_i/P_j) = Z_i - Z_j \tag{2.30}$$

where P_i is now the frequency with which fuel type i is chosen rather than type j in the purchases of a population of identical individuals. The frequency P_i can be measured by the fuel's market share, S_i, and all that remains now is to determine those attributes of each fuel type that determine the probability of its purchase. The Department of Energy (1983) model uses the log of relative fuel price, and the previous value of market share:

35

$$Z_i = \alpha_i + \beta_i \log p_{it} + \gamma_i \log S_{it-1} \tag{2.31}$$

and putting together equations (2.30) and (2.31) for four fuels: coal (C), gas (G), electricity (E) and oil (O) yields a system of equations:

$$\log (SO/SC)_t = (\alpha_O - \alpha_C) + \beta_O \log p_O - \beta_C \log p_C + \gamma_O \log SO_{t-1} - \gamma_C \log SC_{t-1}$$

$$\log (SG/SC)_t = (\alpha_G - \alpha_C) + \beta_G \log p_G - \beta_C \log p_C + \gamma_C \log SG_{t-1} - \gamma_C \log SC_{t-1}$$

$$\log (SE/SC)_t = (\alpha_E - \alpha_C) + \beta_E \log p_E - \beta_C \log p_C + \gamma_E \log SE_{t-1} - \gamma_C \log SC_{t-1}$$

Certain restrictions are implied by the construction of the model: for example, the β_C and γ_C coefficents on the base fuel coal are the same in each equation, but otherwise the model permits considerable flexibility of price and dynamic responsiveness. In practice the Department of Energy imposes additional restrictions on the fitted equations to achieve, in its own words, 'meaningful coefficients'. For the industrial sector in which equations are developed in this form for coal, gas and oil, the most general form is used, but for the domestic sector in which all four fuels are modelled like this, the current version requires all the β coefficients and all the γ coefficents to be identical over all the equations, so that only the intercept term can act like a shift dummy variable to distinguish one type of fuel choice from another.

The long-run elasticities are not constant, and depend on the market shares themselves. For 1980, the Department's results are set out in Table 2.4.

Table 2.4: Some own price fuel elasticities (long-run) from the Department of Energy (1983) model

	electricity	coal	oil	gas
industry	n.a.	−4.6	−1.62	−1.34
domestic space and water heating	−2.88	−2.96	−2.97	−0.32

Source: Department of Energy (1983).

As with some earlier studies, the lagged responses exhibit exceedingly long delays, suggesting that the price effects of the early 1970s were still being observed in the mid-1980s. In particular it is much greater variability of prices in the 1970s that permitted much more precise measurement of their effects. When the data are drawn from earlier parts of the sample, the lack of movement in prices magnifies the standard errors of the coefficients on the price variable.

Case study conclusions

This chapter has focused on the methodology underlying some of the major recent studies of energy and fuel demands, particularly those applicable to the UK. There have been a great many such studies over the last ten years, the majority relevant to the US. Many of these have adopted a relatively pragmatic attitude to model-building, beginning with a basic assumption of constant elasticities and supplementing price and income variables with factors specific to certain end-uses of energy and fuel consumption. The models illustrated here have simply been chosen to illustrate the different approaches possible.

It is clearly dangerous to sum up many different empirical studies in simple terms, but in another earlier survey of Taylor (1976) the following broad conclusions are offered.

● energy consumption is not simply a matter of income and lifestyle;
● for each energy or fuel type, own price elasticity is small but significant in the short run, and much larger in the long run;
● inter-fuel substitution in response to price changes characterises industrial and residential markets.

Conclusions like these emphasise the critical role of prices in energy policy formation.

3

Pricing policy for efficient resource allocation

Most of the analysis in this book concentrates on questions of economic policy in the energy sector, but it is not possible to proceed very far without discussing the basic welfare economics that underlies policy evaluation. This is the concern in this chapter, which begins with a model framework for describing the place of public and private sector fuel producers in the economy. Subsequently the pricing rules for efficient resource allocation in both first- and second-best situations are described, before, finally, equity considerations are brought explicitly into the analysis.

Modelling public enterprises in the economy

We begin with Figure 3.1, which describes the main economic actors to be examined, and the constraints on their behaviour and decision-making. We can imagine a resource base for the economy of basic inputs to be transformed into the commodities supplied to consumers and used by producers. This is represented by the box at the top of Figure 3.1. To transform the resources to final commodities requires producers to adapt the existing technology to achieve the minimum requirements of these limited resources in producing the commodities: hence the box represents the economy's aggregate production constraint. Feeding into this constraint may be a supply of basic resources, such as forgone leisure, from households.

Two types of producers are designated: private and public. Private producers (their outputs are labelled $(X_1 \ldots X_n)$) sell their commodities to households and to the public sector. In doing so they may

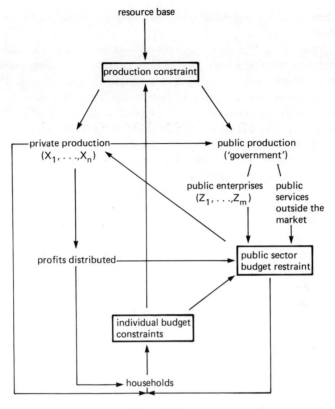

Figure 3.1

make profits over and above the required rates of return to factors employed, and such profits can be thought of as being distributed to households to supplement their income from supplying their own resources.

Public production is divided into services outside the markets, (e.g. state health provision, defence, and so on), and the outputs of public enterprises, labelled $Z_1 \ldots Z_m$. The latter are sold to both private producers and households, and among these outputs are those of the nationalised fuel industries in which we shall be particularly interested.

Households determine their spending and resource supply decisions on the basis of their individual budget constraints, and we can note that the economy will be in an equilibrium position when *all of the individual household budget constraints are satisfied in aggregate.*

Apart from the aggregate production and budget constraints, there is a third which we may want to consider: the budget restraint of the public sector, which it is tempting to symbolise as PSBR. If we ignore the possibility of borrowing from exogenous sources, then public production must be subject to such a PSBR. Indeed, as we shall see in a moment, if the aggregate production and budget constraints are satisfied for the economy, so must PSBR in this simple model. The public sector meets PSBR by paying for the resource requirements of public production from three sources: sales of its products $(Z_1 \ldots Z_m)$ at prices $(p_1 \ldots p_m)$, taxes on the commodities produced $(X_1 \ldots X_n)$ by the private sector at rates $(t_1 \ldots t_n)$, and by taxes on the profits distributed by private producers, Λ, to households.

We can put these ideas symbolically to clarify the sums involved. Let:

R be the total resources available in the resource base,
R_p be the resource requirements of the private sector,
R_g be the resource requirements of the public sector.

Then the production constraint reads simply:

$$R_p + R_g = R \qquad (3.1)$$

Now turn to households and let, for a typical household:

e_p be the expenditure on privately produced commodities
e_g be the expenditure on public sector goods
r be the share of resources owned by the household
n be the net profit income received by the household.

Then the individual household's budget restraint is:

$$e_p + e_g = r + n \qquad (3.2)$$

Aggregate this over all consumers, writing upper case letters for the aggregate amounts:

$$E_p + E_g = R + N \qquad (3.3)$$

and now introduce the definitions:

SR_p: sales revenue in private sector production
PT: tax revenues on profits

so that:

$$N = SR_p - R_p - PT \qquad (3.4)$$

(net profits ≡ sales revenue less resource requirements less profits tax). Now substitute (3.4) and (3.1) into (3.3) so as to obtain:

$$E_p + E_g = R_p + R_g + SR_p - R_p - PT$$

and rearranging:

$$(E_p - SR_p) + PT + (E_g - R_g) = 0 \qquad (3.5)$$

Let us be clear first that (3.5) must hold when (3.1) (the aggregate production constraint) and (3.3) (the aggregate budget constraint) are satisfied. Now (3.5) says that taxes on privately-produced commodities (i.e. the difference between what consumers pay and what producers receive, $(E_p - SR_p)$), plus profits taxes (PT) plus the surplus or deficit in public sector goods and the resource requirements of public sector goods $(E_g - R_g)$ must sum to zero. In other words (3.5) expresses the public sector budget restraint—or alternatively sums to the amount of borrowing from exogenous sources that is required of the public sector in this simple model.

In brief, the aggregate production constraint (3.1), along with the aggregate budget constraint (3.3)—satisfaction of which defines an equilibrium for the economy—implies the satisfaction of a further, third, constraint on the public sector (3.5). In modelling the economy in equilibrium, therefore, satisfaction of any *two* of the constraints (3.1), (3.3) and (3.5) on the flows of commodities, implies satisfaction of the third. This is an example of a well-known phenomenon in general equilibrium economics called Walras' law. This framework will characterise much of our discussion of the public sector energy industries.

Superimposed on this picture of the economy, we want to model the behaviour of some of the public enterprises, those in the energy sector. Thus, we now need to consider policy objectives and policy instruments in this 'government' box. In this theoretical framework we adopt the familiar idea of maximising the economic welfare of individuals in society. Let us pause to recall what conventional welfare economics has to say about this.

The basic criterion is that of a Pareto improvement—a reallocation of resources that results in at least one person being made better off, in his or her own estimation, without any other person being made worse off. We illustrate the idea with the familiar Edgeworth box diagram of Figure 3.2(a) which helps us to locate all the Pareto-optimal or efficient allocations of resources.

In this figure we represent the indifference curves of two individuals for the two commodities, X_1 and X_2, individual consumption

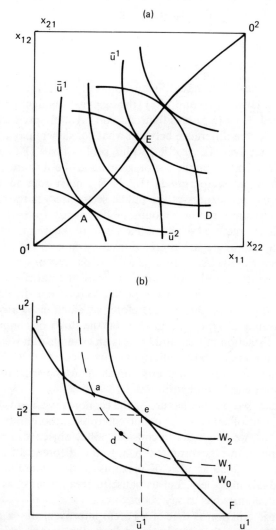

Figure 3.2

being represented by x_{11} x_{12}... etc. By holding the first individual at a pre-specified utility level: e.g. $\overline{U}^1$, we can seek to make the second as well off as possible (maximise U^2 such that $U^1 = \overline{U}^1$). The necessary conditions are given by the familiar equality between marginal rates of substitution, or tangency of indifference curves, such as occurs at points like A and E in Figure 3.2(a).

$$MRS^1 = MRS^2 \tag{3.6}$$

The line, O^1O^2, referred to as the contract curve, traces out all possible points where this equality holds, and in Figure 3.2(b) the points on O^1O^2 are redrawn with respect to the axes U^1 and U^2 along the utility possibility frontier, PF. The fundamental point about PF is that every point on it is optimal or efficient in the sense of the Pareto criterion, because it is not possible to move from a point like a in Figure 3.2(b) to make individual 1 feel better off without lowering individual 2's utility.

However, the Pareto criterion is incomplete as an ethical basis for policy-making because it does not tell us which of two points like a and e is preferable. Indeed, although it can tell us that e is preferable to d in Figure 3.2(b), it cannot determine whether a is preferable to d, even though the corresponding point D is off the contract curve in Figure 3.2(a). Unfortunately many policy decisions do need to determine the desirability of moves from points like d to a or a to e. For example, is it desirable to move from an inefficient allocation of resources to an efficient allocation in the sense of the Pareto criterion? Alternatively, is a project which benefits some consumers but imposes costs on others desirable from society's point of view?

One device which does illustrate a complete ethical basis for policy-making is the social welfare function, which ranks or trades off the utility levels of different individuals in society:

$$W = W(U^1, U^2, \ldots) \tag{3.7}$$

To ensure this is compatible with the Pareto criterion we simply need the restriction that the partial derivatives, i.e. the effect on social welfare of raising one person's utility when everybody else's is held constant, are all positive:

$$\frac{\delta W}{\delta U^j} = w_j > O \qquad j = 1 \ldots J \tag{3.8}$$

In Figure 3.2(b) we have finally drawn three of the indifference contours of a social welfare function (W_0, W_1 and W_2) enabling us to say society finds point e the most desirable, and ranks a and d equally.

In using equation (3.7) we shall never assume that an actual social welfare function (SWF) based, say, on majority voting, could exist in practice for any society. Instead, we use the SWF idea to emphasise the assumptions about weighting the utility levels of individuals that we must make in order to have a complete ethical basis for any policy change. Its role is as a framework for categorising assumptions about the income distribution consequences of alternative economic policies.

For example, consider point e in Figure 3.2(b) again. Here society is at the (constrained) maximum level of social welfare. A useful way of describing this point is to say that at e the *marginal social utility of income of each individual* (α_j) is the same across all individuals. This expression, α_j, measures society's perception of the last £'s worth of income received by individual j. It is possible to make society feel better off by reshuffling income until this criterion is satisfied. In a sense, this is tautological rather than insightful, but it is a useful device for an economist because it enables him or her to consider separately the issues of efficiency in resource allocation and equity, or fairness, in income distribution.

One way of seeing this is to consider a concept, due to Samuelson (1956), known as lump-sum transfers of income. By continually redistributing income whenever policy changes shift us from e, the policymaker could, in principle, always ensure that society returns to points like e. One way of analysing economic policy is therefore to assume that government in the background is (costlessly) able to carry out such lump-sum transfers so as always to ensure that the α_j (marginal social utilities of income) are equalised across consumers. Then, with problems of distribution taken care of, the economist can design policies entirely on the criterion of efficient resource-allocation. Policy, therefore can concentrate on reaching points above the utility frontier, with lump-sum transfers ensuring that society remains at a tangency with a higher SWF contour. Remember, the adoption of a SWF concept along with the hypothetical device of lump-sum transfers is not justified as a description of reality, but as a device to consider the efficiency aspects of policy separately from the equity aspects.

44

In summary, policy prescriptions can be analysed on either of the two bases:

(i) Examine the necessary conditions for finding a Pareto optimum, on the understanding that it will not be possible to evaluate many possible policy options without making interpersonal utility comparisons. On one view (Robbins, 1935) this is as far as economics as a science can proceed.

(ii) Adopt an explicit social welfare function that does make interpersonal utility comparisons, and with the hypothetical device of lump-sum transfers examine all policy prescriptions for their divergence from the conditions for the unique Pareto optimum designated by the constrained social welfare function's maximum value.

In both cases, the technical conditions for Pareto optimality (i.e. either one of the infinite optima under (i), or the unique optimum under (ii)), are legitimate concerns of economic science.

As standard welfare theory shows, the overall condition for Pareto optimality is then given by the equality between the marginal rate of transformation (MRT) between two commodities determined by the technical conditions of production and the availability of inputs, and the common MRS in consumer preferences:

$$MRT_{ij} = MRS_{ij} \qquad (3.9)$$

for each pair of commodities X_i and X_j.

If the second basis for policy is adopted, the social welfare function permits the construction of a unique set of community or social indifference curves, and the optimality condition (3.9) is represented by the tangency between the economy's production possibility frontier (slope = MRT) between any two commodities, and the highest attainable social indifference curve (slope = common MRS), as shown in Figure 3.3.

This tangency then has the familiar concrete interpretations in terms of pricing rules:

(a) for each commodity, price = marginal (social) cost,

or

(b) for each commodity, the (social) value of the marginal product = factor cost.

In analysing the problems of one particular fuel industry, or the

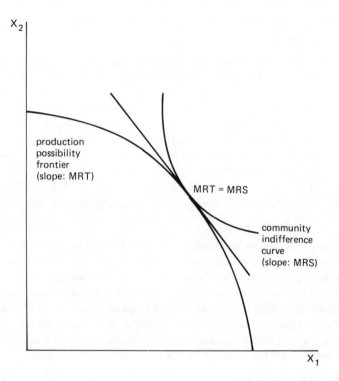

X_2

production
possibility
frontier
(slope: MRT)

MRT = MRS

community
indifference
curve
(slope: MRS)

X_1

Figure 3.3

adoption of one particular fuel supply investment, economists will often want to consider only a partial equilibrium analysis. In this case, conventional cost-benefit analysis often adopts, under policy basis (ii), a very particular form of social welfare function (Crew and Kleindorfer 1979), that has its origins in the old welfare economics of Dupuit and Marshall. This states that social welfare, *ceteris paribus,* is the unweighted sum of aggregate consumer surplus, CS, and the aggregate of total revenues (TR) to producers less total social costs (TC):

$$W = CS + TR - TC \qquad (3.10)$$

This clearly does make interpersonal utility comparisons, in particular using the notion that unweighted money benefits are added up over all those involved in the decision; in other words, it uses the judgement referred to by Samuelson 'a dollar is a dollar is a dollar . . .' regardless of to whom it accrues. However, the necessary conditions for maximising W in (3.10) are the same as those in the rules (a) and (b) above, so this approach is a useful shorthand method for analysing policy on the social welfare function basis (ii), as will be seen below.

Having discussed the objectives of government (a body represented in our model by the taxation authorities and the producers of public sector commodities), we should consider the policy instruments open to them. These are of two kinds: first, the rate of tax on the commodities including work effort in the economy, and on the level of pure profits; and, secondly, the prices of public sector commodities—not counting those excluded from the market. In this model, therefore, gas, electricity and coal prices in the UK, as well as the rates of tax on heating and fuel oil, and motor spirit are all among the instruments of government policy.

We have in this model, the skeleton of a framework for studying the public sector energy industries. We have described the flows of commodities in the economy, the interdependence of aggregate production constraints, individual budget constraints, and the public sector budget constraint, the objectives, and, finally, the instruments of policy-making.

Marginal cost pricing

In this section the marginal cost pricing rule is obtained using the particular social welfare function (3.10) adopted in conventional partial equilibrium cost-benefit analysis.

What we are going to do is treat the decision to charge a price different from marginal cost as if it were a cost-benefit analysis exercise. In Figure 3.4, we have an income-compensated demand curve for commodity X_1. (This may be representative of society's demand curve, or be that of a single individual, since our previous assumptions to remove distributional effects still hold.) Note how we label the compensated demand curve in the figure: X_1^u (p_1; p_2, u) — prices of other commodities, represented here by p_2, and the level of utility along the initial indifference curve are held constant; the amount of the commodity along a given indifference curve is X_1^u, and this depends on p_1. Ignoring the question of who received what amount of resources, the net effect on welfare of lowering price from p_1^0 to equality with marginal cost, MC_1 at

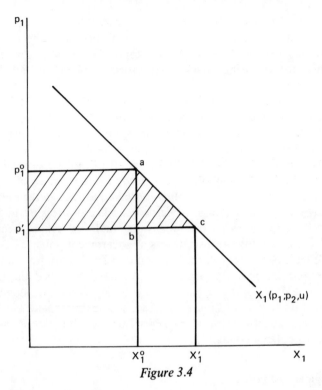

Figure 3.4

p′, is given by the excess of total revenue (TR) over total cost (TC), plus any gain in consumer surplus (CS):

$$\Delta W = \Delta CS + \Delta TR - \Delta TC \qquad (3.11)$$

The gain in consumer surplus is the additional area left of the compensated demand curve that is carved out when price falls (the shaded area in Figure 3.4). Translating (3.11) into prices and quantities produces:

$$\begin{aligned} \Delta W = &\left[p_1^0 X_1^0 - p_1' X_1^0 + \tfrac{1}{2}(p_1^0 - p_1')(X_1' - X_1^0) \right] \\ &+ \left[p_1' X_1' - p_1^0 X_1^0 \right] - \left[p_1' X_1' - p_1' X_1^0 \right] \end{aligned} \qquad (3.12)$$

where the first term in square brackets corresponds to ΔCS, the second to ΔTR, and the third to ΔTC. Cancelling out like terms yields:

$$\Delta W = \tfrac{1}{2}(p_1^0 - p_1')(X_1' - X_1^0) \tag{3.13}$$

the familiar triangle (abc in Figure 3.4) of deadweight welfare loss. Removal of this loss is the net benefit of a move to marginal cost pricing for commodity X_1.

We want to be able to use equation (3.13) in a flexible way to summarise many of the results in the theory of public sector economics. For this reason we shall apply a series of heuristic arguments to it.

The first thing to do is to rewrite (3.13) after multiplying top and bottom by the price change:

$$\Delta W = \tfrac{1}{2}(p_1^0 - p_1') \left[\frac{X_1' - X_1^0}{p_1^0 - p_1'} \right] (p_1^0 - p_1') \tag{3.14}$$

and then to note the following:

(i) $(p_1^0 - p_1') = dp_1 = (p_1 - MC_1)$, where p_1 is the initial price that diverges from marginal cost;

(ii) $\dfrac{(X_1' - X_1^0)}{(p_1^0 - p_1')} = \dfrac{\delta X_1^u}{\delta p_1}$, the inverse of the slope of the compensated demand curve, i.e. its slope with respect to the price axis.

With these definitions, (18) becomes:

$$\Delta W = \tfrac{1}{2}(p_1 - MC_1)\frac{\delta X_1^u}{\delta p_1}dp_1 \tag{3.15}$$

Since $(\delta X_1^u/\delta p_1)$ is the inverted slope of the compensated demand curve, we can give it its proper name: the *Hicks–Slutsky substitution effect,* and (3.15) says that the welfare loss depends on the size of the divergence of price from marginal cost weighted by the substitution effect (which, of course, is taken to be *negative*). Consequently, welfare can be improved until $\Delta W = 0$ by setting price equal to marginal cost for commodity X_1. The conclusion appears to apply only to this commodity, because we have used a partial equilibrium approach based on consumer surplus, rather than the general equilibrium approach adopted earlier.

Let us now try to widen the applicability of the argument summarised by the formula in equation (3.15). Let us suppose there are many goods for which price diverges from marginal cost. Suppose that one of these, say X_k, has a price p_k that is under the control of the government—it is one of the government's policy instruments. When demands are interdependent this price, p_k, will affect all commodities through the cross-price substitution effects:

$$\frac{\delta X_i^u}{\delta p_k}, i = 1 \ldots n$$

By analogy with the argument behind (3.15) we could say that the optimum policy should be to change p_k until the change in welfare that results is zero:

$$\frac{dW}{dp_k} = \sum_i (p_i - MC_i)\frac{\delta X_i^u}{\delta p_k} = 0 \qquad i = 1 \ldots n \qquad (3.16)$$

(Note we have divided both sides by $\frac{1}{2}$ to simplify the formula.) The substitution effect weighted sum of all the price–marginal cost divergences should be zero in order to minimise the total deadweight welfare loss. Clearly a condition that will ensure satisfaction of equation (3.16) is that $p_i = MC_i$ for each $i = 1 \ldots n$; i.e. marginal cost pricing for every commodity.

In summary, we have looked at both general and partial equilibrium arguments for marginal cost pricing. We have made a series of restrictive assumptions in order to achieve the standard rule for efficient resource allocation: set price equal to marginal cost everywhere. Finally we have, in equation (3.16), a measure of the welfare losses from non-marginal cost pricing over a range of commodities.

Second-best pricing in the public sector

Attitudes to the problem of second-best have fluctuated widely amongst economists since the celebrated paper of Lipsey and Lancaster (1956). They had observed that when further constraints (i.e. other than the aggregate production constraint) and especially including constraints on the ability to set price equal to marginal cost *everywhere* were imposed on the objective of welfare maximisation, the standard rule of marginal cost pricing was no longer optimal for any commodity in the economy. Indeed, a policy of piecemeal marginal cost pricing in the public sector, when the private sector did not practise marginal cost pricing, could bring us further from an optimal allocation of resources than the policy of doing nothing at all. Lipsey and Lancaster's general conclusion was that nothing at all could be known about the necessary conditions for optimal resource allocation when constraints on the ability to price at marginal cost everywhere, in addition to the aggregate production constraint, were imposed on policy-makers.

It turns out that the marginal cost pricing rule had become enshrined as the only conceivable policy, and it is arguable that economists over-reacted to the rather obvious conclusion that new policy constraints required new policy rules. Two approaches finally developed to the problem of second-best. On the one hand, economists faced up to the new problem of maximising welfare subject to an aggregate production constraint *and* institutional constraints modelling the real world, and discovered that quite a lot could be said about the appropriate policies, at least in theory. On the other hand, economists also searched for situations and conditions in which the necessary conditions for a first-best problem would do, at least approximately, as the necessary conditions for a second-best problem.

For the moment, we shall concentrate on looking at the theoretical principles behind second-best policies. It is often argued that there is no general underlying principle to the collection of second-best policies discussed by economists—that each is a different response to different, quite separate assumptions about the nature of the policy-maker's problem. This view can be rejected, however, when we examine the nature of the problem of second-best. Consider the following statement of the policy-maker's dilemma:

> maximise economic welfare subject to (i) the technological constraints of the economy to produce commodities, and (ii) the social or institutional limits on the choice of policy instruments.

This is a perfectly comprehensive economic problem, with, in principle, a set of feasible solutions. It is the problem of second-best. The first-best economic problem is then simply the special case that arises when the constraints in (ii) are not effective. We can discuss the general principles of solution to both problems just as easily.

Put in this way, we can see second-best analysis is amenable to solution, with different policies emerging according to the nature of the constraints in (ii).

Among the first to tackle the second-best problem in this way were Green (1961) and later Rees (1968). Since then the subject has expanded enormously, and we can especially mention the work of Diamond and Mirrlees (1971), Mohring (1970) and Feldstein (1972). Baumol and Bradford (1970) established that some of the fundamental ideas had in fact a long tradition pre-dating Lipsey and Lancaster, and including Ramsey (1927) and Boiteux (1956). Green (1975) and Atkinson and Stiglitz (1980) tie together many of the strands.

For most of this section we shall make use of equation (3.16) which showed universal marginal cost pricing (at social, resource or shadow marginal costs) to be the policy rule that minimised welfare losses as measured by Hicksian consumer surplus. We derived that rule by ignoring the social and institutional limits or constraints on policy-makers in choosing policy instruments. It is time to take stock of these constraints and three categories can usefully be named.

1. The prevalence of imperfectly competitive markets so that the private-sector producers can generally be assumed to set price above marginal cost.
2. The necessity of imposing a public sector budget restraint (PSBR) which may lead governments to set excise taxes on commodities which drive a wedge between the price paid by the consumer and marginal cost facing the producer. These taxes include the income tax on work effort which drives a wedge between the MRS of labour input for the output of other commodities, and the MRT between labour input and other commodity outputs. We saw in the second section that the PSBR must be satisfied if there is no public sector borrowing, and aggregate production and budget restraints are to be satisfied.
3. The infeasibility of making lump-sum transfers of income so that at whatever allocation of resources we choose, the marginal social utility of income is the same for every individual; i.e. that a maximum of the social welfare function can be maintained by 'redistribution in the background'. If these transfers are infeasible, and we cannot assume that everybody's marginal social utility of income is unity, then equity or distribution considerations must enter into the details of pricing policy to be traded off against efficiency considerations.

52

We shall take the constraints 1, 2 and 3 in turn, and begin with the analysis of price–marginal cost divergences arising elsewhere in the economy. In other words, we ask how robust is the rule to price at marginal cost in one area of the public sector if other areas of the public or private sector are not pricing at marginal cost.

We shall make use of the fundamental equation (3.16): price–marginal cost divergences must sum to zero when the social welfare function is maximised as a result of pricing policy. The weights are the Hicks–Slutsky substitution effects. To make (3.16) applicable to both public and private sectors, return to our earlier notation in which public sector outputs were lavelled $Z_1, \ldots, Z_m$, and private sector outputs: $X_1, \ldots, X_n$. Income-compensated Hicks–Slutsky substitution effects are labelled with a u superscript to emphasise that each consumer is held on his or her initial indifference curve. Now assume that Z_k is the only commodity whose price can be an instrument of economic policy. All other public and private sector prices are given. It is as if, for example, the government seeks the best allocation of resources simply by manipulating the price of electricity, and relies on cross-price substitution effects to do the rest of the work. With these qualifications (3.16) can be written:

$$(p_k - MC_k)\frac{\delta Z_k^u}{\delta p_k} + \sum_{i \neq k} (p_i - MC_i)\frac{\delta Z_i^u}{\delta p_k} + \sum_j (p_j - MC_j)\frac{\delta X_j^u}{\delta p_k} = 0$$
(3.17)

i.e.:

$$p_k = MC_k - \sum_{i \neq k} a_i(p_i MC_i) - \sum_j a_j(p_j - MC_j)$$
(3.18)

Equation (3.18) says that the optimal price for Z_k is marginal cost, MC_k, corrected for the weighted sum of price–marginal cost divergences elsewhere in the economy. The weights are the *relative* substitution effects, i.e. the cross-price substitution effect divided by the own price substitution effect for Z_k:

$$a_i = \left[\frac{\delta Z_i^u}{\delta p_k} \div \frac{\delta Z_k^u}{\delta p_k} \right] \quad i = 1 \ldots m, i \neq k$$
(3.19)

$$a_j = \left[\frac{\delta X_j^u}{\delta p_k} \div \frac{\delta Z_k^u}{\delta p_k} \right] \quad j = 1 \ldots n$$
(3.20)

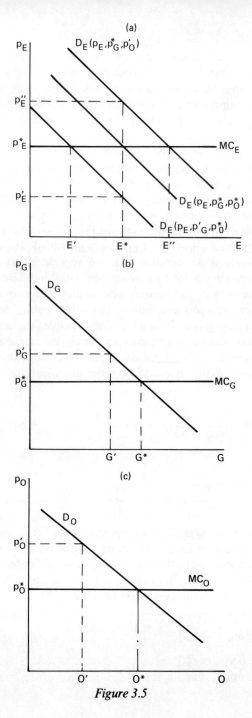

Figure 3.5

We can clarify this idea with the aid of Figure 3.5. Imagine only three commodities: electricity (E), whose price is the policy instrument, electricity using consumer goods (G), and oil (O). Both G and O are produced in the private sector, but the same analysis arises if they are produced in the public sector but their prices are not policy instruments.

In the three parts of Figure 3.5 we have the compensated demand curves D_E, D_G and D_O, respectively and the corresponding marginal cost curves. From equations (3.17) or (3.18) we know that, in the absence of second-best constraints, marginal cost pricing is socially optimal, and hence ideally we look for prices P_E^*, P_G^* and P_O^* with corresponding outputs of E*, G* and O*. In particular note that in Figure 3.5(a) we allow the electricity demand curve to be responsive to changes in the price of G and O: P_G, P_O. In the first-best situation $D_E(P_E, P_G^* P_O^*)$ is the appropriate electricity demand curve.

Now suppose that both oil and electrical goods are supplied in conditions of imperfect competition so that, in fact, their prices exceed marginal cost at P_G' and P_O'. Clearly consumption of these commodities, at G' and O', is below the socially optimal levels of G* and O*. The question is: should the publicly-owned electricity authorities still aim for a price of P_E^* at marginal cost? The answer is negative when allowance is made for the interdependence of electricity demand with other commodities. Suppose the price of oil could be held at P_O^*, and only the price of electrical goods diverges from marginal cost. The appropriate compensated demand curve for electricity takes account of this and is $D_E(P_E, P_G', P_O^*)$. Pricing at P_E^* on *this* demand curve results in consumption of E' well below the first-best optimum level. The reason D_E has shifted is that we can assume electricity demand is complementary with consumption of electrical goods, so that the rise in P_G above MC shifts the electricity demand curve down to the left. To move back towards the first-best optimum level level of electricity consumption, E*, necessitates dropping the price of electricity towards P_E', below marginal cost.

In equation (3.17) the weight attached to the price–marginal cost divergence in the electrical goods market, call it a_G, is *positive:*

$$a_G > 0$$

and this reflects the joint impact of the negative cross-substitution effect from electrical goods price to electricity, arising from complementarity, and the negative own price substitution effect in electricity shown by the negative slope of the compensated demand curve.

Applying equation (3.17) and ignoring all other factors:

$$P_E = MC_E - a_G(P_G - MC_G); a_G > O \qquad (3.21)$$

We can now repeat the analysis for the oil price–marginal cost divergence. Suppose now that oil (e.g. fuel oil for central heating systems) is a substitute for electricity. The appropriate compensated demand curve for electricity in the presence of oil prices above marginal cost at P_O' is $D_E(P_E, P_G^*, P_O')$. At P_E^*, electricity consumption is above the socially optimal first-best level, and to remedy this, the price of electricity needs to rise to P_E''. The appropriate weighting factor, a_0, in the equation is *negative* reflecting the substitutability between oil and electricity, as well as the negativity of the electricity demand curve:

$$P_E = MC_E - a_0(P_0 - MC_0); a_0 < 0 \qquad (3.22)$$

Equations (3.21) and (3.22) combine to produce the general result shown in equation (3.18) itself.

In practical terms the lesson for pricing policy in energy industries is that it is essential to gather information on the demand interdependences amongst complementary and substitute goods. Pricing policy cannot ignore developments in other markets.

We consider now one special case of the above analysis. The basic idea was the necessity of allowing for the interrelationships among price and marginal cost divergences. It may sometimes be the case, however, that a policy-maker in a nationalised energy industry is under a constraint to simplify price structures.

Consider again equation (3.16), and suppose that the only commodities in question are the different outputs of a single public energy industry. Obvious examples are the monthly consumption patterns of the gas industry, or the daily and seasonal consumption patterns of the electricity industry. Z_k is now the output of the industry at time period k, p_k and MC_k are the price charged and marginal cost appropriate to time period k. Equation (3.16) can then be analysed under the constraint that, for example, the same price, p, must operate in every time-period:

$$\sum_i (p - MC_k) \frac{\delta Z_i^U}{\delta p_k} = 0 \qquad i = 1 \dots m \qquad (3.23)$$

56

and solving for p we find it is a weighted average of all the marginal costs involved in a cycle of time-periods:

$$p = \Sigma \, b_i MC_i \qquad (3.24)$$

where the weights are the proportionate cross substitution effects:

$$b_i = \frac{\delta Z_i^u / \delta p_k}{\sum_j \delta Z_j^u / \delta p_k} \qquad i = 1 \ldots m \qquad (3.25)$$

The problem of uniformity or simplicity in tariff structures is worth considering carefully because it brings out many of the issues that the energy supply industries face in practice. We shall apply the analysis of our equations to two simple but prevalent cases and, in doing so, look carefully at three separate issues:

(a)   the reasons given for simplified price structures;
(b)   the welfare losses involved in the second-best optimum; and
(c)   the size and direction of the inevitable cross-subsidisation effects that result.

In the context of point (c) it is worth remembering that many nationalised and regulated utilities are urged to use simple price structures but also to avoid cross-subsidisation: two objectives which are generally incompatible.

To give the analysis some concrete basis we consider two plausible problems. First, imagine a gas or electricity authority subject to fluctuating demand between winter and summer periods. While we investigate the first-best analysis of this in some detail subsequently, we simply assume for the moment that the authority is restricted to charging the same price in both periods. As a second example, imagine again a gas or electricity authority considering the extension of its urban supply network to rural customers, but restricted to charging the same price per unit to both groups, as in Turvey (1968, p. 97). Figure 3.6 outlines the basic arguments.

In Figure 3.6(a) we illustrate the compensated demand schedules for winter and summer fuel demand (D_w and D_s) with their respective marginal costs, MC_w and MC_s. (MC_w is higher because older,

57

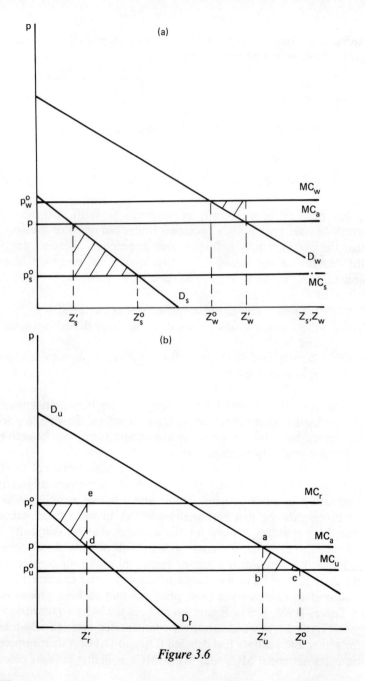

Figure 3.6

less efficient plant and equipment is in use in winter in addition to the up-to-date efficient plant used in summer.)

In Figure 3.6(b) we have the compensated demand schedules for urban and rural consumers (D_u and D_r) with their respective marginal costs, MC_u and MC_r. While $D_r < D_u$ at all prices, $MC_r > MC_u$ because of the extra capacity costs involved in distributing gas or electricity over the wider rural network.

First-best consumption clearly requires price equal to marginal cost, i.e. Z_W^0 and Z_S^0 for winter and summer supplies, while in the rural–urban case, urban consumption is Z_u^0 but there is no supply to rural areas at all.

Consider the motivation for departing from marginal costs. In the periodic winter–summer case it might be that separate metering of the two demands is impossible or unreliable, or that the authority does not believe consumers will understand the difference in prices. In the rural–urban case, it might be that drawing a rural–urban boundary is too arbitrary, or that the authority believes rural consumers 'deserve' to be connected to the gas or electricity network, and charged the same price as urban dwellers.

We already know how to calculate the weighted average of marginal costs according to equations (3.24) and (3.25), and this second-best uniform price is labelled MC_a in both parts of the figure. First, we clarify the impact on the authority's finances. In the first-best case with price set equal to constant marginal (and, hence, average) costs, the authority breaks even. To concentrate on welfare losses alone, we have deliberately chosen demand curve slopes in Figure 3.6 so that the authority continues to break even after uniform pricing is introduced, i.e. the profits raised by charging above marginal cost for either Z_W or Z_u are constructed to match exactly the financial losses incurred by charging below marginal cost for Z_S or Z_r. This is particularly important in the case of Z_r, as we shall see.

Ignoring cross-effects for diagrammatic convenience, the welfare losses are given by applying equation (3.13) above, as:

(a) $\frac{1}{2} (p_S^0 - p)(Z_S^0 - Z_S') + \frac{1}{2}(p_W^0 - p)(Z_W^0 - Z_W')$

and

(b) $\frac{1}{2} (p_u^0 - p)(Z_u^0 - Z_u') + \frac{1}{2}(p_r^0 - p)(Z_r^0 - Z_r')$,

or, in general, half the price change times the consumption change for each commodity whose price has changed. For commodities whose price has risen, (a) summer fuel and (b) urban consumption, the loss is in the form of reduced consumer surplus in excess of the rise in the difference between revenue and costs—the first term in each expression. For the commodities whose price has fallen, (a) winter fuel and (b) rural consumption, the welfare loss is the excess of the difference between costs and revenues over the rise in consumer surplus—the second term in each expression.

Thus, the second-best case of uniform rather than marginal cost-based pricing creates avoidable welfare losses illustrated by the shaded areas in each part of Figure 3.6.

Consider the winter–summer case first. To avoid the costs and difficulties of additional metering, the authority incurs welfare losses by departing from marginal costs in pricing. The practical consequence for society now appears as a need to increase supply capacity to Z_w'. (Obviously this capacity can more than cope with the off-peak consumption level of Z_s'.) This additional capacity ($Z_w' - Z_w^0$) would not be needed if consumers were encouraged to reduce peak (winter) and expand off-peak (summer) consumption by marginal cost pricing. The cross-subsidisation that arises is from one period to another, but since there is no reason to assume in general that winter consumers are different people from summer consumers, there is not generally a transfer of resources from one group of people to another.

Turning to the rural–urban case, the consequence is that rural consumers are now connected to the distribution network instead of having zero consumption, although total consumption at ($Z_u' + Z_r'$) may have risen only marginally, if at all. There has however been a clear transfer of income. In addition to their suffering welfare losses, the profits made from urban consumers are used to pay for the construction of the rural supply network. Here the cross-subsidisation actually transfers income from one group in society to another. As Turvey puts it, society is willing to incur welfare losses (the shaded areas), and to transfer resources in order to provide rural consumers with the consumer surplus arising from consuming Z_r' units rather than doing without the commodity altogether.

Let us check the quantities involved in the rural–urban case. The welfare losses from departing from marginal cost pricing amount to the sum of the triangles (abc) and (p_r^0de). Profits of ($pabp_u^0$) are made on urban supply and these are used to offset the losses involved in extending the supply network with rural areas, $(p_r^0 e dp)$. This transfer of income from urban consumers is received by rural consumers in the form of fuel supplies of Z_r' on which their consumer surplus amounts to $(p_r^0 dp)$.

These two little examples bring out several important points. First, second-best pricing will always give rise to welfare losses absent from marginal cost pricing. Secondly, cross-subsidisation generally transfers income from one group in society to another. Thirdly, since cross-subsidisation redistributes income, the arguments for it will always be based on equity rather than efficiency considerations. The rural–urban case in which rural consumers are felt to have a higher marginal social utility of income than urban-dwellers is a typical example.

We turn now to consider the importance of a public sector budget restraint (PSBR) for optimal pricing policy. In this section we consider an absolute measure of PSBR, leaving to subsequent discussions some of the finer details of regulations and rates of return.

The framework for the analysis is identical to that used earlier. There are several public sector industries with outputs $Z_1 \ldots Z_m$ whose prices can be raised above marginal cost in order to yield a fixed surplus to the government. We saw initially (in equation (3.5)) that such a surplus will be determined exactly by the aggregate production and budget restraints in the event that government borrowing cannot be used to meet the costs of public production. The analysis is similar to that which arises when a system of optimal excise taxes is being designed, and again the objective is to minimise the welfare losses involved when prices are not set equal to marginal costs. As in our analysis of uniform pricing, the procedure involves trading off the consumer surplus changes arising from the constraint and the departure from marginal cost pricing.

Equation (3.16) is no longer the appropriate criterion because it does not recognise the constraint that public sector net revenues must sum to a given number:

$$\sum_i p_i Z_i - \sum_i C^i(Z_i) = R \qquad (3.26)$$

where $C^i(Z^i)$ is the total cost associated with output of public sector commodity Z_i.

To get a clear idea of the important problems to be considered here, imagine the following hypothetical but nevertheless plausible

61

circumstances. The Treasury informs the chairmen of the nationalised industries that their public corporations must collectively achieve a surplus of £y billion in real terms in the coming year. The chairmen are offered two conflicting sets of advice: (a) to raise all public sector prices by the same percentage ($\Delta p_k / p_k$); or (b) to raise prices differentially, but so as to reduce all public sector outputs by the same percentage ($\Delta Z_k / Z_k$). The dilemma is to choose the policy that least distorts the efficient allocation of resources, i.e. minimises the loss of consumer surplus resulting from raising prices above marginal cost.

Consider the following arguments developed by E. J. Mishan (1981). Prior to the price changes we shall assume that inputs are paid the value of their marginal product both in the public and private sector. Recall that this is the rule for the efficient allocation of resources in the absence of second-best constraints. Mishan points out that, to seek an efficient allocation of resources in the public sector, we should seek to maintain this rule. If we are able to assume that, after the price rises, no inputs whatsoever shift out of the public sector, then we can maintain the relative shares of factors in the public sector simply by a common percentage rise in all public sector prices ($\Delta p_k / p_k = \theta$, $k = 1 \ldots m$). This way, the values of the marginal products rise in the same proportion and no 'reshuffling' of inputs takes place in the public sector. The advice of case (a) is then correct.

The assumption of fixed input supplies in the face of relative price changes in the public sector *vis-à-vis* the private sector is however unrealistic. More likely, rises in public sector prices cause a shift of demand to private sector commodities, so that the consumers may escape the price rises, and a consequent movement of inputs out of the public sector and into the private sector. Generally the shift of inputs will reflect the different demand elasticities of goods in both sectors. If we are to maintain the relative input shares in the public sector associated with the pre-price rise situation, then differential price rises that are designed to reduce each public sector output by the same proportion might do the trick. Hence, in this more realistic case, policy advice (b) is appropriate.

The general rule therefore is that when seeking to meet a PSBR requirement, the second-best optimum allocation of resources requires equi-proportionate reductions of consumption along the (compensated) demand schedule for all public sector commodities:

$$\frac{\Delta Z_k}{Z_k} = 0, k = 1 \ldots m \tag{3.27}$$

The rule is illustrated in Figure 3.7.

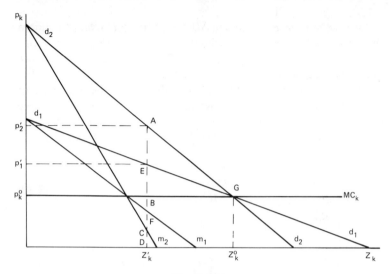

Figure 3.7

In Figure 3.7, d_1d_1 and d_2d_2 are the income-compensated Hicksian demand schedules for two public sector outputs Z_k, $k = 1, 2$. They are assumed to have the same marginal cost, MC_k, and by construction the demand schedules intersect at the point where they cross the MC_k line. Optimum output of both is, therefore, Z_k^0 at price $p_k^0 = MC_k$.

Let us now reduce Z_k^0 by ΔZ_k; by construction both outputs are reduced to Z_k' in order to fulfil the requirement to reduce each by the same proportion. The price that must be charged for Z_1 to achieve this is p_1' while the required price for Z_2 is p_2'. We must now convince ourselves that, subject to meeting the financial surplus requirement of the nationalised industries, consumers would not prefer another price structure. To facilitate this, the marginal revenue curves d_1m_1 and d_2m_2 are also constructed for each industry. Now, the new output of each, Z_k', ensures that the following equality holds by geometric construction:

63

$$\frac{AB}{CD - BD} = \frac{EB}{FD - BD} \qquad (3.28)$$

$$\text{ie.} \frac{AB}{BC} = \frac{EB}{FB} \qquad (3.29)$$

The numerator expressions, AB and EB, measure the required distortion of price from marginal cost ($p_2' - MC_k$ and $p_1' - MC_k$). The denominator expressions in (3.28) measure the difference between marginal revenue and marginal cost for each commodity ($MR_k - MC_k$), i.e. the marginal contribution to the public sector industry's profit, or financial surplus. In other words, by reducing output in the same proportion, θ, we have ensured that the *marginal loss of consumer surplus relative to the marginal contribution to profit* is the same for both industries:

$$\frac{p_1 - MC_k}{MR_1 - MC_k} = \frac{p_2 - MC_k}{MR_2 - MC_k} \qquad (3.30)$$

and with the requirement of meeting the PSBR, consumers cannot achieve a lower loss of consumer surplus by a different price structure. The reader can check the alternative policy advice (a) above by, for example, assuming both Z_1 and Z_2 are priced at p_1' which is the same percentage rise in price above marginal cost for both commodities. It can easily be seen from Figure 3.7 that (3.30) no longer holds, and that by raising the price of Z_2 towards p_2', the marginal loss of consumer surplus relative to marginal profit for Z_2 falls (while, of course, that for Z_1 remains unchanged).

The arguments we have used here turn on the importance of the denominator expression in (3.30) as well as the numerator. This reflects the fact that meeting the PSBR is now a binding constraint on the public sector's attempts to achieve the goal of efficient resource allocation.

We now want to try to generalise (3.27) or (3.30) to a form analogous to our earlier fundamental equation (3.16). If we begin with (3.30), we can derive a useful rule-of-thumb for the policy-maker in a nationalised industry. Write the common ratio of marginal loss of consumer surplus to marginal profit as μ:

$$\frac{p_k - MC_k}{MR_k - MC_k} = \mu, k = 1 \ldots m \qquad (3.31)$$

and using the well-known result relating marginal revenue to price and the elasticity of demand; i.e.:

$$MR = p(1 - \frac{1}{e})$$

(3.31) can be rearranged to yield:

$$\frac{p_k - MC_k}{p_k} = (\frac{-\mu}{1-\mu})\frac{1}{e_k} \tag{3.32}$$

which says that each commodity must be raised in price above marginal cost by a percentage that varies inversely with the elasticity of demand: the greater the elasticity of demand, the lower is the optimum percentage rise in price over marginal cost to yield a financial surplus for the nationalised industries. We should be careful to note that such an elasticity must be derived from the compensated demand schedule incorporating Hicks–Slutsky substitution effects only, and not including income effects, since all of our consumer surplus analysis has been related to the compensated demand schedule.

However, we can obtain a more general result if we work with (3.27) instead:

$$\frac{\Delta Z_k}{Z_k} = \theta, k = 1 \ldots m.$$

Referring again to Figure 3.7 and measuring ΔZ_k by the distance BG, we can see immediately that for both demand curves:

$$BG = \Delta Z_k = (p_k' - MC_k) \div (\text{slope of } d_k d_k), k = 1,2 \tag{3.33}$$

Remembering that the slope of each income-compensated demand curve with respect to the horizontal axis is just the inverse of the Hicks–Slutsky substitution effect allows us to write (3.33) as:

$$\frac{\Delta Z_k}{Z_k} = \theta = \frac{(p_k - MC_k)\frac{\delta Z^u_k}{\delta p_k}}{Z_k} \qquad k = 1 \ldots m \tag{3.34}$$

The one factor absent from our diagrammatic analysis is the cross-price influence of distortions elsewhere in the public sector. These are impossible to show clearly on Figure 3.6. However, when we reflect on the fact that price rises in other parts of the public sector will shift the position of the compensated demand schedule for Z_k, we can see that (3.34) must be extended to allow for the sum of all cross-price as well as own price effects. The object is still equiproportionate decreases in consumption but, allowing for full cross-price effects, the rule must be:

$$\frac{\Delta Z_k}{Z_k} = \theta = \frac{\sum_{i=1}^{m} (p_i - MC_i) \dfrac{\delta Z_k^u}{\delta p_i}}{Z_k} \qquad k = 1 \ldots m \qquad (3.36)$$

This is a very celebrated result in the literature of 'new public economics', and has been discovered independently by, among other economists, F. P. Ramsey, M. Boiteux, Paul Samuelson, P. Diamond and J. Mirrlees. (For a history of this idea the reader is referred to Baumol and Bradford (1970).)

All of our analysis to the present point has maintained a separation between considerations of economic efficiency and considerations of the equity of the resulting outcomes. If you recall, we were able to maintain this separation by using either one of two assumptions: (i) that the social marginal utility of income of every individual is unity ('a dollar is a dollar is a dollar . . .'); or (ii) that the government was, in the background, carrying out, costlessly, lump-sum transfers of income among individuals in order to achieve a given distribution of welfare after every price change.

We suppose now that neither assumption is valid. This means that the policy-maker does differentiate amongst individuals according to the different social marginal utility of income of each of them, but that the device, or set of policy instruments, comprising income transfers is infeasible. This leads to the conclusion, forcibly argued by de Graaf (1957) that discriminatory pricing policy may be the ideal, or indeed only, means of achieving both efficiency and equity objectives simultaneously.

We shall examine this in the context of a public sector attempting to achieve an overall financial surplus or PSBR requirement that we discussed above. We already know that we must expect prices that rise above marginal cost by different percentages in the search for a second-best optimum. There now arises the possibility that in seeking, say, a 10 per cent mark-up on electricity prices, or 20 per cent mark-up on gas prices we might wish to allow for the fact that the two commodities take up different proportions of the budgets of the rich *vis-à-vis* the poor. Since we have already ruled out the possibility of lump-sum redistribution, we now may wish to allow for these mark-ups to be determined partly by the consumption patterns of each public sector commodity across different social classes and income groups.

The implication of using this idea is that the optimal policy when meeting a PSBR changes in a simple but far-reaching manner. We can express the result either in terms of the required percentage reduction in consumption across the public sector or in terms of the required rise in price above marginal cost.

Taking the quantity change first, policy now requires price changes designed to ensure:

$$\frac{\Delta Z_k}{Z_k} = (R_k - 1), \qquad k = 1 \dots m \tag{3.37}$$

i.e. a different percentage change in consumption for each good, rather than the same percentage change across all goods. The parameter that gives rise to this variation is the 'distribution characteristic', R_k, and this arises from aggregating the consumption of different individuals in a very special manner:

$$R_k = \frac{\sum_{j=1}^{J} \alpha_j Z_{jk}}{Z_k} \tag{3.38}$$

Here the individual's consumption Z_{jk} is weighted by his or her *net marginal social utility of income, as a proportion of the shadow price of funds to the government,* α_j. (The word 'net' appears to reflect the fact that the income effects of price changes must be subtracted from our earlier notion of marginal social utility of income before the calculation can be made.) In other words, before determining the required reduction in consumption, we must decide how socially deserving are the persons who predominantly consume the good in question. If a commodity is proportionately more largely consumed by those to whom society wishes to redistribute income, then that commodity should not be reduced in consumption as much as one predominantly consumed by those whom society regards as less deserving. We can clarify this rather complex notion in a moment, but let us first check, in Figure 3.8, the diagrammatic illustration of the idea and its influence on pricing policy.

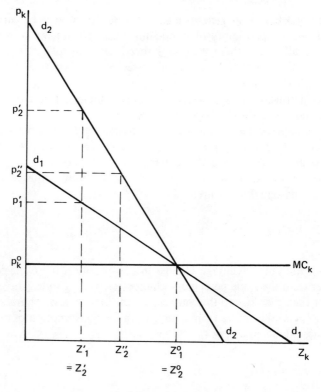

Figure 3.8

Figure 3.8 repeats some of the construction of Figure 3.7. It illustrates compensated demand schedules for two public sector commodities, Z_k, $k = 1,2$, which have the same marginal cost, MC_k. First-best optimal consumption, as before, is at $Z_1^0 = Z_2^0$ at price $p_1^0 = p_2^0 = MC_k$. In the presence of a PSBR requirement, both commodities are identically reduced in consumption to Z_1' $= Z_2'$ by the differential mark-up of price over marginal cost, $(p_1'$ $- MC_k)$ and $(p_2' - MC_k)$.

Now let us suppose that commodity Z_2 has a consumption pattern that means that larger than average amounts of it are consumed by people with high marginal social utility of income (the poor or pensioners, for example). An illustrative good is domestic electricity for space heating. There is some evidence that the less well off, including pensioners, rely more on electricity for space heating than do the better-off groups in society who can obtain the capital resources to instal gas-fired central heating. We would then say that:

$$R_2 > R_1$$

i.e. the distribution characteristic of Z_2 exceeds that of Z_1.

Now note that equation (3.37) can be written:

$$\frac{Z_k^* - Z_k^0}{Z_k^0} = (R_k - 1) \qquad k = 1,2$$

where Z_k^* is the new optimal reduced consumption of Z_k taking equity and efficiency factors into account, and Z_k^0 is the initial level of consumption. Simplifying we have:

$$\frac{Z_k^*}{Z_k^0} = R_k \qquad k = 1,2 \tag{3.39}$$

so that the new optimal consumption as a proportion of the initial level is given by the commodity's distributional characteristic. Now, since we assumed $R_2 > R_1$, we have:

$$\frac{Z_2^*}{Z_2^0} > \frac{Z_1^*}{Z_1^0} \tag{3.40}$$

i.e. the reduction in consumption of the good with the higher distribution characteristic must be proportionately less than for the good with the lower distribution characteristic.

In Figure 3.8, therefore, where $Z_1^0 = Z_2^0$, if Z_1' is still the optimal consumption of Z_1, the optimal consumption of Z_2 must be at a point such as Z_2'' showing a lower reduction for the commodity consumed by the more deserving.

The implication for pricing policy follows immediately. When we imposed a PSBR and looked only for the efficient second-best allocation we adopted a price differential of $(p_2' - p_1')$ reflecting the lower compensated elasticity of $d_2 d_2$. Now, the equity factor must be traded off against this efficiency result, and we have an optimal price differential $(p_2'' - p_1')$ that is smaller. In fact the pricing policy follows directly from (3.37) as:

$$\frac{\Delta p_k}{p_k} = \frac{1 - R_k}{e_k} \qquad k = 1, \ldots, m \tag{3.41}$$

where e_k is the compensated elasticity of demand.

69

Now, just as we did in generalising equation (3.27) to allow for cross-price effects in (3.36), we can generalise (3.37) to allow for cross-price effects by equation (3.42):

$$\frac{\Delta Z_k}{Z_k} = \sum_i (p_i - MC_i) \sum_j \frac{\delta Z_{jk}^u}{\delta p_i} = \frac{\sum_j a_j Z_{jk}}{Z_k} - 1 \qquad (3.42)$$

(Note how (3.42) contains an expression for the sum over all people, $j = 1 \ldots J$, of each person's individual own and cross price substitution effects.)

Conclusion

The object of this chapter has been to bring out the broad approach of second-best theory to public sector pricing. In practice, marginal cost pricing will be the usual starting point of the analysis, with second-best amendments made when a particular type of constraint (equity considerations, PSBR, etc.) seems to be most pressing; in effect the piecemeal approach first criticised by Lipsey and Lancaster (1956).

Nevertheless, the relationship between price and marginal cost is fundamental to policy evaluation, and for this reason a detailed consideration of how marginal costs are to be measured in practice is essential.

4

Marginal costs in practice

The chapter on pricing problems deliberately took a simple, clearcut definition of marginal cost as the derivative of a static long-run total cost function. This allowed us to handle easily a great many welfare analysis constraints in the problem of second-best. It emphasised, in short, the demand side of pricing policy. We turn now to analyse the problem of measuring marginal cost in fuel and energy supplies, forgetting for the moment the intricacies of second-best constraints. Whenever we want to bring in the demand side we shall continue to measure net benefits by the area left of the Hicksian income-compensated demand schedules.

The principal objective of this chapter is to provide the reader with an introduction to the ideas that arise when the economist's concept of marginal cost is confronted with the planner's models of fuel supply technology. We shall find ourselves going far beyond elementary notions of marginal cost defined as the additional expenditure on inputs required when output is expanded by some small amount. We shall want to confront the main areas of economic importance in planning and costing fuel supply.

In the first section to follow, the fundamental ideas of marginal cost are described. Most important among these is the fact that marginal cost is derived from minimising the overall costs of meeting a specified output target. This link between optimisation and the measurement of marginal cost is one that needs to be stressed again and again. Too often it is naively assumed that marginal cost can be measured by looking at past data on a producer's costs. This is quite wrong. Marginal cost is part of the information discovered by trying to find the least expensive way of meeting some future change in output.

These ideas are described in a model familiar to most students of economics in which capital, i.e. plant and equipment, is malleable. It can be reshaped to accommodate different quantities and qualities of other inputs such as labour services, energy and raw materials, and to make use of technological innovation. This is not a model that is familiar to engineers working in the energy field, nor is it one that captures much of the realistic features of problems like when to scrap or retire plant and invest in new equipment. Since such problems are fundamental to important energy policy decisions like the choice between nuclear and alternative energy sources, it is essential that we carry over the ideas of marginal cost to a more realistic model.

To do this, we subsequently adopt a view of technology called the clay–clay concept. This means that on the designer's drawing board plant and equipment can be reshaped, but once installed, its design, operating characteristics and requirements of other factors are essentially fixed. To incorporate new technological features into the stock of capital and equipment, we need new machines in which to embody the technical changes.

Short-run versus long-run marginal cost

A utility supplying a fuel to final consumers or other manufacturers will combine input such as capital, labour, energy and raw materials in the least expensive way consistent with meeting its output targets.

In the highly capital-intensive nature of fuel supply, plant and equipment are the most critical and also the least variable source of input costs. The conventional economic model measures this by constructing short-run marginal cost (SRMC) and long-run marginal cost (LRMC) curves plotted against the output level.

Along the LRMC curve, all inputs including the scale of plant and equipment are free to vary. But at each level of output there is a particular combination of the inputs that ensures total costs are as low as possible. The plant and equipment, corresponding to each level of output, which contribute to this cost minimum are the optimal or efficient scale of capital for that output level. If, in the short run, this plant level is fixed, then the cost of expanding output must be measured along the particular SRMC curve cutting through LRMC at the given level of output, as shown in Figure 4.1.

It will always be the case that expanding along SRMC is more costly than expanding along LRMC. This is so because as soon as output rises above the level for which the given plant and equipment minimised costs, then it must be true that a bigger level of plant and equipment is needed. This is not available and the output increment must be met by working the existing level of plant and equipment more intensively. Hence, the conventional cost model of the firm has each SRMC curve cutting LRMC from below and rising more steeply than LRMC, irrespective of whether LRMC itself shows increasing, constant or decreasing returns to scale.

The result has many implications for investment policy. We can see immediately, for example, that suppliers will behave differently according to whether output is expanding or contracting. Suppose the energy utility is at q_2 in Figure 4.1. If forced to contract to

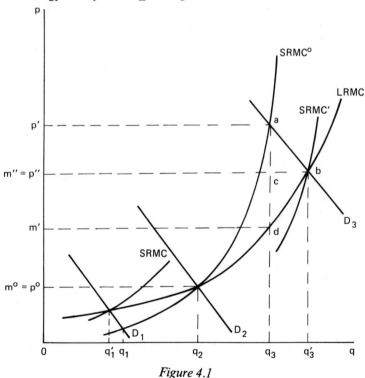

Figure 4.1

q_1, total costs can be reduced more speedily by moving down $SRMC^0$ instead of LRMC: hence labour-shedding with plant size unchanged is often a first response to contracting demand. On the other hand, an expansion of demand to q_3 can be more cheaply accommodated by moving along LRMC, so that investment in new plant and relatively slow taking-on of labour and other variable inputs, may characterise the move out of recession.

In the long run, of course, a contraction or expansion of plant size will lead to a new SRMC curve intersecting further down or higher up the LRMC curve.

Suppose the initial output level is q_2 with an optimal scale of capital K^0, and the supplier's LRMC and $SRMC^0$ curves intersect above q_2 at marginal cost m^0, so that price is set at p^0 along D_2. Now suppose demand expands by an outward shift of the demand schedule to D_3. In the short run the supplier's only response can be to move up the $SRMC^0$ curve to the intersection with D_3 at a; the output target is q_3 and, if priced at short-run marginal cost, it is sold at p'. Consider now the benefits and costs of expanding output from q_3 to q_3' along LRMC. Capital equipment would rise to K', SRMC would shift right to $SRMC'$, and output will be q_3' at a price p'' equal to short-run and long-run marginal cost, m''. We can calculate the net benefits using the expression:

$$\Delta W = \Delta CS + \Delta TR - \Delta TC \qquad (4.1)$$

Taking these in turn produces:

$$\Delta CS = p'acp'' + abc; \quad \Delta TR = p''cq_30 + cbq_3'q_3 - p'acp'' - p''cq_30$$

and,

$$\Delta TC = cbq_3'q_3 - dbc$$

where the last expression, ΔTC, is measured as the additional area under LRMC between q_3 and q_3'. The net benefit measure, shown in Figure 4.1, is therefore:

$$\Delta W = abc + dbc$$

and this has several useful interpretations:

$$\begin{aligned}
\Delta W &\cong \tfrac{1}{2}[(p' - m'') + (m'' - m')][q_3' - q_3] \\
&= \tfrac{1}{2}[(p' - m')][q_3' - q_3] \\
&= \tfrac{1}{2}[SRMC - LRMC][q_3' - q_3] \qquad (4.2)
\end{aligned}$$

74

and in the last equation SRMC and LRMC have both been calculated for the base level of output, q_3. This last expression is particularly useful since it emphasises that, under a first-best pricing policy, investment appraisal can be done entirely in terms of marginal cost measurements.

As additional plant is installed along LRMC, new short-run total and marginal cost curves are traced out corresponding to the new level of plant and equipment; in the final outcome, therefore, price is set at SRMC and LRMC simultaneously, as illustrated in Figure 4.1. In this model we have two alternative statements of optimal plant size;

(a) we can price at SRMC, and expand or contract the scale of capacity along the LRMC curve as long as there are positive net benefits (represented by SRMC–LRMC) from doing so.

or

(b) we can price at LRMC, to choose the appropriate scale of plant.

The outcome of both procedures is the same: we choose a scale of plant at which finally:

$$p = SRMC = LRMC \qquad (4.3)$$

There have been many classical statements of this proposition, including the celebrated paragraph 21 of the UK government's White Paper on *Nationalised Industries* (Cmnd. 3437, 1967), but the first and most concise is by Boiteux (1949): 'Provided there is an optimal investment policy, short term pricing is also long term pricing, and there is no longer any contradiction between the two.' This textbook analysis of marginal cost calculation produces two fundamental conclusions which we can now apply in a more general framework of choosing plant size:

(1) Marginal cost calculations result from the operation of minimising cost subject to the requirement of meeting an output target.

(2) The long-run optimal scale of plant is characterised by an equality between SRMC and LRMC reflecting the alternative decision rules (a) and (b) above.

These fundamental ideas can now be carried over to a more

easily recognisable description of the technological opportunities facing energy utilities. In contrast to the idea of capital plant and equipment used above, i.e. a form of putty which can be remodelled to suit the different labour energy and raw material requirements of each different industrial process, we adopt a description of capital that emphasises its fixed requirements of other inputs.

Marginal cost with fixed capacity equipment

The analysis of this case will be the central concern of this chapter, and it needs to be flexible enough to cover several possibilities. A basic minimum of examples consists of:

(i)   One type of plant operating for one period,
(ii)   One type of plant operating for two periods, and
(iii) Two types of plant operating for two periods.

These basic cases are treated as if the periods were of equal length, and at first storage of output is not assumed feasible for cases (ii) and (iii). Subsequently, storage possibilities are considered as part of the analysis.

These cases then cover, at least in essence, most of the important economic results so that the further generalisation to many plant types and unequal length periods is relatively trivial. However, since more than one time-period is involved, the necessity of discounting will eventually have to be incorporated into the analysis.

Of most initial importance is the definition of the cost concepts involved:

c: the cost of installing one unit of capacity
r: the cost of operating one unit of capacity for one period

where the planning horizon in the analysis is, for example, one year, c must be the annual equivalent repayment on capacity purchased for many years of use. When the analysis is subsequently applied to short time-periods, the definitions of c and r will need to be reconsidered.

Begin with the case of one plant installed to meet demand for one period ahead (Figure 4.2). The horizontal axis in Figure 4.2 measures both the capacity installed, q, and the rate of output from that capacity. In the context of electricity supply, capacity, q, is in kilowatts, and output is also in kilowatts with an hour's

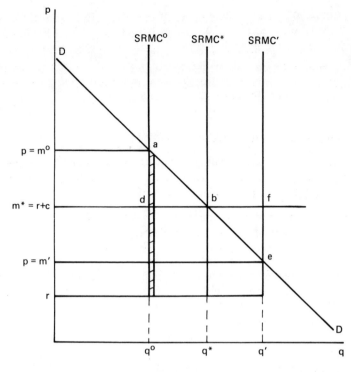

Figure 4.2

usage of capacity yielding q kilowatt hours. In gas supply the equivalent terms are q therms per day for capacity, and q therms for a day's usage of capacity.

Whatever level of capacity is installed, its unit running cost is the horizontal labelled r up to the capacity rating; beyond q, no further output is possible irrespective of the value of r, and the corresponding SRMC curve rises vertically. Each larger capacity level has a corresponding SRMC curve horizontal at r up to q, and vertical beyond, displaced to the right as capacity rises. Each SRMC must cut LRMC from below, and LRMC has no capacity rating limit, being simply the sum of running cost r, and capacity cost c for each further unit of capacity:

$$LRMC = r + c \qquad (4.4)$$

In Figure 4.2 application of the rule p = LRMC immediately

determines q* as the optimum plant size with price = m* = r + c. Any other size of plant offers net benefits to scrapping or further investment given by:

$$\Delta W = \tfrac{1}{2}(SRMC - LRMC)(q^* - q) \qquad (4.5)$$

$$= \tfrac{1}{2}(m - m^*)\Delta q$$
$$= \tfrac{1}{2}(m - r - c)\Delta q \qquad (4.6)$$

where m is the price that rations demand to capacity on whichever SRMC curve corresponds to the non-optimal q. Demand is given by the income-compensated demand schedule, DD. Along DD, too low a plant size, q^0, with corresponding $SRMC^0$ requires a price equal to m^0 to ration demand to capacity, and therefore yields net benefits of abd if increased to q*. Conversely, demand can be met by price equal to m' at capacity q" leaving fbe as a measure of the net benefits of scrapping (q' − q*) units.

An alternative way of expressing the investment rule is to take the capacity change unit by unit. The very first extra unit of capacity in Figure 4.2 beyond q^0 yields an increment of welfare of approximately:

$$\frac{dw}{dq} = m^0 - (r + c) \qquad (4.7)$$

so that this marginal investment is in general worthwhile as long as:

$$(m - r) > c$$

Now (m − r), i.e. the narrow shaded segment in Figure 4.2, can be interpreted as the excess of willingness to pay for another unit of capacity over its running cost, r, and as long as this exceeds the capacity cost, c, the marginal investment is warranted.

A final, more technical interpretation of (m − r) is given by the mathematical programming version of this cost-minimising investment problem. If the utility constructs LRMC by minimising total cost (i.e. the sum of running plus capacity costs):

$$rq + cq^*$$

subject to the two constraints that:

(i) output cannot exceed installed capacity:
$$q \leqslant q^*$$

(ii) output must be as large as the demand forthcoming at what-
      ever price is charged

$$q \geqslant demand$$

then the mathematical programming solution attaches shadow
prices to these two constraints. The shadow price on the first represents the benefit of marginally relaxing the capacity constraint and
therefore must be $(m - r)$, while that on the second represents
the benefit of marginally relaxing the need to ration demand and
therefore must be m (i.e. price) itself. This shadow price interpretation will always underlie the analysis of investment and pricing
policy.

Finally, it is worth noting that the expression $(m - r)$, i.e. the
difference between the price along the SRMC curve needed to ration
demand to capacity, and the running cost of that capacity has
received a number of different names in the literature on capital
theory: quasi-rent, Marshall, optimal amortisation, Turvey (1969),
true depreciation, Hotelling (1925), and opportunity value, Wright
(1968).

In terms of Figure 4.2 every additional unit of capacity brings
marginal cost along SRMC closer to running cost, r, and so it
will be convenient to use the term *running cost savings* of capacity,
when referring to $(m - r)$.

Bringing together the analysis of this one period–one plant case,
the relationship between the short-run marginal cost pricing rule
and the long-run marginal cost investment rule becomes clear in
practice. The long-run rule is given as before:

$$p = LRMC = c + r$$

while the short-run rule consists of:

(a) $p = SRMC = m$,
(b) invest or scrap according as $(m - r) \gtrless c$ at the margin
     so that net benefits of $\frac{1}{2}(m - r - c)\Delta q$ are realised.

Marginal cost with differing demands: peak loading

An important extension of the ideas of marginal cost pricing arises
when demand fluctuates steadily over a number of periods. If output
is expensive or difficult to store, then capacity must be available
to meet the largest of the demand levels, and may be idle at other

times. This is the classic peak loading problem and is characteristic of nearly all fuel supply industries.

Consider at this stage a model with only one plant type, as in the previous section, and assume for simplicity that the demand level fluctuates over two periods of equal length: winter and summer periods of six months each, or day and night periods of twelve hours each. Terminology can remain unchanged, but the time-periods involved need careful definition.

The timescale for capacity to be available is at least several of the equal length sub-periods, and so define:

c: cost of installing a unit of capacity for a cycle of equal length sub-periods,
r: cost of running a unit of capacity for one sub-period.

Capacity is still expressed in units available per cycle, and demand is at a given rate per sub-period, e.g. twelve hours. These definitions which prevail in the literature are convenient for cycles of equal length sub-periods.

There are two equivalent LRMC measures:

$$\text{cycle LRMC} = c + 2r \qquad (4.8)$$
$$\text{sub-period LRMC} = (c/2) + r \qquad (4.9)$$

(where in the latter the effect of discounting for time within the cycle is, for the moment, ignored).

This model is the basis of the peak-load pricing problem in economics and the essential question is how to allocate prices and costs to the two periods and how to plan the size of system capacity.

Boiteux (1949) once again provides the essential solution to the problem, though his results were foreseen by Lewis (1941). Other classic treatments of the problem are those of Houthakker (1951), Steiner (1956), Hirschleifer (1958), Williamson (1966) and Little-child (1970). The fundamental ideas used are the same in every case, though the diagrammatic treatment used by Steiner and Hirschleifer is particularly useful (Figure 4.3).

Along the horizontal axis measure the demand per sub-period, q_1 and q_2, corresponding to the off-peak and peak-compensated demand schedules, D_1D_1 and D_2D_2. SRMC curves are horizontal at running cost, r, up to capacity, and then vertical and cycle LRMC is shown as $c + 2r$. There are now two measures of marginal willingness to pay for capacity corresponding to the demand in

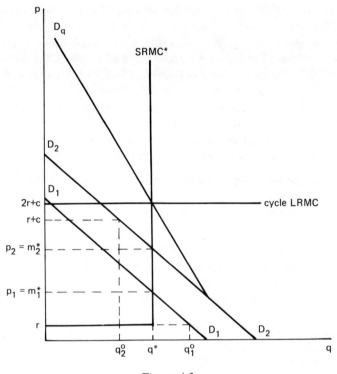

Figure 4.3

each sub-period, and the investment rule would seem to indicate that it is the sum of these prices that should be set equal to cycle LRMC:

$$p_1 + p_2 = c + 2r \qquad (4.10)$$

This is explained as follows. The first need is to identify the SRMC-based prices that ration demand to capacity; since the *same* capacity is available and used in *each* sub-period, the demand curves can be summed along the vertical axis. In other words, the off-peak use of capacity does not render any of it unavailable for subsequent peak use. This vertical summation makes sense because the investment decision requires consumers to put a value on the total demand for capacity over both sub-periods.

The vertical summation of D_1D_1 and D_2D_2 is labelled D_q in Figure 4.3, and the optimum level of capacity is q* where D_q intersects cycle LRMC, so fulfilling equation (4.10) above. Individual sub-period demands are then priced at levels where each sub-period demand schedule intersects the SRMC curve corresponding to optimal capacity, q* in Figure 4.3. In this way both sub-period demands contribute to the recovery of capacity costs on the marginal unit. The prices that ration demand to q* along SRMC* are m_1^* and m_2^* in off-peak and peak periods, respectively, and from equation (4.10):

$$(m_1^* - r) + (m_2^* - r) = c \qquad (4.11)$$

with the running cost savings term $(m_t^* - r)$ representing the willingness to pay over r for more capacity being larger for the peak period. Once again the equivalence of long-run and short-run pricing rules is established:

short-run pricing: $p_t = m_t;\ t = 1,2$
long-run pricing and investment: $\Sigma(m_t - r) = c$

This is a general result which will handle all equal-length sub-period cases in the peak loading problem, and it has several useful extensions. Its essence is that the capacity cost is loaded onto sub-period prices in proportion to the strength of demand. An early version of the result is used in Houthakker's (1951) classic paper in which all the capacity cost is included in peak period prices:

$p_1 = r$
$p_2 = r + c$

That this result is not general enough for the present analysis can be checked in Figure 4.3, because at such prices (p_1' and p_2') peak demand has dropped to q_2^o below off-peak demand q_1^o. The peak has shifted. The characteristic of the more general Boiteux solution is that with optimal pricing the peak disappears since demand in each sub-period is then equal, $q_1^* = q_2^* = q^*$. Whenever the peak is eliminated the outcome can be referred to as a *shifting peak solution;* and whenever the peak period demand continues to exceed off-peak demand, the outcome can be called the *firm peak solution.*

Before leaving the one plant case, consider finally the size of the differential between peak and off-peak prices. This follows simply from rearranging equation (4.10) above:

$$p_2 - p_1 = c - 2(p_1 - r) \qquad (4.12)$$
$$= c - 2(m_1^* - r) \qquad (4.13)$$

This reflects the following fact: installing one more unit of capacity at the peak costs, c, but yields the cycle equivalent of the running cost savings of a unit of capacity in the off-peak period. Where there is a shifting peak solution and off-peak demand needs to be rationed to capacity, this additional benefit for the so-called base load, i.e. off-peak demand, is an offset to the cost of expanding capacity to meet peak demand.

Two plant–two period peak loading

Within the peak loading problem, there are quite complex invest-ment, scrapping, load scheduling and pricing decisions, and these can be treated in principle by assuming two plants are available to meet demand in each of the two sub-periods in the planning cycle.

An obvious example is the choice of nuclear or coal-fired elec-tricity generating equipment, or two alternative processes for syn-thesising natural gas, or even the choice between maintaining an old established pit for coalmining for which all capacity costs have virtually been eliminated, and the sinking of a new pit where the promise of cheaper mining costs may outweigh the capital costs of setting up the project. This example, therefore, can cast much light on the nature of the competing investment decisions found in energy industries. The essential factor in considering two types, or two vintages, of equipment is the comparison between running and capital costs. By vintage is meant the date of commissioning of the plant in question, and it is possible to treat two plants of different vintage as two different types of plant.

There are several reasons for this. First, the older the plant the more 'wear and tear' it will have experienced, and this is represented by expecting older plant to show higher unit running costs. Secondly, such plant is more likely to experience 'forced outages', i.e. the necessity of switching plant off for unforeseen maintenance and repair—again this is represented by higher operating costs. Finally, new plants will embody the latest design improvements and technical advances: this embodied technical progress will ensure that up-to-date plant has the cheapest operating costs per unit. This factor in itself casts interesting light on the concept of marginal cost.

Consider, therefore, two types or vintages of equipment where

83

the installed capacity of each is labelled q^1 and q^2. The plant types differ in their running costs per unit of output, r^1 and r^2, and their capacity or installation costs per unit of output, c^1 and c^2. From now on, assume:

$$r^1 < r^2 \tag{4.14}$$

Plant type 1 (e.g. nuclear generating capacity) is therefore cheaper to operate than plant type 2 (e.g. coal-fired generating capacity), but plant type 1 is more expensive to instal or set up:

$$c^1 > c^2 \tag{4.15}$$

Were this not the case, there would be no point in even considering type 2 plant. The first consideration is the condition under which it makes sense to use both types of plant. This is quite independent of the size of demand in the different sub-periods, and depends only on the comparative costs of the two plant types as long as it is assumed that plant is completely divisible, and unit operating costs are constant.

Output can be labelled according to the type or vintage of equipment, (first subscript 1 or 2) and according to the sub-period in which it is produced (second subscript 1 or 2), and output can never exceed the rated capacity installed, giving four constraints of the form:

$$q_{11} \leqslant q^1; q_{21} \leqslant q^2$$
$$q_{12} \leqslant q^1; q_{22} \leqslant q^2$$

As before, unit capacity cost is defined for the whole cycle of two sub-periods, while unit running cost is measured per sub-period, so that the total system cost is:

$$C = c^1 q^1 + c^2 q^2 + r^1 (q_{11} + q_{12}) + r^2 (q_{21} + q_{22})$$

Total system costs are therefore the sum of installation and operating costs in each period. This assumes both types of plant are built and operated in one or both periods. Suppose, since plant type 1 is cheaper to run, only this type was installed and all of plant 2's load was shifted to type 1. Total system cost would be:

$$C' = c^1 (q^1 + q^2) + r^1 [q_{11} + q_{12} + q_{21} + q_{22}]$$

where $(q^1 + q^2)$ of plant type 1 is installed. The difference in costs is the saving or loss associated with *not* installing and operating plant 2:

$$C - C' = (c^2 - c^1)q^2 + (r^2 - r^1)[q_{21} + q_{22}]$$

Remembering that the capacity constraints include:

$$q_{21} \leqslant q^2 \text{ and } q_{22} \leqslant q^2$$

add these together and obtain:

$$q_{21} + q_{22} \leqslant 2q^2$$

and inserting this inequality into the expression for the difference in costs gives:

$$C - C' \leqslant (c^2 - c^1)q^2 + (r^2 - r^1)2q^2 = [(c^2 - c^1) + (r^2 - r^1)2]q^2$$

Now for $(q^2 > 0)$, it will be the case that:

$$C - C' \leqslant 0, \text{ if } (r^2 - r^1) \leqslant (c^1 - c^2)/2$$

But $C - C' \leqslant 0$ tells us that system costs fall by leaving plant 2 out and switching load to plant 1. Hence the condition that ensures that both types of plant will be used, i.e. the condition that ensures costs rise if plant 2 is left out, must be:

$$\frac{(c^1 - c^2)}{2} < (r^2 - r^1) \tag{4.16}$$

Thus, whether or not there is an optimal mix of plants or exclusive use of one type depends on relative capacity and running costs, and on the number and length of sub-periods represented here by the 2 in the denominator of the capacity cost difference.

Now introduce demand considerations. Diagrammatically, these are represented by two sub-period income-compensated demand schedules, D_1D_1 and D_2D_2 (Figures 4.4–4.6 below), along which demand will be rationed to capacity by short-run marginal cost pricing. Suppose for the moment that the sub-period demand levels that emerge at SRMC-based prices along the demand schedules are labelled X_1 and X_2, respectively. Each can be supplied from two capacity types so that rationing by SRMC pricing ensures:

$$X_1 = q_{11} + q_{21}; X_2 = q_{12} + q_{22}$$

Before looking at a general diagrammatic approach, it is possible to isolate the crucial factors in determining the plant mix in different sub-periods, often referred to as the load scheduling or load despatching problem in gas and electricity supply. There are three vital factors: the merit order (equation (4.14)), the optimal mix condition (equation (4.16)) and the firm peak condition; these are summarised in Table 4.1.

Table 4.1: Load scheduling in the two period–two plant model

condition:	merit order	optimal mix	firm peak	shifting peak
	$r^2 - r^1 > 0$	$r^2 - r^1 > (c^1 - c^2)/2$	$X_2 > X_1$	$X_2 = X_1$
result:	$q_{11} > 0$	$q_{22} > 0$	$q_{21} = 0$	$q_{21} > 0$
	$q_{21} > 0$			

The merit order condition ($r^2 - r^1 > 0$) reflects the fact that since plane 1 is cheaper to operate it will always be used first to produce output, regardless of whether it is in the off-peak or peak period. Hence the system has base load from plant 1, $q_{11} > 0$, and at least some peak load, $q_{12} > 0$. More generally, once plants are constructed, they will be used in ascending order of their unit operating costs up to the rated capacity of each, until the sub-period demand is met.

The next condition refers to the optimal mix of plants based on the comparative operating and installation costs. If this condition ensures both plant types will be built, then plant 2 will at least be used to meet some peak load, $q_{22} > 0$.

Whether or not plant 2 (lower down the merit order since its operating costs are higher), will be used for base load in the off-peak period depends on whether there is a firm or shifting peak. In the firm peak case, as has already been seen, demand in the off-peak period remains below that in the peak period, $X_2 > X_1$, and there is no incentive to stop installing plant 1 capacity short of X_1. Thus off-peak demand is met entirely from base load plant 1, and output of plant 2 in period 1 is zero, $q_{21} = 0$. In the shifting peak case, demand in the two periods is equalised, and since the optimal mix condition is satisfied, plant 2 will be used in both sub-periods— that which was initially 'off-peak' as well as that which was initially 'peak'.

These are the general principles governing the load scheduling decision: comparative costs determine the merit order and whether more than one plant type is used, while demand conditions determine whether plant lower down the merit order is used, along with the most efficient plant, to supply load in each period.

Now consider the diagrammatic analysis of the pricing and investment decisions. Since the idea of the running cost savings from a particular plant in any sub-period will continue to be of critical importance, it is helpful to have separate notation for these. Consequently, use the expressions:

$$k_{11} = (m_1 - r^1); k_{12} = (m_2 - r^1) \tag{4.17}$$

$$k_{21} = (m_1 - r^2); k_{22} = (m_2 - r^2) \tag{4.18}$$

where m_1 and m_2 will be the SRMC-based prices that ration demand to capacity in each sub-period, and r^1 and r^2 are the unit running costs on each capacity type (assumed constant over time, although a more general analysis would permit r^1 and r^2 to rise from period 1 to period 2).

If the analysis were to be done in a mathematical programming framework, the $k_{11} \ldots k_{22}$ terms would be the shadow prices associated with the four capacity constraints described previously.

Several cases are considered in Figures 4.4, 4.5 and 4.6, but in each, c^1, c^2, r^1 and r^2 are chosen in such a way that the optimal mix condition is fulfilled, and both capacity types q^1 and q^2 are at least partially used.

Begin with a firm peak situation in Figure 4.4. Along the horizontal axis, the capacity levels can be summed horizontally, since total capacity available in each period will be $(q^1 + q^2)$. Suppose the amounts q^1 and q^2 have been installed, so that the stepped line indicates the system SRMC schedule reflecting the merit order of running costs.

In the firm peak situation, with the off-peak demand schedule D_1D_1, only q^1 is used as base load capacity, and the SRMC-based price that rations demand to q^1 is m_1. This in turn represents the sum of type 1 capacity running cost r^1 and the running cost savings available for period 1, i.e. the marginal willingness to pay over running cost for another unit of type 1 capacity in period 1:

$$\text{off-peak price} = m_1 = r^1 + k_{11} \tag{4.19}$$

Since $m_1 < r^2$, there is no output in period 1 from q^2 capacity: the marginal willingness to pay over r^2 in period 1 for type 2 capacity is negative.

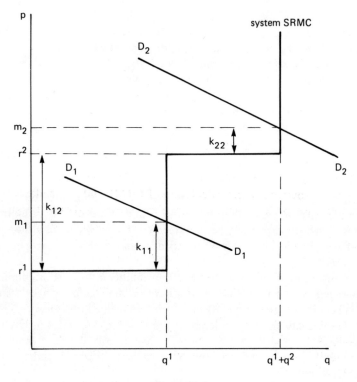

Figure 4.4

In the peak period, demand, represented by $D_2 D_2$, is rationed to $q^1 + q^2$ by the SRMC-based price, m_2 and this provides running cost savings to both types of capacity, with those for type 1, whose running cost is lower, being greater:

$$\text{peak price} = m_2 = r^1 + k_{12} = r^2 + k_{22} \tag{4.20}$$

Having established the short-run pricing rule, it now remains to look at the investment rule to determine whether q^1 and q^2 are indeed optimal. To do this, the marginal running cost savings associated with each plant type over the cycle of sub-periods are compared with their unit capacity costs, and investment carried on until the following results hold: for type 1 capacity:

$$
\begin{aligned}
k_{11} + k_{12} &= (m_1 - r^1) + (m_2 - r^1) \\
&= c^1
\end{aligned}
\tag{4.21}
$$

and for type 2 capacity, (where $k_{21} = 0$):

$$k_{22} = (m_2 - r^2)$$
$$= c^2 \qquad\qquad (4.22)$$

At this long-run equilibrium, it will then be the case that:

$$\text{off-peak price} + \text{peak price} = m_1 + m_2$$
$$= (r^1 + k_{11}) + (r^1 + k_{12})$$
$$= c^1 + 2r^1$$
$$= c^2 + r^2 \qquad\qquad (4.23)$$

which looks rather similar to the one plant definition of cycle LRMC. However, direct calculation of LRMC did not make sense in this case because without the price-based short-run marginal cost approach it would not have been easy to guess that type 2 capacity was not to be used in period 1.

Thus, while the procedure is still equivalent in the end to LRMC pricing, as it should be when investment policy is optimal, the basic sense of the analysis is more usefully done in terms of the SRMC-based prices. When the amount of capacity is optimal, then it can be seen that the off-peak and peak prices are observationally equivalent to the sub-period long-run and short-run marginal costs.

Figure 4.5 provides generalisation of this firm peak case. Both types of capacity are present, but only q^1 is in use in the off-peak period for base load, since m_1 being less than r^2 ensures no output from q^2, $q_{21} = 0$.

Short-run marginal cost-based prices are:

off-peak: $\quad m_1 = r^1 + k_{11}$ $\qquad\qquad$ (4.24)

peak: $\qquad m_2 = r^1 + k_{12}$

$\qquad\qquad\quad = r^2$ $\qquad\qquad\qquad\qquad$ (4.25)

Since q^2 is only partly used in period 2 its running cost savings are zero ($q_{22} < q^2$ means $k_{22} = 0$). Since $k_{21} = k_{22} = 0$, we can ask why q^2 is there at all. The reason can only be that $c^2 = 0$, in other words q^2 is some capacity inherited from the past, whose capacity costs are long since sunk and of no relevance to current investment and operating decisions. Plant q^2 plays the role of the marginal plant, and its running cost alone, r^2, is the marginal cost on the system in period 2. The only decision is whether to operate q^2 at all, and should m_2 drop below r^2, operation on it will cease.

Finally in Figure 4.6, there is an example of a shifting peak

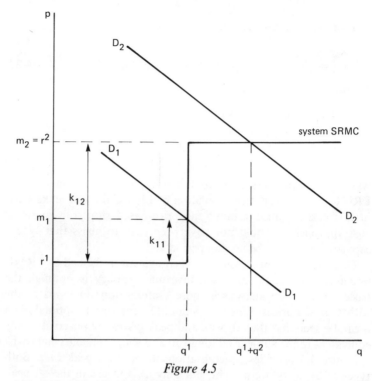

Figure 4.5

with total output in both periods being equalised by the peak load-ing signals in SRMC based prices:

$$m_2 > m_1$$

Both plants are used to capacity in both periods and have positive running cost savings in both periods, $k_{11} > 0$, $k_{12} > 0$, $k_{21} > 0$, $k_{22} > 0$. As expected the running cost savings on q^1 ($m_1 - r^1$ and $m_2 - r^1$, respectively), are greater than those on plant q^2 in order to justify incurring q^1's greater capacity cost.

Once the SRMC-based prices for installed capacity are deter-mined, the investment decisions to instal or scrap capacity proceed until:

$$\begin{aligned} \text{off-peak price} + \text{peak price} &= m_1 + m_2 \\ &= r^1 + k_{11} + r^1 + k_{12} \\ &= c^1 + 2r^1 \\ &= r^2 + k_{21} + r^2 + k_{22} \\ &= c^2 + 2r^2 \end{aligned} \qquad (4.26)$$

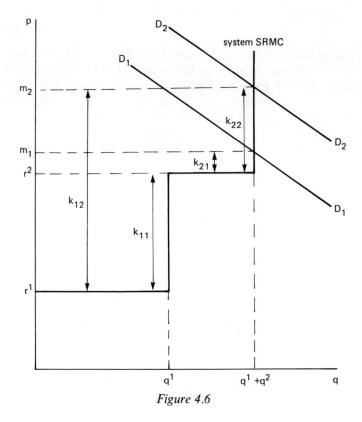

Figure 4.6

At the optimal capacity combination it will then be possible to observe in SRMC-based prices, their LRMC equivalents.

Finally, it is useful to consider what determines the maximum differential between peak and off-peak prices at the long-run optimal capacity level combining both plant types. Taking equation (4.26) above, the differential is:

$$\begin{aligned}
\text{(peak price–off-peak price)} &= m_2 - m_1 \\
&= c^1 - 2(m_1 - r^1) \\
&= c^2 - 2(m_1 - r^2)
\end{aligned} \qquad (4.27)$$

in other words the marginal cost of capacity, of whichever type, less its running cost savings when operating on base load accumulated over the cycle. In the firm peak case there is no running cost saving to offset against c^2, and the expression simplifies to:

$$(m_2 - m_1) = c^1 - 2(r^2 - r^1)$$
$$= c^2 \qquad (4.28)$$

which not only reflects the optimal mix condition, but also measures what is sometimes referred to as the *net effective cost* (NEC) of capacity. For q^1 (base load capacity), this is capacity cost less the cycle savings on running cost arising from its replacing type 2 (or peaking) capacity. The NEC on type 2 capacity, used only for peaking purposes, then has no running cost savings offset.

Suppose the system were now in disequilibrium with a firm peak, and it was the case that:

$$c^1 - (2r^2 - r^1) \leqslant 0 \leqslant c^2 \qquad (4.29)$$

then several results are clear:

(i)   type 1 capacity has a negative NEC and should be installed immediately in preference to type 2;

(ii) if type 2 is inherited capacity ($c^2 = 0$) then it should immediately be scrapped and replaced by type 1;

(iii) the positive benefits of installing type 1 capacity will, at equilibrium, permit an expansion of demand in one or both periods, and this will be reflected in new SRMC-based prices.

These results underlie amongst other things the cost-benefit analysis of nuclear power examined in Chapter 5 below.

Peak load pricing with variable running cost

The two period–two plant model encapsulates almost all the essential principles of the load scheduling and capacity investment decisions likely to be met in practice, but it is worthwhile generalising these briefly to the case of a system with a concentration of old plant of different ages to emphasise the role of the variable running cost assumption.

This can be done quite simply by assuming that the constant running cost element, r, applies only to *new* plant and equipment. All older plant is ranked below this in the merit order, and this older plant exhibits a rising running cost schedule as it is brought on stream. Figure 4.7 illustrates this by having the older plant's running costs rising in a smooth linear fashion along $SRMC^0$ to the capacity of the system, at which m* is the running cost of the oldest plant.

This linear segment of the running cost schedule $SRMC^0$ between q^0 and $q*$ summarises all the stepped gradations like those between r^1 and r^2 in Figure 4.6. (This type of running cost representation is found in Millward (1971) and Gravelle (1976).)

Consider first a one period demand model, represented by the single demand schedule, DD, and it can be seen that at the demand level q_1, q^0 is supplied by new plant at running cost, r, and $(q_1 - q^0)$ by old plant, with the last unit in use being that with running cost, m_1.

Suppose it was proposed to replace all of the capacity $(q_1 - q^0)$ by N units of new capacity; under what circumstances would the decision be warranted?

The installation of N units of new capacity must shift the SRMC

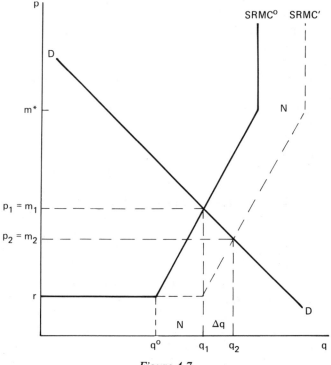

Figure 4.7

schedule to the right, giving SRMC^1. If the size of the scrapping and replacement programme is sufficiently large (as it is in the diagram), system marginal running cost drops to m_2, and if price is based on SRMC, demand itself expands by Δq from q_1 to q_2. The components of $(\Delta CS + \Delta TR - \Delta TC)$ are as follows:

(i) $\Delta CS + \Delta TR = p\Delta q \cong (\frac{p_1 + p_2}{2})\Delta q$, if a large change occurs

(ii) $\Delta TC = m\Delta q \cong (\frac{m_1 + m_2}{2})\Delta q$, if a large change occurs

      plus $(Nr + Nc)$, i.e. new capacity costs

      less $(Nm) \cong (\frac{m_1 + m_2}{2})N$, if N is large; i.e the saving

      on marginal units scrapped

In summary,

$$\Delta W = (\frac{p_1 + p_2}{2})\Delta q - (\frac{m_1 + m_2}{2})(\Delta q - N) - Nr - Nc \quad (4.30)$$

(Note that the effects of large changes are measured by taking averages of the initial and final values of the price and running cost variables.)

Equation (4.30) is based on a very celebrated treatment of the marginal cost pricing basis of cost-benefit analysis in Turvey (1964). By assuming $p_1 = m_1$ and $p_2 = m_2$ (SRMC-based prices) and $N = \Delta q = dq$ is infinitesimally small, equation (4.7) is recovered from (4.30).

Now consider peak load pricing in Figure 4.8.

A firm peak is illustrated with the peak demand schedule, D_2D_2, intersecting the vertical arm of SRMC, while off-peak demand, D_1D_1, requires a level of old and new plant below the capacity of the system. Off-peak price is based on SRMC, at:

$$p_1 = m_1 \quad (4.31)$$

While peak price is based on the running cost of the oldest (most marginal) plant, m^*, plus a rationing element to restrict demand to the capacity of the system at peak:

$$p_2 = m^* + k \quad (4.32)$$

However, k will be less than the cost of a unit of new capacity. To see this, consider that k measures the marginal benefit less

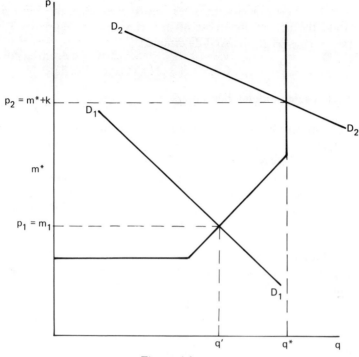

Figure 4.8

running cost of a unit of new capacity, but that if such a unit was now added to the system it could replace output from the marginal unit of plant in the peak period, thus saving $(m^* - r)$, and could also replace output from the marginal unit of plant in the off-peak period, saving $(m_1 - r)$. Therefore,

$$p_2 = m^* + (c - [m^* - r + m_1 - r]) \qquad (4.33)$$

and the maximum peak–off-peak price differential becomes:

$$p_2 - p_1 = (m^* - m_1) + (c - [(m^* - r) + (m_1 - r)]) \qquad (4.34)$$

This means the difference between peak and off-peak prices is no longer dependent solely on the need to cover capacity costs, but also on the difference between peak and off-peak running costs.

The importance of this variable running cost assumption is that even with a steady demand or a firm peak, the demand level itself determines running costs and, hence, the running cost savings on

95

a unit of new capacity. In other words, even when there is a firm peak, the net effective cost of new capacity, $c - (m^* - r) - (m_1 - r)$, is partly demand-determined.

Peak loading with feasible storage

The essence of the peak loading problem is that it arises when output is difficult to store from one period to another. However, there may be cases when storage is feasible, if expensive. Certainly gas supply makes use of several types of storage including variable pressure in the national transmission system and liquefied natural gas (LNG) storage near demand centres. In the case of the Central Electricity Generating Board, the Dinorwic pumped storage scheme takes advantage of the low opportunity cost of night-time electricity to move water uphill so that it can run down through turbines at peak day-time periods for load balancing at times of high opportunity cost.

It is worth analysing, therefore, the combination of storage and further capacity expansion in meeting peak demand, and an important general result emerges relating marginal storage costs to the maximum differential between peak and off-peak prices. As an example, adopt the one plant–two period model, with constant running cost, r, although the results carry over to the more general cases.

For storage costs, the simplest possible assumptions are made, following Gravelle (1976): storing a unit of output in the off-peak period costs v per sub-period, and if s is the amount of storage then system storage costs are: vs.

Consider first the firm peak solution shown in Figure 4.9, which is analogous to Figure 4.3, for the one plant–two period model.

Imagine, initially, that storage is not considered, and a capacity level of q^* is installed with peak and off-peak prices set at $p_2 = r + c$ and $p_1 = r$, respectively. Now it is clear from the comparison of output levels, q_1 and $q_2 = q^*$, that storage of off-peak output may be attractive. Suppose a form of storage is now developed that costs v per unit. If some storage, s, is carried out in sub-period 1:

$$s \leq q^* - q_1 \tag{4.35}$$

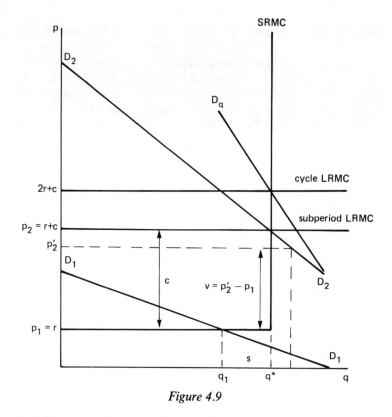

Figure 4.9

then this output has a marginal cost in the peak period of:

$$p_2 = r + v \tag{4.36}$$

which can be compared with the marginal cost of peak demand when no storage is available:

$$p_2 = r + c \tag{4.37}$$

Storage will be preferred, therefore, for supplying peak demand at the margin if:

$$v \leqslant c \tag{4.38}$$

and this is the condition for an optimal mix of storage and capacity in the firm peak case. Now if all costs are treated as constants, then it may always be the case that $v < c$. If so, then, although some capacity must be available to make storage feasible, the firm

97

peak solution in Figure 4.9 will not be a long-run equilibrium, since it will always be preferable to meet peak demand at the margin from storage of off-peak output. After the development of the storage option, therefore, capacity will be scrapped at the margin and replaced by storage, until the firm peak in production is eliminated. The signal to do this is that on comparing equations (4.36) and (4.37) it is clear that the marginal cost of storage sets an upper limit to the differential between peak and off-peak prices, so that in long-run equilibrium:

$$p_2 - p_1 = v$$

Thus after storage is introduced in Figure 4.9 as an alternative to capacity installation, the knowledge that $v < c$ will encourage a movement towards identical *production* in both sub-periods and a reduction in capacity compared with the initial no storage equilibrium. Naturally, the difference in *consumption* between peak and off-peak periods—the willingness to pay for which is represented by the marginal cost of storage—will remain.

Now consider the shifting peak analysis for this case of one plant and two periods. It is clear that if storage is feasible, then there must be an optimal mix of storage and capacity expansion to meet peak demand. Two conditions together determine the complete solution:

$$p_1 + p_2 = c + 2r = \text{cycle LRMC} \qquad (4.39)$$

$$p_2 - p_1 \leqslant v \qquad (4.40)$$

The first is the usual optimal investment rule aggregating marginal willingness to pay over the two periods and setting this equal to cycle LRMC. The second sets the marginal cost of storage as the ceiling on the peak–off-peak price differential. The interpretation of this second rule is that storage or further capacity expansion are two alternatives for meeting a peak demand increment, and the cheaper option will be chosen at the margin. From equation (4.12) above, recall that without storage the peak–off-peak price differential was $c - 2(p_1 - r)$ so that output from storage is preferred, at the margin of peak demand, to output from new capacity if:

$$v \leqslant c - 2(p_1 - r) \qquad (4.41)$$

To enable further storage to be done, off-peak demand must

be restricted by raising p_1, so that a long-run equilibrium mix of storage and capacity expansion is achieved when:

$$p_2 - p_1 = v = c - 2(p_1 - r) \qquad (4.42)$$

Figure 4.10 shows this analysis in detail. Without storage, assume peak and off-peak prices are p_2' and p_1' to ration both peak and off-peak demand to capacity, and these are given by the intersection of D_2D_2 and D_1D_1 with SRMC. If storage of output from period 1 is available at marginal cost of storage of v, then the $(p_2 - p_1)$ differential must be reduced to the distance, v. Compared with the no storage outcome, off-peak demand is restricted below capacity, q^*, by the rise in p_1:

$$q_1 = q^* - s \qquad (4.43)$$

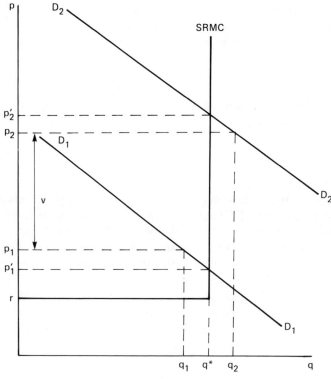

Figure 4.10

while peak demand can expand beyond the capacity limit, q^* (as the peak price drops) to the level:

$$q_2 = q^* + s \qquad (4.44)$$

Now production in both sub-periods remains unchanged at the maximum capacity level of q^*, but there is a trade-off effect on consumption between sub-periods 1 and 2 to take advantage of the storage possibility. This trade is advantageous to consumers because the marginal willingness to pay for peak period consumption exceeds that of off-peak consumption.

Comparing the firm and shifting peak solutions in this fixed running cost (r) case, several results emerge. First, the criterion for the use of storage was at first less demanding in the firm peak case when there is spare capacity in period 1, compared with the criterion in the shifting peak case (compare equations (4.38) and (4.41)). This is because in the shifting peak case, off-peak demand already presses on capacity, and making room for storage of off-peak output involves a loss of consumer surplus at the margin. Secondly, the capacity decision with storage will produce a different result from the case without storage because there are always now two investment options. Finally, a short-cut to determining the optimal peak and off-peak prices is provided by the pair of equations (4.39) and (4.40) when the second is an equality, at equilibrium. Solving for p_1 and p_2:

$$p_1 = (c/2) + r - v/2 = \text{sub-period LRMC} - \tfrac{1}{2}v \qquad (4.45)$$

$$p_2 = (c/2) + r + v/2 = \text{sub-period LRMC} + \tfrac{1}{2}v \qquad (4.46)$$

The storage option can easily be included in the two plant model over two periods. It would be expected that storage will always involve the output of the base load rather than the peaking capacity plant, i.e. will always be from the plant with lower running cost. At the margin, therefore, an expansion of peak demand in the firm peak case implies the comparison of three different marginal cost items:

v: marginal cost of off-peak storage

c^2: marginal cost of a unit of peak capacity

$c^1 - 2(r^2 - r^1)$: marginal cost of a unit of base load capacity

and if v is the lowest item, storage will proceed until there is no longer a firm peak in production.

Finally, the assumption of variable running cost reflecting a mix

100

of old and new equipment leaves the basic principles unchanged, except that since marginal running cost rises smoothly and continuously, an equilibrium with storage and with a firm peak in production, as well as consumption, becomes a possibility. In this case, the marginal condition for an optimal mix of storage and new capacity is (from (4.34)):

$$v = m^* - m_1 + c - (m^* - r) - (m_1 - r)$$

Discounting for time in marginal cost analysis

In all the two period models used so far, there has been an implicit assumption that the periods are short enough to render irrelevant the possibility that waiting for the running cost savings until demand has reached a peak could involve any opportunity cost. However, if the basic analysis is extended to cover a planning horizon involving many different peak and off-peak cycles, stretching perhaps over several years, then the need to wait for subsequent running cost savings to justify the installation of new capacity involves losing the opportunity to invest now in more immediately attractive projects. This factor must be accounted for by discounting the future running cost savings over the lifetime of the plant involved.

Consider, for example, the most elementary model, the one period, fixed capacity case, where the marginal net benefit to expanding capacity is (from (4.7)):

$$\frac{dW}{dq} = m - r - c$$

and suppose that over many years of the life of capacity this marginal net benefit is steadily forthcoming every period. Each year's benefit needs to be discounted by the factor $(1 + i)^{-t}$ where i is the *social discount rate* (SDR), providing a net present value welfare measure:

$$PV(\frac{dW}{dq}) = PV(m - r - c)_t$$
$$= \sum_{t=0}^{n} (m - r - c)_t/(1 + i)^t$$
$$= \Sigma(m - r)_t/(1 + i)^t + K \qquad (4.47)$$

Here, PV represents the discounted present value procedure, and the present value over the lifetime of plant of each year's capacity cost, c, is the total cost of installing the investment, K.

This basic idea can be rephrased in several useful ways, including one that indicates the importance of the SDR in determining LRMC.

To begin with, consider the very first year (or sub-period), 0, of operation of a marginal unit of new capacity that will last for many years. In equilibrium, the following results will hold:

$$
\begin{aligned}
p_0 &= SRMC_0 \text{ (i.e. } m_0) \\
&= LRMC_0 \\
&= r + (m_0 - r) \\
&= r + [K - \sum_{t=1}^{n} (m_t - r)/(1 + i)^t]
\end{aligned}
\tag{4.48}
$$

In other words, the first year's price is the sum of running cost, r, and the first year's running cost savings. The latter is the difference between the cost of a unit of capacity and the present value of all future running cost savings. Clearly, therefore, the SDR, i, is a critical ingredient of this measure of LRMC.

Now assume i rises. This must devalue all the discounted future running cost savings, so requiring more of the capacity cost to be recovered by the first year's output and price than was previously the case. Put another way, if this marginal capacity investment is to remain worthwhile, the willingness to pay for it now in year 0, as signalled by the present sub-period LRMC, must also rise.

A rise in SDR can be interpreted in several ways, of which perhaps the easiest is to state that the social opportunity cost of capital has risen to reflect the fact that saving done today will produce a higher income in the future. Any current individual project has therefore to compete on harder terms with all the alternative uses of capital; a fact signalled to the consumers of that project's output by a rise in its long-run marginal cost.

This role for SDR = i is equally applicable to the case where each year contains cycles of peak and off-peak sub-periods. An essential ingredient in the calculation of LRMC is the discount factor determined by i, and representing the social rate of return that can be obtained on alternative uses of the capital tied up in any particular project.

Price guidelines for the energy industries

Reference has already been made to the White Paper on the UK nationalised industries (Cmnd. 3437, 1967), which is regarded as the apotheosis of the marginal cost pricing idea in UK policy-making. Experience with the 1967 guidelines (which included a stipulation that a test discount rate be applied universally across the public sector) was mixed, and a study by the National Economic Development Office (1976) found that the use of marginal cost pricing was either not understood or not widely practised in the nationalised industries.

There is a variety of reasons why this happened, including the use of public sector prices in an anti-inflation policy (Millward 1976), but in any case, the Treasury issued new guidelines in Cmnd. 7131 (1978). Interpretation of these has been less clearcut than with the earlier instructions, but the Treasury's own views (1979) are that they essentially restate the marginal cost pricing doctrine.

The most important idea in Cmnd. 7131 (1978) is the Treasury's signal of the social opportunity cost of capital to be used for discounting future costs and benefits, labelled RRR (required rate of return). This was set at 5 per cent, to mirror achieved post-tax rates of return on comparable private sector industrial investment. (The earlier test discount rate had been set at private sector projected rates of return rather than achieved rates.) This RRR was to be achieved on the amount of new investment as a whole in any one year, thus permitting some revenue-raising projects to be evaluated at a higher rate in order to permit the supply of some social service facilities—an example is the urban–rural electricity subsidy discussed in Chapter 3.

By stipulating RRR, the Treasury argued that it was setting the most important common ingredient in the LRMC of public sector output, and could subsequently leave precise LRMC calculations to individual industries, although it noted that those constrained to operate in world markets might or might not behave as price-takers according to market circumstances.

Certainly it is the case, as will be seen in Chapters 5 and 6 below, that prices based on the idea of LRMC appear to rank first in the consideration of the electricity and gas supply industries. Nevertheless, there is a substantial emphasis in Cmnd. 7131 on the role of financial targets, reflecting a return to a preoccupation with profitability that characterised public sector policy before the 1967 guidelines were issued. In principle, the financial target guidelines were designed to reflect each industry's forecasting ability.

Suppose that LRMC-based prices (incorporating i = RRR as shown above) are set for a number of periods ahead. Revenues based on these prices, p_0, p_1 ... etc., can be forecast using a model of the industry's demand. Subtracting from these forecast revenue flows, p_0q_0, p_1q_1, ... etc., the accounting operating costs, OC, and depreciation provisions, D, applied in the particular industry's annual accounts, therefore provides a forecast accounting profit, AP^*_t, for each year before interest:

$$AP^*_t = p_tq_t - OC_t - D_t$$

This forecast was then to be the basis of the industry's financial target.

The target therefore becomes, in principle, an incentive to forecast correctly, minimise costs so as to determine LRMC, and to apply LRMC pricing. There is no indication that the industries should use Ramsey pricing to meet their targets, though the Central Electricity Generating Board has certainly indicated that it uses Ramsey pricing ideas (see Chapter 6).

In practice, however, this version of the financial targets idea did not last very long, and by 1983 it was clear that the Treasury, at least, viewed the setting of financial targets as a means of raising taxes. In principle, of course, there is no reason why public sector prices should not be used as a tax instrument, though the debate on the issue showed up several misunderstandings.

By the beginning of 1984, substantial excess capacity was apparent in UK electricity supply and the CEGB was clearly not at its long-run equilibrium. As Figure 4.2 suggests in that case, SRMC-based prices cover only running costs, and capacity is scrapped until once again price = SRMC = LRMC. However, Rees (1983, 1984) argues that the Treasury would have found the financial losses involved in only covering SRMC based on running costs to be politically unacceptable. In consequence, the Treasury appears to have argued to the select committee on energy, not that it wanted to raise the tax on SRMC-based prices, but that its calculation of the equilibrium LRMC was too low, and that higher prices for the domestic consumer were justified. (In fact, domestic tariffs should be related to the SRMC of the area board distribution authorities anyway.)

It appears therefore that the principle of marginal cost pricing (i.e. SRMC-based prices along with appropriate investment decisions until SRMC = LRMC), has received some lip-service in Treasury guidelines to the nationalised industries, but that in practice macro-economic policy considerations have continued to dominate the pricing constraints. In the 1970s these macroeconomic constraints took the form of price freezes, while in the 1980s they have taken the form of excise taxes to reduce the public sector budget deficit.

Cmnd. 7131 also contains a relatively new control on the public sector industries: external financing limits (EFLs). These are prede-termined ceilings on the amount that the Treasury will lend to an industry from the National Loan Fund (NLF) in order to top up revenue financed investment. (The Treasury itself does all the public borrowing for the nationalised industries.) In effect, this means that each industry must achieve a given net cash flow in order to finance its investment programme from year to year, since its borrowing from the NLF is determined in advance, largely by considerations of monetary policy.

In practice, the EFLs came to be the dominant control on the nationalised industries over the 1979–84 period, and Heald and Steel (1981) report that this was having the effect of permitting only very short-term investment projects to have priority.

With the idea that public sector energy prices can be seen simply as excise taxes, and the ceilings on borrowing irrespective of how many projects pass an RRR test when price = LRMC, it is clear that over the early 1980s the practice of public sector pricing may have diverged very widely from the first- or second-best theoretical basis. Nevertheless, the essential ideas of marginal cost pricing characterise almost all the day-to-day supply decisions in the public sector energy industries, and subsequent chapters consider several detailed case studies of these.

5

Nuclear versus coal-fired generation of electricity

Introduction

This chapter examines in detail a particularly important case study of investment in the UK energy sector: the choice between coal-fired generation and nuclear power generation of electricity. The objective will be to set out the issues in the cost-benefit analysis, using as examples the figures that featured in the UK government's decision to proceed with a public inquiry into the siting of a pressurised water reactor (PWR) at Sizewell. At the time of writing, this inquiry is still in progress, and most of the issues discussed in this chapter are being aired at considerable length.

The first task is to set out the theoretical investment analysis discussed in Chapter 4 in a way that is amenable to separate cost-benefit analysis of a particular project. This will clarify the way in which the Central Electricity Generating Board (CEGB) has presented the nuclear case over a number of years. As a concrete example, the CEGB's calculations for adopting nuclear power presented in 1980 to the House of Commons select committee on energy (SCE) are used to illustrate the ideas. This case study raises several important issues, such as the nature of demand forecasts, the reliability of electricity supply, sensitivity to different assumptions and the means of pricing electricity in practice. These are examined in turn, using as a framework the critique of the CEGB case presented by the 1981 report of the Monopolies and Mergers Commission. Subsequently, the wider issues of nuclear cost-benefit analysis are considered.

Optimal plant mix in electricity generation

This section sets out the incremental cost-benefit analysis usually applied to generating programme decisions. The theoretical framework was set out in Chapter 4 above, and now a concrete application is needed. While the economic ideas remain unchanged, they are often set out in a particular framework, and this requires some description.

First, the basic problem is one of cost-minimisation, i.e. the analyst is *not* deciding on whether there are net social benefits from offering electricity for sale at the current long-run marginal cost; instead, the purpose is to find the cheapest way of supplying that electricity. So fundamentally cost-benefit analysis is an incorrect description, cost-effectiveness being more accurate.

In full, the objective is to find the plant construction programme that minimises the discounted present value of system (capital and operating) costs of meeting specified output targets. The key ingredients are:

(i)   a discount rate,
(ii)   output target forecasts,
(iii) capital and operating cost data, and
(iv)   a means of investigating uncertainties in (ii) and (iii).

The earlier analysis worked exclusively in demand and supply diagrams, but can be conveniently restated in terms of load curves and load duration curves. Figure 5.1(a) illustrates a load curve, and Figure 5.1(b) a load duration curve.

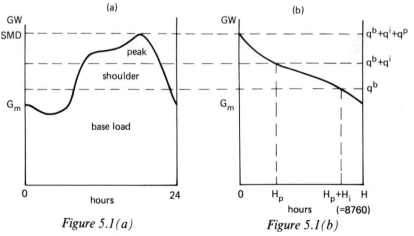

Figure 5.1(a)   Figure 5.1(b)

In Figure 5.1(a), the system load in gigawatts (gW), i.e. 10^6 kilowatts, is plotted for each hour of the daily cycle, and three demand periods—base load, shoulder and peak—are distinguished. The daily load curves can be summed over the year and plotted as a load duration curve in Figure 5.1(b) (which for simplicity has assumed all 365 load curves are identical). The horizontal axis now measures the number of hours during the year for which each individual level of load lasts. The minimum load on the system, Gm, lasts for all 8760 hours, while the highest peak load, the system maximum demand, SMD, is shown to last for only an instant (in practice the basic time unit is a $\frac{1}{2}$ hour).

As we already know, such time-varying demands may be met by different types and vintage of generating plant, and on the right-hand vertical of Figure 5.1(b) three types are distinguished: base load capacity, q^b, intermediate capacity, q^i, and peaking capacity, q^p. Typical candidates for q^b are new nuclear and coal-fired plant, for q^i new oil-fired plant or older coal-fired plant, and for q^p gas turbines.

To begin with, assume there is no old inherited plant, and consider the decision to invest in any or all of q^b, q^i and q^p to meet next year's demand. The demand target to be met is the whole load duration curve, so a forecast of every point on it, i.e. each hour's demand for the next 8760 hours, is needed. The crucial forecast of course is SMD, since there must be at least enough capacity to meet this system maximum demand:

$$\text{SMD} = q^b + q^i + q^p \tag{5.1}$$

As we already know, there will be a mix of plant types as long as they can be ranked differently in terms of annual unit capital and running costs (c and r, respectively):

$$c^b > c^i > c^p \tag{5.2}$$

and

$$r^b < r^i < r^p \tag{5.3}$$

so that base load capacity is most expensive to instal (at a unit cost of c^b), but least expensive to run (at a unit cost of r^b), and hence highest in the merit order of operation.

The units of measurement of c and r are important. In this discussion running cost, r, is measured in pence per kilowatt hour (p/kWh) generated, and c is measured as the annual equivalent of installing a unit of capacity, in pounds per kilowatt per annum. Therefore c is the result of applying an annuity calculation to the actual construction cost of an electricity generating set with associated equipment, and dividing by the capacity installed in kilowatts. The annuity factor will be based on an assumed life for the plant, and the social discount rate—the government's required rate of return (RRR) in the case of the CEGB.

From Figure 5.1(b) it is clear that as higher and higher load is experienced (lasting for fewer and fewer hours), load increments are met by adding intermediate and then peaking capacity to the plant at the top of the merit order of operation–base load plant. To see why, consider in Figure 5.1(b) a load increment that is going to last for H_p hours of the year. Comparing the marginal costs of a unit of intermediate or peaking capacity, the system planners will only be indifferent between the two types when:

$$c^p + r^p H_p = c^i + r^i H_p \tag{5.4}$$

when running q^p for H_p hours at the high running cost r^p just offsets the saving on capital cost over intermediate capacity. Hence for load lasting less than H_p hours, it is cheaper to switch in peaking capacity because of its low capital costs. The critical H_p is then given by:

$$H_p = \frac{c^i - c^p}{r^p - r^i} \tag{5.5}$$

which can immediately be recognised as an application of equation (4.16), the condition for optimal plant mix.

Similarly, for loads lasting $(H_p + H_i)$ hours in Figure 5.1(b), planners will be indifferent between base load capacity, q^b, and intermediate capacity q^i, if their marginal costs are equal:

$$c^b + r^b(H_p + H_i) = c^i + r^i(H_p + H_i) \tag{5.6}$$

so that the critical switching point from base load to intermediate capacity is:

$$(H_p + H_i) = \frac{c^b - c^i}{r^i - r^b} \tag{5.7}$$

By equating these cost increments, the planners are sure of minimising the system costs of meeting the constraint in (5.1).

109

We can adapt the formulae in (5.4)–(5.7) to provide us with the *marginal capacity cost* of each type of plant. (This is not the marginal cost of output in the usual sense.) Suppose SMD rises by one unit, remembering that SMD lasts for an infinitely short duration in our simple model. It could be met by installing one more unit of peaking capacity, costing

$$c^p \tag{5.8}$$

On the other hand, it could be met by a unit of intermediate capacity which can immediately, as well as meeting the SMD increment, displace a unit of peaking capacity that would have run for H_p hours. The cost effect is:

$$c^i + (r^i - r^p)(H_p) \tag{5.9}$$

where the second expression is an offset to the first in terms of running cost savings.

Finally, another unit of base load capacity could have been used to meet the SMD increment, but at the same time displacing both a unit of intermediate capacity for $(H_p + H_i)$ hours and a unit of peaking capacity for H_p hours. It would cost net:

$$c^b + (r^b - r^i)(H_p + H_i) + (r^i - r^p)H_p \tag{5.10}$$

Here there are two sources of cost saving arising from the displacement down the merit order of both one unit of q^i and one unit of q^p.

When there is an optimal plant mix, then each of the marginal plant costs (5.8)–(5.10) must be the same, which is another way of stating the conditions (5.5) and (5.7):

$$c^b + (r^b - r^i)(H_p + H_i) + (r^i - r^p)H_p = c^i + (r^i - r^p)H_p =$$
$$c^p = \text{NEC} \tag{5.11}$$

This common marginal plant cost is usually referred to as the *net effective cost* of new capacity (written NEC in equation (5.11)).

It is now necessary to consider NEC when the system has not yet reached its optimum. In this case, system costs are not at a minimum (which would be the case if (5.11) did hold), and hence there are potential cost savings to be made by an appropriate scrapping and investment policy. In Figure 5.2, the actual plant mix is given by q_a^b, q_a^i and q_a^p, and the current load durations are G_p and $(G_p + G_i)$ hours for peaking and intermediate capacity. It

110

is apparent that, compared with the optimal H_p and $(H_p + H_i)$, there is insufficient base load capacity q^b relative to the amounts of q^p and q^i.

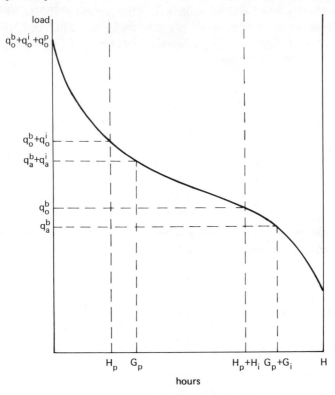

Figure 5.2

Using (5.11) as a benchmark, and noting $G_p > H_p$ and $(G_p + G_i)$ $> (H_p + H_i)$, it is now apparent that:

$$NEC^b = c^b + (r^b - r^i)(G_p + G_i) + (r^i - r^p)(G_p) \qquad (5.12)$$
$$>$$
$$NEC^i = c^i + (r^i - r^p)(G_p) \qquad (5.13)$$
$$>$$
$$NEC^p = c^p \qquad (5.14)$$

Hence the cost signal is to expand installation of q^b and q^i relative to q^p until (5.11) is re-established. Note that whereas in (5.11) we

111

would expect the common NEC to be a positive number (expressed as pounds per kilowatt per annum), it need not be the case that out of equilibrium, each of the NEC terms in (5.12)–(5.14) is positive. Clearly NEC^p will be positive (it is the common NEC to which the others rise as equilibrium is established), but NEC^i and NEC^b might at any time be negative—they only have to be less than NEC^p out of equilibrium.

Suppose we had the situation:

$$NEC^b < 0 < NEC^i < NEC^p \qquad (5.15)$$

This would suggest:

(i)   instal more base load capacity immediately because in so doing total costs will fall (and scrap some q^p in the process);
(ii) if it were then the case that $0 < NEC^b = NEC^i < NEC^p$, a demand increment should not be met by installing q^p, but by preferring q^b or q^i.

(Note that carrying out an investment policy reaps the available cost savings so that the subsequent NEC^b calculation is a higher number.)

Now finally we can allow for the use of capacity inherited from the past. Suppose only q^b and q^i are new, and that peaking plant, at the bottom of the merit order, is made up of old inherited capacity, the running costs of which are highest because it is obsolescent, but the capital costs of which are zero since they are sunk, $c^p = 0$.

In addition, another simplifying assumption, that SMD lasts only for an infinitesimal amount of time, can also be dropped, and we can now assume SMD lasts for H^* hours. The net effective cost calculations are in equilibrium:

$$\begin{aligned} NEC &= c^b + (r^b - r^i)(H_p + H_i) + (r^i - r^p)H_p + r^pH^* \\ &= c^i + (r^i - r^p)H_p + r^pH^* \\ &= r^pH^* \end{aligned} \qquad (5.16)$$

and all are equal to a common figure. Each term has added to it the running costs of meeting SMD from old peaking capacity, r^pH^*. The switch points H_p and $(H_p + H_i)$ are determined exactly as before (except that $c^p = 0$).

Consider the role of old capacity. Its availability is a benefit to the system and scrapping it is the only investment option. The cost effect of scrapping this old capacity is to save the last term in (5.16), r^pH^*, which is then referred to as the net avoidable cost (NAC) of inherited capacity. At a long-run optimal mix, increments in SMD can be met as cheaply from old as from new capacity, and NEC = NAC.

Now suppose the system is out of equilibrium and it is the case that:

$$0 < NAC < NEC^b = NEC^i \tag{5.17}$$

then an SMD increment should be met by once more postponing retirement of old capacity rather than investing in new. The important items in the coal *vs.* nuclear case therefore amount to:

(1)   Which is lower: NEC of new nuclear or NEC of new coal?
(2)   If one is negative, adopt it immediately, even if demand is not forecast to rise.
(3)   If both are positive, and as large or larger than NAC, then a demand increment should be met by postponing retirements rather than new investments.
(4)   As investment proceeds, potential cost savings are realised, and long-run equilibrium plant mix is characterised by:
$$NEC^b = NEC^i = NEC^p = NAC \geqslant 0.$$

The discount factor in NEC calculations

An expression for the net effective cost of capacity is critical to the analysis of the investment decision, and it is worth stopping at this point to compare (5.11) with the other forms of NEC calculation used in Chapter 4. In particular these were:

(i)   In the two periods–two plant model of (4.28)
$$NEC = c^2$$
$$= c^1 - 2(r^2 - r^1).$$

(ii)   In the two period variable running cost case of (4.34)
$$NEC = c - (m^* - r) - (m_1 - r)$$

Both of these versions measured capacity cost, c, in annual equivalent terms, and otherwise ignored discounting, while in the discounted present value model of (4.47):

(iii) $NEC = K - \Sigma(m - r)/(1 + i)^t$
$$= K - PV(m - r)$$

where PV stands for the discounted present value calculation, and K is actual installation cost.

In each case, NEC consists of the capacity cost of the equipment offset by its running cost savings over whichever equipment it displaces in the merit order of operation. The NEC terms of (4.28), (4.34) and (5.11) are all calculated only for the next cycle of demand (represented in the case of (5.11) by the whole annual load duration curve), and the terms labelled c^1, c^2, c, c^b all represent the capacity cost chargeable to this cycle alone. In contrast, (4.47) adopts as the cycle of demand sub-periods the whole lifetime of the plant's operation, with discounting at the rate i applied over the stream of cost savings. In (4.28), (4.34) and (5.11) it is this discount factor i that is used to calculate the cycle capacity cost terms, c.

In using (5.11), therefore, the analysis will need to be repeated for each year of a plant's life and the NEC term in (5.11) should be taken only as a typical year's calculation. More properly, in practice, the NEC terms will be calculated as discounted present values over the lifetime performance of the plant along the lines of (4.47).

The problem now arises of comparing plants with unequal working lives. Suppose the typical life of q^b plant is twenty years, but the typical life of q^i is thirty years; it would then be wrong simply to calculate NEC on the basis of 4.47 for each plant. Suppose NEC^b came out larger on this lifetime present value basis, and a unit of q^b is preferred to q^i. After twenty years, another plant must be installed, but if q^i had been chosen, no replacement investment is needed. In other words, it is wrong simply to compare the net present values when one plant supplies electricity for ten years less than the other. To compare with a unit of q^i, more than a unit of q^b is needed in this case.

One way out of the problem would be to take a common lifetime that incorporates several plants of each type, e.g. a 60-year investment programme would compare three identical, consecutive q^b units with two identical, consecutive q^i units. In this case (which is only an approximation since it is unlikely that worn-out plant will be replaced by identical new units after 20 or 30 years' technical progress), a short-cut calculation is provided by finding the annual equivalent of the discounted present value of a single unit's NEC for each plant type. Comparing these annuity factors for a single plant is equivalent to comparing sequences of plants, with a common programme lifetime, in net present value terms.

Adopting the convenient notation A[x] to represent the calculation of an annuity that has the same present value as the sum x, (5.11) can be written:

$$NEC = c^p$$
$$= c^i + A[(r^i - r^p)H_p]$$
$$= c^b + A[(r^b - r^i)(H_p + H_i) + (r^i - r^p)H_p]$$

and, of course, $c^b = A[K^b]$ when K^b is the actual installation cost (or its present value if incurred over several years), and similarly for the other capacity cost terms. The annuitised running cost terms, e.g. $A[(r^i - r^p)H_p]$, are now to be taken as the typical term in one year of the plant's life. The important point is that when such annual equivalent NEC terms are compared, as they are in Table 5.1 below, the role of the discount factor takes on critical importance. This is because the timing of the cost savings, if any, of each plant type will probably differ significantly among different plant types.

As with most of the rest of the analysis in this book, the discount factor is taken simply as the social opportunity cost of capital as signalled by the UK government's required rate of return on nationalised industry investments. Nevertheless, it remains a critical choice in the investment decision.

The CEGB analysis of nuclear generated electricity

The example of an incremental cost-benefit analysis of nuclear electricity generation that we shall examine is that used by the CEGB in 1979–80. This coincided with the case for the use of PWR as the basis of a new nuclear programme. Subsequent analyses have appeared at the Sizewell 'B' Public Inquiry held through 1983 and 1984.

Having developed its demand and cost forecasts, and having examined both nuclear and coal-fired stations as base load capacity in the simulation of load duration curves many years ahead, the CEGB calculated the net effective costs (NEC) of these capacity types to be the figures shown in Table 5.1.

These calculations form the principal evidence submitted by the CEGB to the House of Commons select committee on energy for its report on the government's interim statement on the new nuclear programme (SCE, 1980–81).

115

Table 5.1: Net effective cost (NEC) of nuclear and coal-fired generating stations (£/kW per annum, 1980 prices)

	Nuclear	Coal-fired
capital charges	77	36
fuel costs	34	113
other operating costs	12	10
total generation costs	123	159
less fuel saving from displacing less efficient plant	148	143
NEC	−25	+16
(lifetime average load factor, per cent)	63	54

Source: CEGB *Annual Report and Accounts,* 1979–80.

Consider their details: the basic NEC is calculated as an annual equivalent sum for each programme and divided by the total size of each programme to obtain comparable marginal cost estimates in £ per kW per year. The first row of the table describes the capital cost element (c^b in our notation) and of the two candidates, coal-fired stations have much lower capital and construction costs. This item has to include interest during construction, since installation takes several years. For nuclear plant it must also include the distant, and therefore heavily discounted, cost of decommissioning the still highly radioactive reactor at the end of its life.

The second row describes the fuel component of direct operating costs, and clearly nuclear appears to have the advantage over coal in this case. This item must clearly be sensitive to forecasts of both coal and uranium prices, and the CEGB essentially assumes it will always buy UK coal from the National Coal Board, and uranium on the world market. These fuel costs include, for nuclear plant, the cost of the fabricated elements (fuel rods, and so on), local storage of irradiated fuel, transport of irradiated fuel with its own special problems, reprocessing, intermediate long-term storage, vitrification of the spent fuel, and ultimate waste disposal. Similarly for coal, it includes ash handling and disposal.

The third row refers to all direct operating costs other than fuel, and includes wages and salaries, repair, rent, rates and administration costs.

Finally, the credit item: fuel savings from displacing less efficient plant down the merit order is added to arrive at the NEC in the form discussed above. These fuel savings are larger for nuclear

116

than for coal because nuclear plant will remain high on the merit order for a larger part of its life than the coal-fired generating stations, and this is shown by the forecasts of lifetime average load factor given for each plant: nuclear, 63 per cent; coal, 54 per cent.

The negative NEC for nuclear plant therefore arises because its forecast fuel savings and lower fuel costs more than outweigh the capital cost advantage of the coal-fired generating plant. The background parameters of this analysis are that nuclear plants have a life of 25 years, while coal-fired plants have a life of 30 years, and the discount rate is 5 per cent: the government's required rate of return.

The figures refer to what the CEGB calls the basic NEC estimates for a nuclear *vs.* coal programme. Note that nuclear NEC does not distinguish the PWR case from the AGR. The phrase 'basic NEC' means that some background variables (e.g. coal prices) are set at the mean of the forecast range of possibilities, while plant-specific factors, construction time and so on, are set at the CEGB's target levels, and therefore may differ from past experience.

Two areas of the CEGB case for the 1980–81 nuclear programme were clearly critical: the demand assumptions and the cost assumptions, and the criticisms applied to these warrant discussion. The next two sections consider the demand forecasts, and then the sensitivity analyses associated with different cost assumptions are examined.

Overall demand forecast

The CEGB has to forecast system maximum demand beginning about 6–8 years ahead and proceeding from that point, though the more distant the forecast, the less critical it is since the system planners have more time to adjust the investment programme. Two aspects of the demand forecast have been singled out as important. First, the economic assumptions underlying the level of the forecast of maximum demand and total generation. Such assumptions cover economic growth rates, the trend of energy prices, elasticities of demand, and so on. Secondly, the maximum demand forecast is multiplied up by a factor that allows for uncertainty and risk of supply failures. This planning margin itself is of roughly the same magnitude as the proposed nuclear programme, and hence the economic case for a particular size of planning margin needs to be examined.

We begin with the forecasting assumptions in this section.

In presenting a case for the nuclear programme to the select committee on energy, two sets of demand forecasts were used, produced separately by the Department of Energy (1979), and the CEGB (1980). The Department of Energy projections which we can refer to as M16 (the memorandum number in the select committee's evidence), were an updated version of the Green Paper (Cmnd. 7101), using essentially the same planning assumptions.

(a) Economic growth in two scenarios: higher and lower. In the higher case GDP was assumed to grow at a little under 3 per cent to the end of the century (in fact 3 per cent to 1990, and 2.4 per cent thereafter, equivalent to 2.8 per cent overall).

In the lower case, GDP would grow at about 2 per cent to 2000 (M16, para. 2).

(b) Crude oil prices, treated as the marginal cost of energy would rise by about $2\frac{1}{2}$ times in real terms reaching \$30 per barrel in 1977 prices by 2000 (M16, para. 2).

(c) Conservation allowances that represent a reduction in demand for useful energy of around 20 per cent below what it might otherwise have been (M16, para. 8).

These assumptions then generate overall primary energy demand figures for the year 2000, which represent annual growth rates of energy of 0.9 (lower) to 1.5 (higher) per cent (M16, para. 9).

Pearce (1980) has suggested an ingenious way of testing the implicit elasticities underlying these assumptions. Since we know the exogenous growth rates of GDP and energy prices (g_y and g_p, respectively) and the final endogenous growth rate of energy, g_e, we could impose the convenient economic structure:

$$g_e = \varepsilon_y g_y + \varepsilon_p g_p$$

to obtain the elasticities for income and prices, ε_y and ε_p implied by the M16 projections. (Note there is no presumption that the Department of Energy used a model of this nature, it is simply one implication of the assumptions of M16.) The assumptions (a) and (b) above contain one anomaly, the price escalation of $2\frac{1}{2}$ times quoted in M16, para. 2 is greater than would be needed

118

to raise 1977 crude oil prices of \$14 a barrel to the assumed \$30 a barrel, so let us take g_p as 3.4 per cent a year, which does produce \$30 a barrel by 2000. With the higher case GDP growth of 2.8 per cent and the lower case of 2.0 per cent, we have two equations to obtain ε_y and ε_p:

higher: $1.5 = \varepsilon_y(2.8) + \varepsilon_p(3.4)$
lower: $0.9 = \varepsilon_y(2.0) + \varepsilon_p(3.4)$
yielding: $\varepsilon_y = 0.75$, and $\varepsilon_p = -0.18$

(In Pearce's own calculations he assumed $\varepsilon_y = 0.88$ and obtained $\varepsilon_p = -0.3$.) Thus, when M16 talks about conservation allowances of 20 per cent, it is by implication assuming that the long-run price elasticity of energy demand lies somewhere near -0.18.

Critics of the M16 forecasts have concentrated on the assumptions about g_y and the implied ε_p values. As Pearce points out, periods when the UK growth rate has averaged 2–3 per cent over thirty years are very rare in this century anyway, and with the prolonged recession following the publication of the M16 forecasts, these assumptions are already wildly optimistic. Secondly, critics have argued that the assumed long-run price elasticity is significantly below the values found in other research work (see Chapter 2 above), and probably leads to an underestimate of the price-induced conservation in energy over the next twenty years. It is certainly below the conservation potential analysed for example in Leach (1977).

The CEGB produced its own set of demand forecasts for the select committee, in its memorandum M17, and used growth rate assumptions of 1.5–3.5 per cent. Clearly, the criticisms of optimism were applied even more strongly to this range than to the Department of Energy. The CEGB reported to the Monopolies and Mergers Commission (1981) that it did not think electricity demand very responsive to price changes and judged the overall price elasticity of electricity demand to be about -0.1. In fact, as MMC (1981) shows, the CEGB had rather a poor record of forecasting in the 1970s, having consistently overestimated system maximum demand, sometimes by as much as 40 per cent. M17 indicates that the CEGB forecast of the *new* plant requirement for 1998 to allow for its growth forecast and plant retirement, was between 18 and 49 gW on its low and high growth assumptions. These are enormous requirements, and the Department of Energy had used a central forecast of around 33–6 gW new *nuclear* capacity, (M16, para. 17) by 2000, while the CEGB itself wanted 15 gW new *nuclear* capacity by 1992 (M17, para. 14). This implied building one or two nuclear plants of 1.5 gW capacity each year to the end of the century—a plant construction programme far in excess of anything ever attempted, let alone achieved in the UK. The select committee took the view that these forecasts were both overoptimistic and unrealistic.

The planning margin for supply failure

Apart from the forecasts of system maximum demand implied by these forecasts of overall demand, we must also consider the second aspect of demand forecasts, the inclusion of a margin of spare capacity.

The CEGB applies two steps in arriving at its 'planning plant margin': (i) the adoption of a security standard, and (ii) the translation of the standard into the plant margin.

Consider the peak demand constraint (5.1) above, and write q $(= q^b + q^i + q^p)$ as total installed capacity:

$$(q - SMD^*) \geqslant 0 \tag{5.18}$$

When uncertainty is present, the demand forecast is the mean of a range that depends on weather conditions, and we use the symbol SMD^* to represent the forecast maximum demand for average weather conditions.

However, forecasts may be wrong, and although both q and SMD^* are fixed numbers, the critical constraint in practice is:

$$(P - X) \geqslant 0 \tag{5.19}$$

where P is *actual* capacity available, and X is the *actual* SMD that the system must meet $(P - X)$, the actual (plant–load) margin is a random variable, and its assumed distribution (e.g. the normal) is shown in Figure 5.3.

The variance, σ^2, of this actual margin will be known from experience and will reflect three sources of error:
1. unexpected non-availability of plant,
2. errors in the SMD^* forecast,
3. weather variability.

Consider now a simplified analysis of the CEGB procedure (based

120

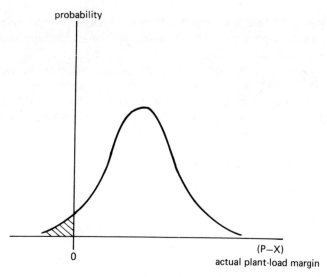

probability

(P–X)
actual plant-load margin

0

Figure 5.3.

on Bates and Fraser (1974), Ch. 6). We need to determine a value for q (installed capacity) that accounts for the random variation in (P–X). The system planner must set an acceptable maximum level of risk, r, that (P–X) the actual (plant–load) margin will be in deficit:

$$\text{prob} [(P-X \leqslant 0)] = r \tag{5.20}$$

and this is shown as the shaded area in Figure 5.3. Reading from tables of the normal distribution, we find the corresponding Z value (standard normal deviate), i.e.:

$$\text{prob} [(Z_r \leqslant (0-\mu)/\sigma)] = r \tag{5.21}$$

allowing us to write:

$$\mu = Z_r\sigma \tag{5.22}$$

for this critical value, Z_r. Remembering σ is known, we must now consider μ. By definition μ is the expected value or mean of the actual (plant–load) margin, (P–X):

$$\mu = \text{mean } (P-X) = \text{mean } (P) - \text{mean } (X)$$
$$= E(P) - E(X)$$

Now the mean availability of plant, $E(P)$, is simply installed capacity multiplied by the mean percentage non-availability, α, itself known from past experience:

$$E(P) = \alpha q$$

and the expected load, $E(X)$, is just the already determined forecast of system maximum demand in average weather conditions, SMD*, so that (5.22) becomes:

$$\mu = (\alpha q - \text{SMD*}) = Z_r \sigma \qquad (5.23)$$

or

$$q = \frac{Z_r \sigma}{\alpha} + \frac{\text{SMD*}}{\alpha} \qquad (5.24)$$

The first part of the formula allows for the combined variability due to the three independent sources of error described above, while the second allows for the mean non-availability of plant due to 'forced outage'. Clearly, as more stringent security standards are chosen (lower values for r in (5.24)), the Z_r value in (5.24) and hence the value of q must rise. The margin is usually expressed in ratio form, as m, the planning plant margin:

$$m = \frac{q - \text{SMD*}}{\text{SMD*}} \qquad (5.19)$$

and Figure 5.4 shows the relationship between m, the plant margin, and r, the security standard. There are two curves, because there are two equivalent definitions of a deficit. At full load there may be load-shedding in the form of reduced voltage. This provides one (m, r) curve. Beyond $7\frac{1}{2}$ per cent voltage reductions disconnections will occur when there is a deficit, and this gives a second (m, r) curve linked to the first. The single security standard can be set as a risk level, r, along either curve: e.g. the current CEGB standard is:

  risk, r, of some load shedding in 20 winters in 100
and, risk, r, of disconnections in 3–4 winters in 100

These together imply a plant margin on the current CEGB system of 28 per cent spare capacity. This margin itself has risen substantially since the mid-1960s, although the security standard has not changed. This is because as larger generating sets are installed, a single breakdown leads to a much greater capacity loss than

122

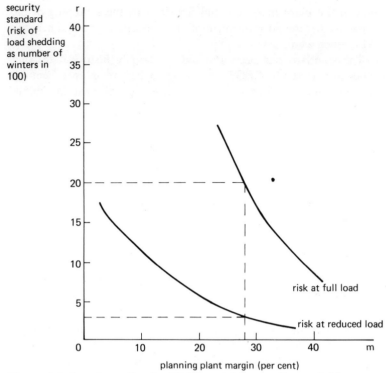

Figure 5.4 (based on Berrie (1968) and Monopolies and Mergers Commission (1981))

was the case 10 or 15 years ago. In a sense, this is a risk-based diseconomy of scale, and is referred to by engineers as a *rise in the loss of load probability* (LOLP).

While the need for a planning margin in demand forecasts is incontrovertible, much criticism both from official and academic commentators has been directed toward the arbitrary choice of security standard adopted. The select committee on energy advocated a lower standard and an attempt to improve reliability, while the Monopolies and Mergers Commission have reported considerable pressure on the CEGB from the Treasury to reduce the standard or the margin. The rise from the 1968 level of 17 per cent to the 1983 level of 28 per cent alone amounts to about 4 gW at the 1968 capacity level, or more than three AGRs equivalent to the latest under construction (Heysham II). (Of course, a reduction in the plant margin would first lead to the scrapping of old capacity, not the postponement of new capacity that had a negative NEC, such as nuclear.)

The standard has been adopted for largely historical reasons, reflecting what the CEGB has come to believe is an acceptable risk of supply disruption, in the sense of not arousing public hostility.

Cost-benefit analysis of the security margin

Critics of the CEGB, however, have advocated the application of cost-benefit analysis to the setting of the security standard itself. The essential point is that the CEGB clearly applies a very high standard of security of supply to its sales to area boards, and these in turn apply high reliability standards to their transmission and distribution networks. But how can we decide whether these standards are too high? Two calculations are necessary: first, the marginal cost of reliability implied by the current plant margin must be calculated; and, secondly, some estimate made of the marginal social benefit associated with a reliable electricity supply. Neither calculation is straightforward, though valuable insights have been offered by Webb (1977), Munasinghe (1979), and the Monopolies and Mergers Commission reports on the CEGB (MMC, 1981) and the Yorkshire Electricity Board (MMC, 1983; Cmnd. 9014).

Take the implied marginal cost of security first. The typical consumer loses very little electricity due to supply interruptions on the national grid, and the vast bulk of the hours lost over the last twenty years has been due to industrial disputes or distribution failures rather than shortage of generating capacity. The MMC report (1981) mentioned an Electricity Council calculation that in 1978 the last gas turbine plant served to prevent the need for two hours of disconnections at system peak.

The MMC report estimated both the NEC of gas turbine (peaking) capacity and the NAC of low merit inherited capacity at approximately £10 per kW p.a. Hence the marginal reliability cost of the two hours' disruption saved at current reliability levels could be approximated at 1981 prices as:

$$\text{NEC}^p/(\text{hours saved}) = \frac{£10/\text{kW}}{2} = £5/\text{kW hour.}$$

124

To determine whether this standard is excessive, the marginal value placed on rescued electricity at this standard of reliability needs to be calculated. This is a complex idea, but note first that the MMC report rejected arguments by both the CEGB and the Yorkshire Electricity Board that security was supplied cheaply because the costs of the plant margin divided by total kW hours generated in a year was a negligible percentage of consumers' bills. This is simply a crude averaging of revenues and is no guide to marginal valuations.

What is needed is an estimate of what consumers are willing to pay to avoid an unexpected disruption or supply outage. This will clearly vary with the type of consumer (residential, industrial, commercial), the duration of disruption, whether it occurs at night or at a system peak, and whether advance warning was given. For investment in generating capacity, to meet forecast SMD, we require the marginal value per kWh at time of system peak for a short duration interruption averaged over all consumers.

For residential consumers, it might appear that the obvious starting point is the consumer surplus from electricity consumption, but this has several drawbacks arising from the difficulty of measuring the item required.

To begin with it is necessary to distinguish between willingness to pay for planned consumption and willingness to pay to avoid an unexpected outage. The latter is likely to far exceed the former, but it is only the former item that is measurable from the usual econometric studies of observed demand functions. We would expect therefore the marginal willingness to pay to avoid an unplanned outage to be many times the price of the last unit consumed, so that the average price of electricity makes a very poor candidate even as a lower bound.

Secondly, even where models are able to construct *expected* welfare measures that allow for random shortages of supply capacity, the calculation itself depends on the way in which load shedding or rationing is applied. This can be made clear with the aid of Figure 5.5, based on Crew and Kleindorfer (1979), p. 70.

Since price cannot be altered when a sudden unexpected outage occurs, it is kept fixed at $\bar{p}$ throughout the supply disruption. Suppose that due either to a random surge in demand or to a random outage of the generating supply, capacity available at $\bar{p}$ is $\bar{q}$, so that Δq units will be lost, i.e. demanded but not supplied. The

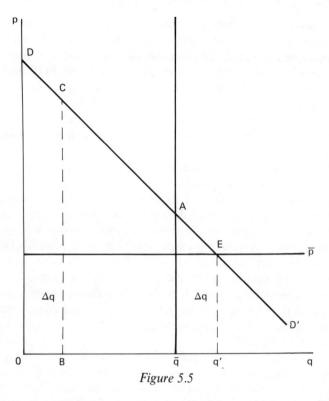

Figure 5.5

question is which consumers are cut off. If those with lowest willingness to pay are cut off (rationing in order of willingness to pay)
then consumer surplus plus total revenue is given by ODA$\bar{q}$. But
such rationing may not be possible if, for example, part of the
distribution network has failed. In any case, it is highly unlikely
that the supplier could be aware of the rankings of willingness
to pay of individual consumers. It may be the case, therefore, that
those with highest willingness to pay are cut off, leaving consumer
surplus plus total revenue of BCEq' only.

Without knowledge of which form of rationing to apply, and
without allowing for the costs of administering the appropriate
rationing scheme, using the idea of expected consumer surplus measures becomes impracticable as a guide to valuing lost or rescued
electricity.

For reasons like these, many economists prefer not to use an
expected consumer surplus approach, and have developed alterna-

126

tive measures. Munasinghe (1979) has provided the most detailed analysis of electricity supply reliability and his analysis is worth considering in some detail. For both residential and industrial sectors he treats electricity as an input in the production of household or firm outputs rather than as a commodity that enters utility functions directly.

Let us consider residential and industrial outage costs separately in turn. The model of residential consumption identifies three household outputs partly dependent on electricity: housekeeping, nutrition and leisure. The first two, it is argued, show significant substitutability between outage-dependent processes and outage-independent processes: i.e. much housekeeping can be rescheduled away from periods when supply is disrupted, and alternative means of cooking and/or purchasing meals are available. However, certain types of leisure are heavily dependent on electricity, (e.g. television viewing, evening reading) and these are usually confined to a critical number of evening hours (typically 19.30–22.00 p.m.). Munasinghe argued, therefore, that the chief outage cost of residential supply disruption is the loss of a critical period of evening leisure which is electricity-dependent. The willingness to pay to avoid this loss of leisure output is measured by the opportunity costs of the factors involved in producing the leisure output, to provide a measure of residential outage cost, OC^R:

$$OC^R = w\Delta t + p\Delta e + b\Delta k$$

i.e. the opportunity cost of the time lost, Δt, valued at the wage or income-earning rate, w, plus the cost of electricity, $p\Delta e$, plus the opportunity cost of the appliances left idle, $b\Delta k$—this might be measured for example by 1 hour's depreciation of a television set or hi-fi equipment, where b is the income forgone to purchase the hour's usage. Since the electricity lost will not be charged for, and the idle appliance cost will usually be negligible in the usual time-periods involved, the dominant item in residential outage costs is the opportunity cost of lost leisure time as measured by the wage rate, w.

In an empirical test of this hypothesis, Munasinghe described a World Bank survey of Brazilian consumers which confirmed that outage avoidance was highly valued by households for a critical period of evening leisure, and given negligible valuation for short daytime durations. Three critical questions from the survey were:

127

- During what hours is electricity essential for the enjoyment of your leisure?
- If an unexpected outage occurred during these critical hours. . . . how much extra would you be willing to pay to avoid:

  (a) a 1-minute interruption

  .   .

  .   .

  .   .

  (f) a 2-hour interruption.
- How much would you pay to avoid an unexpected outage outside these critical hours.

The sample indicated a critical mean 1.5 hours in the evening (with low s.d.) in response to the first question, a zero valuation in response to the third question, and a rising valuation in response to the second, which correlated closely with the household's hourly earnings.

As an example, suppose that 1 hour's outage in the critical evening leisure period was valued at a 1984 UK hourly earning rate of £3.50, and that the average household consumed 6 kWh per hour in winter evenings: then it could be argued that the willingness to pay to avoid a winter evening outage is £(3.5/6) per kWh = £0.58 per kWh. This can be compared with the average unit price of residential electricity in the UK in 1984 of 4.99p per kWh making the avoidance of unexpected losses of residential electricity in winter evenings 12 times as valuable as the unit price of uninterrupted supply.

Turning now to industrial costs, the important relationship is between output and inputs. The competitive firm's profit level is:

$$\pi = py - \Sigma p_i x_i - p_e e$$

where p is the price of its product, y is output, x_i are inputs with prices p_i, and $p_e e$ is expenditure on electricity. If use of each input depends on the supply of electricity, then the effect of an unexpected outage is:

$$\frac{\Delta \pi}{\Delta e} = \Sigma (p.MP_i - p_i) \frac{\Delta x_i}{\Delta e} - p_e$$

where MP_i is the marginal product of the ith factor of production.

In the short run, factors might have zero opportunity cost, p_i, if they cannot be re-employed in other work during the outage, and the resulting loss is called the idle factor cost, IFC:

$$\text{IFC} = \Sigma p.\text{MP}_i \frac{\Delta x_i}{\Delta e} - p_e = p\frac{\Delta y}{\Delta e} - p_e$$

In addition some inputs (i.e. materials and products) in processes may be ruined by the outage (e.g. in the food industry), and an additional term, spoiled product cost (SPC) must be added. Depending on the duration of the outage, d, some of the lost value added associated with idle factors may be recoverable during subsequent slack periods, though possibly only by paying an overtime premium, ρ. This gives industrial outage costs for a year as:

$$\text{OC}^1 = \sum_{j=1}^{f} \text{SPC}(d_j) + \sum_{j=1}^{f} \text{IFC}(d_j) - \sum_{j=1}^{f} \text{RC}(\rho,d_j) - \sum_{j=1}^{f} E(d_j)$$

where f is the number of outages in a year, RC is the amount of IFC subsequently recovered, and E is expenditure saved on electricity. Each term depends on the outage durations and RC depends on overtime costs as well.

Having developed this model of industrial outage costs, Munasinghe (1979) was able to use it to devise a questionnaire for industrial consumers in Brazil who had experienced outages. It is important to recognise that by developing a model of the outage costs, the design of the questionnaire could be made much more precise and productive. In Munasinghe's case, short duration outage costs amount to $1-3\frac{1}{2}$ times the analogous costs claimed by residential consumers for their evening leisure periods.

Once outage costs have been established in theory and estimated in practice by survey work, they can be incorporated into an investment decision such as that of choosing the type of generation system. Both Munasinghe and Turvey and Anderson (1977, Chapter 14) have shown how this might be done. Munasinghe drew up a set of possible investment programmes with different levels of generating and transmission reliability—this would correspond to different planning margins in the context of the CEGB's nuclear *vs.* coal decision. Reliability was measured by:

$$R = 1 - \frac{\text{(expected present value of lost electricity)}}{\text{(expected present value of total electricity supplied)}}$$

and generating and transmission systems with different plant and capacity margins could then give different future supply capacities according to the reliability index. Naturally higher reliability added to system supply costs (SC), as shown in Figure 5.6, but at the same time, higher reliability reduced consumers' outage costs OC^R + OC^I with these being zero for $R = 1.0$. Munasinghe then argued that rather than choose a supply system that minimised SC, the public utility should choose one with a reliability index that minimised total cost, TC:

$$TC = SC + OC^R + OC^I$$

i.e. the costs of supply *and* outages. This gives the reliability level R_M in Figure 5.6, and this might, for example, be lower than some arbitrarily imposed reliability standard as in the CEGB's planning margin. (It was in the case of Munasinghe's Brazilian utility case study.) The condition for minimising TC is that the marginal reduc-

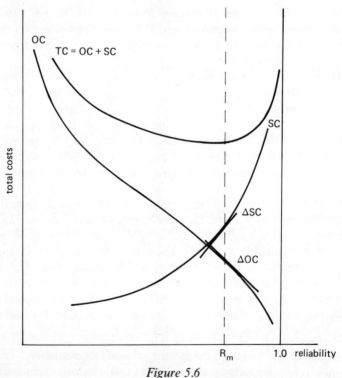

Figure 5.6

tion in outage cost from higher reliability should equal the marginal increase in system supply cost from higher reliability:

$$| \Delta(OC^R + OC^I) | = | \Delta SC |.$$

This rather extended discussion of the costs and benefits of reliability has taken us away from the precise details of coal *vs.* nuclear generation in the UK. But the discussion is important to that decision, for two reasons:

1. At present, a large part of the demand for new capacity (the security margin) is arbitrarily determined, when a cost-benefit analysis would be practicable.
2. The CEGB's objective—the minimisation of system supply costs—is clearly not the only possibility, since minimisation of supply and outage costs raised another possible criterion.

Both MMC (1981) and Webb (1977) in the UK case, argue that where cost-benefit analyses of security margins have been carried out, the marginal benefits of added security fall short of the implicit marginal costs of the current security standard—compare, for example, the marginal security cost figure of £5/kWh by MMC (1981), and mentioned at the outset of our discussion, with the value of £1.30/kWh which MMC (1981) reports as the Electricity Council's informal estimate of consumers' willingness to pay to avoid outages. Both MMC and the select committee took the view that the overall CEGB planning margin was excessive, and hence the demand forecasts in the nuclear case needed to be revised downward.

Cost assumptions in the nuclear case

The probable costs of nuclear power have caused considerable controversy as well as the demand forecasts. We now turn to examine these in the context of the sensitivity analyses applied by MMC and SCE to the CEGB case. The cost assumptions fall into three broad areas: (1) fuel prices and availability; (2) construction costs and time; and (3) plant performance variables. These are taken in turn.

Two types of fuel price must be forecast, coal prices (both for the UK National Coal Board (NCB) and in world coal markets), and the nuclear fuel cycle costs. The CEGB has for many years been the NCB's chief customer, currently buying about 78 million tonnes a year, and for much of the last 10 or 15 years this 'coal burn' was set at an uneconomically high level in order to mitigate the decline of the NCB, which began in the 1950s and was only arrested in the late 1970s. In its nuclear case, the CEGB expected coal prices to rise at approximately 4 per cent a year until the 1980s, and subsequently at about 1 per cent as new pits were developed. In the late 1970s it had believed these price rises would keep UK and world prices in step; but by 1980, the CEGB had revised this assumption to one in which world coal prices outstripped UK prices by up to 40 per cent by 2000, even after assuming the gradual phasing-out of coal subsidies by the government. The MMC found these forecasts 'highly implausible', and felt that rising world coal prices that reflected international marginal production costs would pull up UK prices. Although this would favour the nuclear case, the MMC appeared to take the view that implausible forecasting of coal prices cast doubt on the CEGB's other forecasting efforts.

For the nuclear fuel cycles (nfc) there are four categories of cost: procurement of uranium, enrichment of the fissionable isotopes, fabrication of the nuclear fuel elements, and managing the irradiated fuel (including waste disposal, reprocessing and long-term storage). Rises in the first two components would, the CEGB believed, be offset by falling costs of fabrication leaving a net overall increase of 1.7 per cent per year in nfc costs. Nevertheless, the absence of settled technologies and cost analyses of reprocessing, disposal and storage meant there were major uncertainties in these fuel cost estimates.

For fuel cost variables, the CEGB had generally adopted mean estimates from a likely range, but had taken a different approach to the plant related variables: construction costs and times and plant performance. In its nuclear case these were usually set at the target rather than likely levels, leading the MMC to criticise the use of the phrase 'basic NECs' in Table 5.1, since it implied something much more optimistic than average forecast NEC.

For construction costs, the CEGB was in the habit of adding $17\frac{1}{2}$ per cent allowances for all types of plant to allow for cost over-runs. But as the MMC pointed out, their experience of previous nuclear programmes amount to at least 100 per cent cost over-runs in construction. On construction time, the CEGB assumed a target 72 months for nuclear stations, despite actual experience that suggested average construction times of 100 months for coal-fired stations, and 157 months (13 years) for nuclear stations.

In terms of plant performance, the critical assumptions were how quickly, if at all, would new plant reach its designed capacity (usually 1500 mW) and what would be its average availability allowing for maintenance and refuelling (either while on-load or while not delivering electricity).

The MMC expressed dissatisfaction with the CEGB case-sensitivity analyses in two ways. First, it felt that likely rather than target assumptions should be adopted; and secondly, it pointed out that in presenting the nuclear case to the government and the public (e.g. in evidence to the select committee) the CEGB had not provided calculations that showed NECs when more than one assumption broke down at once, preferring to allow for only one wrong forecast at a time. To counter this 'appraisal optimism', the MMC asked the CEGB to recalculate the NECs under a combination of fresh assumptions, as set out in Table 5.2.

In drawing up these alternative assumptions, the MMC wanted to see the effect of:

(i) lifetime capacity ratings reflecting the likely current AGR programme values;

(ii) average availability reflecting the difficulties experienced in current AGR on-load refuelling;

Table 5.2: The CEGB's basic estimates and alternative assumptions (March 1980 prices)

		CEGB	Alternative
(i)	nuclear fuel cycle (nfc) costs	£40/kW	£48/kW (+20%)
(ii)	plant-related factors		
	(a) nuclear capital cost	£78/kW	£86/kW (+10%)
	(b) nuclear construction time	6 years	8 years
	(c) coal capital cost	£35/kW	£37/kW (+5%)
	(d) coal construction time	6 years	7 years
(iii)	plant performance		
	(a) nuclear annual average availability	66%	65%
	(b) nuclear winter peak availability	86%	85%
	(c) nuclear lifetime capacity rating	100%	95%
	(d) build up to nuclear full rating and availability	3 years	4 years

Source: Adapted from MMC (1981) p. 104, Table 5.13.

(iii) construction time estimates closer to actual experience;

(iv) nfc costs that allowed for uncertainty in reprocessing nuclear fuel.

The key factor in these assumptions was that they tried to reflect the limited actual experience of the CEGB with its current AGR stations, in order to discover the robustness of the nuclear case to different assumptions. Table 5.3 shows the outcome of the combined sensitivity analyses, and makes it clear that the CEGB case for the nuclear programme was very vulnerable to assumption changes. Combining the allowances results in the nuclear NEC exceeding the net avoidable cost associated with postponing investment and retaining old plant, while reducing the nuclear advantage over new coal-fired plant by a factor of more than five.

The CEGB itself had carried out one combined sensitivity analysis which was not shown to the Department of Energy or the select committee, but was first published by the MMC itself (1981, p. 94

Table 5.3: Results of the sensitivity assumptions of Table 5.2 (£/kW per annum, March 1980 prices)

		NEC of typical AGR nuclear plant	NEC of typical coalfield plant	NAC of inherited capacity
1.	CEGB	− 18	+ 22	+ 10
2.	MMC alternative assumptions	+ 18*	+ 25	+ 10
Contributory factors in 2:				
(i)		+ 8	—	
(ii)	(a)	+ 8	—	
	(b)	+ 13	—	
	(c)	—	+ 2	
	(d)	—	+ 1	
(iii)	(a)	+ 2	—	
	(b)	+ 0.5	—	
	(c)	+ 4	—	
	(d)	+ 0.3	—	
		35.8	3	

* Rounded up.

Source: Adapted from MMC (1981), p. 107, Table 5.14.

Table 5.11). Assuming that a repeat of all the over-runs and de-ratings experienced with the first AGR programme would character-ise any future AGR or PWR programmes, this analysis showed that new coal-fired plant had an NEC lower than that of the PWR, and nearly half that of the AGR.

On the basis of these sensitivity analyses, used to allow for un-certainty, and the observation that the basic NECs used in the CEGB case contained optimistic plant performance forecasts not correlated with past experience, the MMC argued that it was not convinced that the CEGB had demonstrated a robust case for its nuclear programme.

In summary, we have seen the development up to 1981 for the CEGB's assessment of the nuclear power programme, and the areas of the analyses open to criticism. In 1979, the CEGB arguments had convinced the government that there was a reasonable basis for its proposed nuclear programme, although the only commitment made was to allow design work and planning for the first station (Sizewell 'B') to be begun. It was decided that Sizewell 'B's public inquiry would be used to question all the assumptions behind the CEGB case. The MMC and select committee reports cast quite severe doubts on the economic case put up by the CEGB, with the consequence that in arguing its case once again before the Sizewell 'B' public inquiry, the CEGB was compelled to try to find a more rigorous justification for the nuclear programme than it had succeeded in doing previously.

Broader issues in nuclear cost-benefit analysis

In this final section, we turn to consider some very broad back-ground issues that have been raised in the context of the nuclear *vs.* coal cost-benefit analysis, though we shall only mention them rather than do them justice.

Once of the clearest treatments of the broader issues is that by Pearce (1979), who seeks to discover the value of cost-benefit analysis in the nuclear case. We already know from Chapter 3 the nature of the value judgements involved in looking at potential Pareto improvements, and Pearce emphasises that these are particu-larly restrictive and narrow in the case of a nuclear power pro-gramme, the consequences of which are spread over many gen-erations. This is highlighted by the way in which calculation of

135

present values using a positive social discount rate involves us today in imposing our preferences on generations who experience the costs and benefits of a long-lived nuclear future without being present to have their willingness to pay counted. This is true, of course, of any long-lived programme, but Pearce is arguing that such consequences may be less reversible in the nuclear case.

In addition, the nuclear cost-benefit analysis involves the estimation of the social costs of as yet undiscovered technologies (e.g. in the long-term disposal of radioactive waste as opposed to its short-term storage). Other unknowns include the possible costs of low-level radiation damage involving human life valuations, as well as the impact of low-probability but high-cost nuclear accidents. None of these issues is, in principle, only associated with nuclear power and no other cost-benefit analysis, but the practical difficulties of the nuclear cost-benefit analysis may be of an enormously higher order of magnitude.

Pearce argues, however, that nuclear power does raise issues—such as the defence of civil liberties in a nuclear society, or the problem of weapons proliferation when nuclear enrichment processes become more widely available—which are simply not amenable to cost-benefit analysis at all.

Conclusion

This chapter has focused on some of the issues raised by the choice between nuclear and coal-fired electricity generation. The case study details date from the CEGB's estimated figures for 1980, but these are less important than the analytical issues raised. In terms of the cost-benefit analysis, these are (1) the nature of the demand forecasts, including the allowance for a security margin for supply reliability; and (2) the nature of the cost assumptions. Where possible we have looked at alternative critical analyses to those used by the CEGB, though restricting the detailed critiques to those voiced by other arms of government itself: the Monopolies and Mergers Commission and the select committee on energy.

6

Electricity and gas prices in practice

Introduction

Chapters 3 and 4 set out the theoretical basis of marginal cost pricing in energy supply, and now it is time to consider the implementation of these ideas in the UK electricity and gas industries. The analysis will focus on the treatment of the peak load problem and the consequent definition of prices and quantities by *time of use* (tou). In earlier chapters the price term is unambiguously the cost per unit consumed, but in the fuel industries it is customary to have two definitions of demand, and hence two types of price. The straightforward price per kilowatt hour (kWh) which is all that is necessary to the theoretical peak load pricing solution in electricity supply is still to be used, and is referred to as an *energy charge*. However the fuel industries also refer to the demand level in kilowatts (kW), as the power available at a point in time, so that 1 kWh is 1 kW used for 1 hour, and hence have developed the idea of a *demand charge* in £ per kW. Although the economist's theoretical solution need not make any use of kW demand charges, they are used in practice and must be analysed as an alternative to tou prices, which will usually be expressed in kWh terms. If, for example, the industry were certain that each consumer's maximum demand occurred simultaneously at system peak then a demand charge based on the individual's maximum kW might be an alternative way of penalising peak consumption. The analogous terms in gas supply (sometimes referred to as capacity and commodity charges instead of demand and energy charges), are expressed in £ per therm per day for the demand charge and pence per therm for the time of use energy charge.

This chapter first examines the basic empirical work on the price elasticity of peak demand, before considering, in turn, a method for designing gas and electricity tou prices in the absence of detailed demand information, and actual electricity and gas charges in recent UK experience.

Time of use (tou) studies

Most of the empirical work on energy economics has concentrated on annual or quarterly sales, but this is an inadequate reflection of the importance of the peak load problem. It is essential to measure peak as well as average demand responses in order to evaluate the benefits of peak load pricing net of metering costs, and to measure the benefits of base load as opposed to peaking capacity investments.

Begin with a very basic question: should we expect a difference between price elasticities for peak and off-peak demand; if not, then estimates from annual sales data might be usable in peak load studies. Figure 6.1 shows that there is likely to be a fundamental difference in the elasticities, but that its magnitude depends on whether or not peak load pricing is already in operation.

Taking a polar case to sharpen the analysis, Figure 6.1 shows parallel off-peak (D_1D_1), and peak (D_2D_2) demand curves for equal length sub-periods. Suppose a uniform price, $\bar{p}$, is charged in both periods, so that peak demand q_2^0 exceeds off peak demand, q_1^0. It follows that at $\bar{p}$, elasticity of peak demand is smaller in absolute terms than off peak demand:

$$| \varepsilon_2 | < | \varepsilon_1 | \qquad (6.1)$$

This reflects the fact that fuel 'need' is greater at, for example, times of extreme weather, so thermostats stay on in a cold spell. Equation (6.1) should characterise samples of uniform prices. This is important for forecasting, since if the fuel supplier raises his uniform price for both periods, peak demand will fall less than off-peak demand, and the suppliers' load factor (i.e. the ratio of actual sales over the cycle to maximum sales in the cycle) will decrease. In Figure 6.1, load factor is $[(q_1 + q_2)/2q_2] \times 100$ per

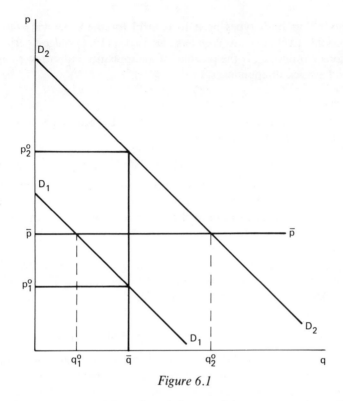

Figure 6.1

cent, and the elasticity of load factor with respect to the uniform price is:

$$\frac{q_1 (\varepsilon_1 - \varepsilon_2)}{q_1 + q_2}$$

If *time of use* (tou), pricing was in operation, so that peak demand was charged p_2^0 and off-peak p_1^0, and the peak was eliminated: $q_1 = q_2 = \bar{q}$, then the reverse of 6.1 would hold:

$$|\varepsilon_2| > |\varepsilon_1| \tag{6.2}$$

since economic theory predicts elasticity will rise with price along the demand curve. This will reflect on the measurement of the net benefits from any further alteration in the ratio of peak to off peak prices, p_2/p_1, and (6.2) will characterise samples for which tou pricing is applied.

Studies of tou pricing have used both econometric and survey methods, but both types need to control for the other variables that could affect demand. Wenders and Taylor (1976) suggest periodic consumption, q_i, is the product of an appliance utilisation rate, h_i, and a stock of appliances, k:

$$q_i = h_i k \qquad i = 1,2 \tag{6.3}$$

with the utilisation rate being determined by economic factors including price, and other variables, e.g.:

$$q_i = (\alpha_{1i} + \alpha_{2i}y + \alpha_{3i}p_1 + \alpha_{4i}p_2 + \alpha_{5i}p + \alpha_{6i}t)k \tag{6.4}$$

for i = 1,2, where y, p, and t are respectively income, other prices and temperature. Hence, p_1 and p_2 are the time of use prices and we might be interested in both the own price effects, α_{31}, and α_{42}, and the cross-price effects of, say, off-peak price on peak demand, α_{32}, etc.

If, instead of tou prices, we had a tariff structure that signalled a uniform energy charge, p_0, and a demand charge, F, related, say, to the consumer's previous maximum demand, $q_2 (t-1)$, then (6.4) becomes:

$$q_i = (\beta_{1i} + \beta_{2i}[y - Fq_2(t-1)] + \beta_{3i}p_0 + \beta_{4i}p + \beta_{5i}t)k \tag{6.5}$$

and we find that it is the income elasticities of peak and off-peak demands that may measure the impact of the demand charge.

Allowing for such effects imposes large information requirements on tou studies. Among the most ambitious and important is that carried out by the UK Electricity Council (1974) over the period 1966–72. 3420 domestic consumers spread over six area boards were recruited to take part in the survey. They were split into four broad groups, and their consumption monitored closely. Three of the groups were offered specially designed tariffs (with associated meters), while the fourth acted as a control. The groups were chosen so as to exhibit approximately the same ownership of appliances, availability of gas as an alternative, and social class (but not income), although none had less than 3000 kWh annual consumption. At the time, most domestic consumers including the control group faced energy charges that were uniform over time but declined with kWh consumed. However, restricted hour tariffs that permitted the use of cheaper electricity only for night storage heaters and water heaters were also widely available throughout the study period, so that the impact of the experimental tou prices was super-

140

imposed on a partial peak/off-peak differential that already existed.

The three novel tariffs all used energy charges in pence per kWh that differed from the uniform kWh rate available under standard tariffs as faced by the control group (the 'standard rate').

1. *Seasonal:* metering changed by a date switch. From December to February, the energy charge was 155 per cent of the standard rate, while for the rest of the year it was 72 per cent of the standard rate. Consumers in this group could still use standard restricted hour tariffs as well.

2. *Seasonal time of day:* metering changed by date and time, and three energy charges applied to all electricity consumption:
   (i) winter weekdays 08.00–13.00 and 16.30–19.30; rate: 324 per cent of standard;
   (ii) night 23.00–07.00 all year; rate: 40 per cent of standard;
   (iii) all other hours of the year; rate: 78 per cent of standard.

3. *Load rate:* consumers subscribed for a basic level of kW demand at £5 per kW per annum and also paid 62 per cent of the standard rate for kWh when kW demand lay below this level, and 148 per cent when it lay above. Overload meters indicated the kW demand in the house at any time.

The percentage deviations from the standard rate energy charges reported above are averages of two values, since each sample group was divided in two and each part given marginally different p/kWh charges, so that linear demand curves could be interpolated between the paired observations of prices and consumption.

The consumption patterns of experimental and control groups differed substantially; for example the group on the seasonal time of day tariff consumed about 24 per cent less at winter peak hours than the control group, even though their total annual consumption was about 2 per cent higher than the control. Each experimental group showed higher load factor than the control, with those on the seasonal tariff (with access to standard restricted hour tariffs as well) showing a 10 per cent rise in load factor.

The new tariffs were evaluated using the detailed kWh consumption charges observed when compared with the control group by summing the net welfare charges over each of the new tariff periods, exactly in line with equation (3.13) of Chapter 3:

$$\Delta W = \Sigma \tfrac{1}{2} \, \Delta p . \Delta q \qquad\qquad (6.6)$$

(i.e. half the consumption change times the price change for each 'good') and comparing the observed annual ΔW with the annual metering cost for each tariff. Despite the evidence of substantial demand response to the new time of use prices, ΔW net of metering costs came out negative for each tariff type.

The Electricity Council survey is clearly important as the first large-scale cost-benefit analysis of peak load or tou pricing in the domestic sector, and it was a well thought-out and comprehensive study. Wenders and Taylor (1976) have, however, indicated some criticisms.

The Electricity Council did not begin with a fully articulated model of consumer behaviour such as equation (6.4) which might have indicated which variables to control for—in particular, the groups were not matched for permanent income, which clearly does affect electricity consumption. In addition, the method of determining price responses by paired observations is much too crude compared with the full-scale econometric estimation which could have been used. This would also have permitted estimation of the cross-price effects which were left out of the ΔW calculation in (6.6), and therefore understated the benefits of tou pricing (compare equations (3.13) and (3.16)). Finally, the control group was itself allowed access to restricted hour tariffs for some uses of electricity. A preferable control (if it were possible) would have been the consumption patterns of the experimental groups before they had access to tou prices.

After the oil price rises of the 1970s with their consequent effects on gas and electricity prices, considerable international interest in European experience of peak load pricing developed. Mitchell, Manning and Acton (1978) showed that the CEGB and Électricité de France, by leading the trend towards tou pricing, had achieved considerable improvements in system load factor—including complete peak elimination in certain sectors of industry such as petroleum refineries and cement manufacture. The US Federal Energy Administration set up several residential tariff experiments in different electricity utilities, and many of the regulatory bodies imposed tou pricing structures on the utilities' industrial consumers. A considerable amount of econometric research has been devoted to these events and is worth summarising here. Some of the important elasticities are shown in Table 6.1.

The residential experiments were generally on a much smaller

Table 6.1: Some US studies of tou pricing of electricity

Sector		*off-peak period kWh with respect to own price*	*peak period kWh with respect to own price*	*max kW demand with respect to energy charge*	*max kW demand with respect to demand charge*	*Source*
				Elasticities		
residential	(i)	−0.59[1] −0.38[2]	−0.33[1] −0.60[2]	—	—	Lawrence & Braithwait (1979)[3]
	(ii)	−0.2−−0.6[2]	−0.6−−0.8[2]	—	—	Atkinson (1979)[3]
industrial		—	—	−1.91	−0.78	Henderson (1983)[4]
total system		—	—	−0.44	−0.08	Spann & Beauvais (1979)[5]

Notes: 1. Before tou pricing.
2. After tou pricing.
3. Pooled time series and cross-section.
4. Cross-section sample.
5. Time series sample.

143

scale and of a much shorter duration than the Electricity Council's study. Most involved the replacement of uniform energy charges by time of use prices. Lawrence and Braithwait (1979) obtained the predicted theoretical results of equations (6.1) and (6.2) with a linear expenditure system model that restricted the elasticities to lie between 0 and -1. These elasticities are comparable to those based on annual sales data and the pooled time series cross-section sample suggests they reflect some long-term adjustment. Atkinson (1979) obtains similar results for a different group using the translog model of Pindyck (1979) described in Chapter 2. However these are gross own price elasticities, and when Taylor (1979) obtained net elasticities after eliminating the income effect for the same sample, the elasticities were insignificant.

In industrial sales, maximum demand charges are important and the studies by Henderson and Spann and Beauvais measure the separate effect of energy and demand charges on peak demand. Henderson's results are based on a cross-section sample and hence probably reflect long-run adjustments unlike the smaller short-run elasticities of the Spann and Beauvais model. There are severe problems associated with specifying demand relations when demand charges are important but the econometric evidence as well as the survey evidence has produced a fair degree of unanimity that there are load-shifting possibilities in tou tariffs, and indicates a sensitivity of peak demands to penalty charges.

The design of tou tariffs for electricity and gas supply

The theoretical models of marginal cost pricing clearly establish the equilibrium tou prices. In practice, however, a utility does not have the market overview represented by intersecting demand and marginal cost curves. It must use a marginal cost model allied to the net effective cost (NEC) of capacity determined in its cost-minimising investment decisions. This usually has to be done for specific demand targets. The process of costing a demand increment, setting a price and then re-forecasting the demand target, must be done in a sequence of steps aiming to converge on the unknown equilibrium. In such circumstances, where several types of plant will be operated on a merit order, the principle of long-run marginal cost (LRMC) pricing stills leads to tou prices, but there may not be a unique item called LRMC. We need a model of how a utility

144

can derive tou prices on the LRMC principle in the absence of detailed information on its tou demand functions, and with no unique LRMC.

Such a model has been developed by Turvey (1968) and Wenders (1976), and it extends the load duration curve analysis of NEC that was used to examine nuclear investment in Chapter 5. Figure 6.2 shows the forecast load duration curve for the next year facing an electricity supply authority. The optimal switch points from base load to intermediate capacity ($H_p + H_i$) and from intermediate to peaking capacity (H_p) are shown as before, and these depend

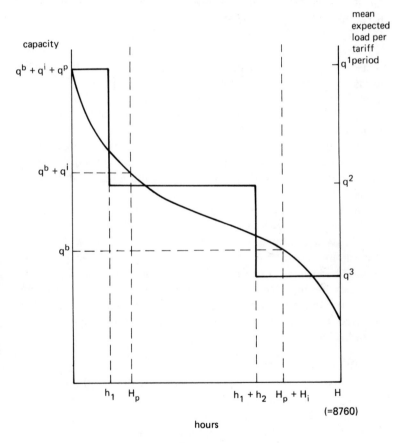

Figure 6.2

only on the annual capital costs, c, and running costs, r, and are independent of the level of demand:

$$H_p = \frac{c^i - c^p}{r^p - r^i}$$ (5.5 above)

$$H_p + H_i = \frac{c^b - c^i}{r^i - r^b}$$ (5.7 above)

where b, i, and p represent base load, intermediate and peaking capacity, respectively. The derivation of these results is given in Chapter 5.

Suppose the electricity supply authority had distinguished three tariff periods for the bulk supply tariff. The peak accounts for h_1 hours in the year, the standard day time rate for h_2 hours, and the off peak rate for $(H - h_1 - h_2)$ hours, where $H = 8760$ is the total number of hours in the year. To calculate tou marginal costs, the authority will devise a synthetic total cost function in terms of the mean expected load for each tariff period. Thus load level q^3 (in kW) is the mean expected load at night and demand will not be forecast to fall below this level in any of the total H hours; q^2 is the mean expected daytime load and occurs for $(h_1 + h_2)$ hours, while q^1 is the mean expected peak load occurring for h_1 hours. The tariff periods and mean expected load levels therefore form a stepped approximation to the actual load duration curve.

Suppose there is a forecast rise in mean expected off peak load, q^3. Figure 6.2 indicates that for such a load lasting H hours, running more base load capacity, is preferred at the margin with capital and running costs of $c^b + r^bH$. However an extra unit of q^b can be used to meet a unit of expected mean daytime load of q^2. Since this lasts for $(h_1 + h_2)$ hours, less than the $(H_p + H_i)$ for which q^i is marginal, it is a unit of intermediate capacity which can then be saved. Hence the marginal cost of an increment in mean expected night load, q^3, is:

$$MC_3 = c^b + r^bH - c^i - r^i(h_1 + h_2)$$ (6.7)

i.e. the cost of the extra base load unit less the saved cost of the displaced intermediate unit, defined in terms of the tariff period durations to which expected load levels apply. Extending this analysis yields marginal costs of daytime and peak expected load increments:

146

$$MC_2 = c^i + r^i(h_1 + h_2) - c^p - r^ph_1 \qquad (6.8)$$

$$MC_1 = c^p + r^ph_1 \qquad (6.9)$$

(Note that each MC term has been defined for the prespecified duration of the tariff periods and for the expected load levels averaged over the numbers of hours in each tariff period.)

Now rewrite (6.7)–(6.9) using the formulae for the optimal switch points H_p and $H_p + H_i$ and NEC given by equations (5.5), (5.7) and (5.11).

$$MC_3 = r^b(H - H_p - H_i) + r^i(H_p + H_i - h_1 - h_2) \qquad (6.10)$$

$$MC_2 = r^i(h_1 + h_2 - H_p) + r^p(H_p - h_1) \qquad (6.11)$$

$$MC_1 = NEC + r^ph_1 \qquad (6.12)$$

Night off-peak and daytime time of use marginal costs simply amount to a weighted combination of the running costs of the capacity types that are marginal for any load increments in the hours $(H - h_1 - h_2)$ and h_2, respectively. The peak period is the only one that bears any capital cost in this firm peak simulation, and it shows the cost of a unit of peaking capacity, c^p, equal to the common NEC of all capacity types in the optimal plant mix. This last fact emphasises that c^b and c^i are themselves implicitly signalled in (6.12), but after offsetting the associated running cost savings.

This model assumes load increments always require new capacity. If we now assume that some capacity is inherited from the past (e.g. some old q^i represented by coal-fired plant), then the NEC in (6.12) can be replaced by the equilibrium NAC, net avoidable cost of retaining inherited capacity.

Equations (6.10)–(6.12) now yield tou kWh prices for the three tariff periods:

off-peak: $p_3 = MC_3/(H - h_1 - h_2)$ \qquad (6.13)

standard: $p_2 = MC_2/h_2$ \qquad (6.14)

peak: $p_1 = MC_1/h_1$ \qquad (6.15)

These can be fed into the authority's econometric model to forecast demand, and should there be changes in the demand forecasts, a new investment solution can be calculated. In this way, the authority can draw up tou prices in the absence of fully-formulated demand functions.

What is important to realise is that (6.10)–(6.12) are calculated on the basis of a pre-set number and duration of tariff periods. If the authority changes the number or durations then it may change the plant types preferred at the margin for a given kW load increment, and hence change the calculated synthetic tou marginal costs.

Now consider a demand increment of 1 kW lasting for all H = 8760 hours of the year. Call the associated marginal cost 'Permanent increment marginal cost' (PIMC). This 1 kW load will be charged either p_3 or p_2 or p_1 depending on the hour being metered, so that the total bill over the year is:

$$PIMC = p_1h_1 + p_2h_2 + p_3(H - h_1 - h_2)$$

$$= \sum_{j=1}^{3} MC_j$$

$$= NEC + r^pH_p + r^iH_i + r^b(H - H_p - H_i) \qquad (6.16)$$

Here the abitrary tariff periods are cancelled out, and the 1 kW increment is charged the precise NEC and running costs associated with the marginal plant in any hour of the year.

All of the analysis so far has examined capacity increments, and hence exhibited LRMC pricing principles. We know LRMC pricing need not yield a unique item called LRMC when there is a mix of plant types in the system. Nevertheless, the reader should be aware that some commentators refer to (6.16) as LRMC itself, a usage we have avoided by the term PIMC.

This model can be applied to gas pricing as well as electricity, in which case the option of storage is important. In Figure 6.3, the load duration curve of the gas industry is shown, with load in therms per day and duration in days.

In this model, consider the simplest storage possibilities. Base load capacity is q^b (e.g. North Sea supplies) while q^0 is the outlet capacity from storage (i.e. the capacity for evaporating gas from store to mains supply) assuming storage is in the form of liquefied natural gas (LNG). The stored LNG is assumed to come from q^b in summer months, and storage is used on H_s days out of the total H = 365 in the year. Three quantities are critical:

   s: supply (in therms) actually taken from storage,
   v: supply taken directly from base load capacity,
   w: excess base load capacity available for storage.

Clearly, to have any storage facility at all, the load factor on q^b must be less than 100 per cent, so that w is positive:

$$\frac{v}{v + w} = \frac{v}{(365)q^b} < 1 \tag{6.17}$$

but the binding constraint requires that storage cannot exceed availability:

$$0 < s < w \tag{6.18}$$

Suppose the industry distinguishes only two tariff periods: summer (off-peak) and winter (peak). The stepped load duration curve representing these is superimposed on Figure 6.3, with q^2 represent-

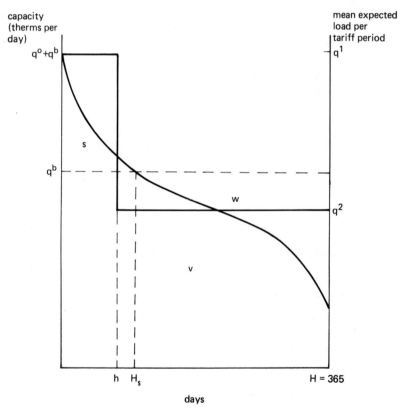

Figure 6.3

ing mean expected summer load, and q^1 mean expected winter load lasting for h days.

Ignoring the storage availability constraint (6.18) for the present, tou marginal costs can be determined exactly as in the case of electricity. A rise in mean expected summer load met by acquiring one more unit of base load capacity to operate for H days would permit the industry to save a unit of supply from storage in the peak tariff period:

$$MC_2 = c^b + r^bH - c^0 - r^sh \qquad (6.19)$$

In (6.19) c^0 is the annual unit capital cost of storage outlet capacity, while r^s is the unit running cost of supply from storage. This r^s term depends on several factors:

(i)   running cost of outlet capacity,
(ii)   capital and running cost of the store,
(iii)   cost of liquefaction of LNG,
(iv)   running cost of base load gas put into storage.

Winter peak tou marginal cost will be:

$$MC_1 = c^0 + r^sh \qquad (6.20)$$

As before, these expressions can be written in terms of the cost-minimising number of days for which storage is used:

$$H_s = \frac{c^b - c^0}{r^s - r^b} \qquad (6.21)$$

to give:

$$MC_2 = r^b(H - H_s) + r^s(H_s - h) \qquad (6.22)$$

$$MC_1 = NEC + r^sh_1 \qquad (6.23)$$

where (6.23) uses the common value of the net effective cost of capacity at the optimal plant mix:

$$NEC = c^o = c^b + (r^b - r^s)H_s \qquad (6.24)$$

Finally, a permanent increment of 1 therm per day for each day of the year gives the permanent increment marginal cost as PIMC = ΣMC:

$$PIMC = NEC + r^sH_s + r^b(H - H_s) \qquad (6.25)$$

Now suppose that the limited availability of storage from base load capacity, represented by (6.18), does form a binding constraint. In terms of Figure 6.3, there needs to be a price signal that tells consumers to move away from peak consumption so that demand pressure on storage is relieved. This move would then be equivalent to having more base load capacity. In Figure 6.4 two switch points are shown: for H_s days storage availability is limited, but for T_s days it is not, and the effect is as if more base load capacity were available. If the optimal switch point could be set at T_s instead of H_s as determined by (6.21), there would be marginal running cost savings of $(r^b - r^s)$ on every day between H_s and T_s. Offering this as a *discount* on summer time of use marginal cost is therefore

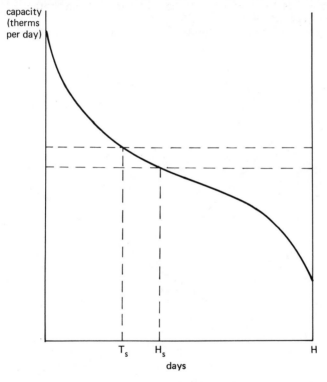

T_s : storage availability constraint not binding

H_s : storage availability constraint is binding
shadow price = $(r^b - r^s)(H_s - T_s)$

Figure 6.4

151

the signal to consumers that storage availability is limited. The tou marginal costs are then:

$$MC_2 = r^b(H - H_s) + r^s(H_s - h) + (H_s - T_s)(r^b - r^s) \quad (6.26)$$

$$MC_1 = NEC + r^s h \quad (6.27)$$

$$PIMC = NEC + r^s H_s + r^b(H - H_s) + (H_s - T_s)(r^b - r^s) \quad (6.28)$$

One point remains to be emphasised in the use of this model. The forecast load duration curve is taken as given, which means for one part of the decision-making process demand is assumed insensitive to price. This is illustrated in Figure 6.5, which shows simple single-period demand and marginal cost curves. In effect, the supply authority forecasts a demand q_0 on the basis of the current price p_0; q_0 represents a point on the forecast load duration

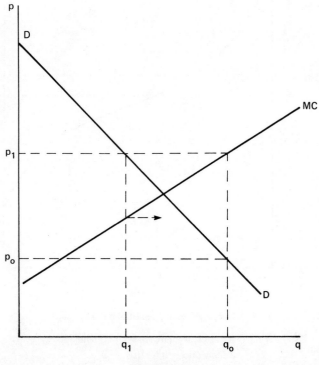

Figure 6.5

curve. The corresponding MC is calculated and price set at p_1. This must produce a new demand forecast q_1 (i.e. a new load duration curve when p_1 represents a revised MC based tariff structure). This in turn requires a revaluation of MC, and so on. Convergence to equilibrium follows the usual cobweb process as long as marginal cost rises less quickly when output rises than the price falls along the demand curve. However, iteration is a necessary part of this tariff setting model. It is not enough to forecast q_0, set price at p_1, and then stop. This would amount to assuming that demand was unresponsive to price, in which case there are no welfare gains to LRMC pricing anyway. Unfortunately, this incorrect one-stage process is often used in practice, as the subsequent discussion will indicate.

UK electricity and gas tariffs

The electricity and gas industries are organised differently in the UK, though both make up part of the nationalised fuel sector.

The Central Electricity Generating Board (CEGB) sells electricity in bulk through the national grid to twelve area boards (ABs) in England and Wales. Its price structure, the bulk supply tariff (BST) is one of the most important fuel prices in the economy. The CEGB has its own financial targets and borrowing controls so does not sell its output on a pure marginal cost-based transfer price system, as might be used between the branches of a vertically integrated industry. The area boards sell to individual consumers through a lower voltage distribution system on their own retail tariffs (RTs), and they too are subject to financial targets and borrowing constraints.

The British Gas Corporation (BGC) does behave more like a vertically integrated industry, and its retail tariffs (which differ in some respects among regions) are determined centrally. However, there is an unpublished BGC bulk supply tariff which is used to signal costs when the regions nominate the amount of storage and North Sea supplies they will want in the coming year.

All these different price structures at least pay lip-service to the principle of LRMC pricing as set out in Cmnd. 7131 (1978) and can be examined principally as tou price structures but also for their financial target recovery.

Bulk supply tariff of the CEGB

This price structure, part of which is set out in Table 6.2, is the most celebrated and debated in the UK economy. There are three elements (two of which appear in Table 6.2), to concentrate on:

1. a set of demand charges in £/kW,
2. a set of energy charges in p/kWh varying by time of use, and
3. a set of load management rebates for any load shut off at the CEGB's request, varying according to the notice given (anything between 24 hours and 15 minutes).

Criticism and debate have raised questions about the level and the number of the demand charges, the calculation of the energy charges, and the relationship between the BST and the NEC of new capacity.

A mixture of demand and tou energy charges (rather than the pure tou marginal costs of equations (6.10)–(6.12)) can be explained by looking at (6.16), the PIMC of a permanent demand increment. Since (6.16) is composed of a NEC term and running cost terms, it is reasonable to argue that the NEC, in £/kW, can be captured by a demand charge, and the energy charges can reflect the running costs of the marginal plant type in different hours of the year. This seems to be the basic philosophy behind the BST.

Table 6.2 indicates a very large variety of energy charges with winter–summer, weekday–weekend and hourly differences. Prior to the 1984–85 version, there had been only four separate energy charges with no summer or weekend distinctions. However, a report by the consultants Coopers & Lybrand, subsequently released by the Department of Energy (1984), argued that the original four energy charges contained considerable averaging over different plant types, vintages and operating procedures, and in response the CEGB has adopted one of the most tou-differentiated tariffs in the world. Although area boards are unlikely to be able to offer more than a day–night differential to many of their present customers, it was argued that by providing much more detailed tou information in the BST, the area boards would be able to get closer to optimal second-best combinations of the energy charges for their own tou prices.

It is the demand charges that have attracted most attention, however. In particular, why is the 'peak' charge below the 'basic'

Table 6.2: The CEGB's 1984-85 bulk supply tariff

Basic capacity charge: £31 per kW taken on average at times of basic demand (the average system demand when the latter is within the band 90–91% of chargeable peak system demand).

Peaking capacity charge: £24 for each kW by which the average kW take at times of chargeable peak system demand exceeds the average kW taken at times of basic demand.

Unit rates: p/kWh

times	weekdays		times	weekend and public holidays	
	summer	*winter*		*summer*	*winter*
24.00–01.00	1.59	1.74	24.00–01.00	1.61	1.72
01.00–04.00	1.17	1.34	01.00–03.00	1.13	1.24
04.00–06.00	1.17	1.24	03.00–07.00	1.13	1.17
06.00–08.00	1.93	1.93	07.00–08.00	1.47	1.39
08.00–13.00	3.33	2.74	08.00–13.30	2.22	2.25
13.00–16.00	2.47	2.74	13.30–14.00	2.22	2.04
16.00–18.00	2.74	2.74	14.00–16.30	2.04	2.04
18.00–21.00	2.33	2.74	16.30–17.00	2.04	2.04
21.00–24.00	2.33	2.38	17.00–24.00	2.16	2.22

In addition a peak surcharge of 2.28 p/kWh applies in the half hour of highest system demand in the period 08.30–23.30 and in each immediately adjacent half hour on each day except summer weekdays.

Source: Adapted from CEGB (1984).

155

charge, and why are there two demand charges when (6.16) indicates only one NEC term in the marginal cost of a permanent demand increment? First of all, consider how the charges operate, in the context of Figure 6.6.

At the end of the winter, the CEGB looks back at the pattern of system demand and superimposes on it the synthetic load durations shown in the diagram. For each area board, two kW levels are important:

1. The board's average load at those times when system demand was in band B, 'basic demand'.
2. The board's load when system demand was at the level P, 'chargeable peak system demand'.

In the 1984–85 BST, band B was 90–91 per cent of P, but this fraction has varied over the years. Under 1, the board is charged

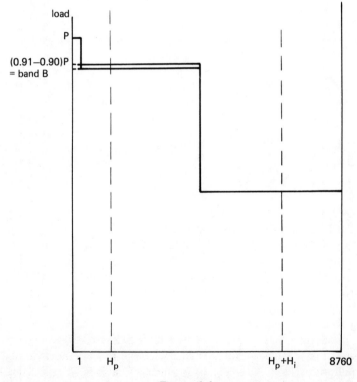

Figure 6.6

156

£31/kW, the basic capacity charge, and under 2, it is charged £24/ kW, the peaking capacity charge, on the difference between its load under 2, and its load under 1. Since the hours that count for P and band B are not determined until the end of the winter, boards do not know their total demand charges until after the peak has passed.

If we assume that these capture the NEC item in (6.16), why are there two such charges? The CEGB's explanation in its 1984–85 BST (an explanation which differs from earlier ones), seems to indicate that it is the basic capacity charge which reflects the common NEC of new capacity: 'for demand increments which are sustained there is likely in the long run to be a need to build new plant'. Band B, basic demand, is therefore taken to represent the broad plateau of winter peak demand. The CEGB has indicated, in evidence to MMC (1981), that the basic capacity charge is set at the level NEC would be expected to reach at a long-run equilibrium plant mix. It seems closest to current estimates of NEC[i], represented by new coal-fired plant, remembering that current estimates reflect a non-optimal plant mix.

However, at any one time there will be some old plant on the system about to be retired. For short-term 'needle peaks' lasting a few hours and not representative of the broad winter demand peak, old plant would simply be retained rather than new plant installed. The current estimate of NAC is therefore the basis of the peaking capacity charge. It is clear, therefore, that for the next year's demand forecast, the CEGB cannot be at an exact optimal plant mix since NAC < NEC. But this is only for one year ahead, and for longer sustained peak demand growth, retaining old plant is not a viable prospect, so that it is NEC that is relevant. The CEGB believes that its 'needle peak' is simply a random extreme observation, and that the important estimate of peak demand is the broad winter plateau at about 90 per cent of the random needle peak. It is the basic capacity charge, therefore, which is the important signal of NEC for permanent demand increments, and the peaking capacity charge could just as well be signalled by one of the tou energy charges.

This explains why there are two demand charges, though the use of the so-called peaking capacity charge reflects short-run disequilibrium (NAC < NEC), while the basic capacity charge reflects long-run equilibrium plant mix. If a pure set of tou prices were

157

used instead, it is NEC that would be used in MC_1 for peak demand increments believed to be permanent.

The distinction between equilibrium and non-equilibrium plant mix was highlighted in their critique of the BST by Slater and Yarrow (1983), who raised the question: if the CEGB's investment policy suggests nuclear NEC is negative, why is this not signalled in the BST? The CEGB's response would presumably be that in long-run equilibrium as more nuclear plant is constructed its marginal net benefits decline until its NEC rises to the common positive NEC of the optimal plant mix. This idea of pricing at what would be the marginal costs of the optimal plant mix is exactly what Boiteux (1949) and Turvey (1964) recommend for tariff stability. But in that case, Slater and Yarrow argue, the energy charges should also reflect the optimal plant mix, whereas they are in fact calculated on the basis of the current plant mix.

The problem is analogous to that illustrated in equation (6.28), which calculated PIMC for gas supply when there was a constraint on the optimal mix of base load and storage. In the electricity case, the current plant mix is not optimal since cost-minimising investment policy suggests there ought to be a higher concentration of base load nuclear capacity. This discrepancy should be signalled by a discount on off-peak time of use marginal cost (as it was in (6.28)) to persuade consumers to switch towards off-peak periods, and this discount ought to reflect the cost advantage of nuclear power at the present time. Slater and Yarrow's conclusion is that by combining a long-run equilibrium NEC with short-run disequilibrium energy charges, any increments of demand that are spread evenly throughout the whole year are penalised more heavily than they should be.

Despite these criticisms it is fair to say that the CEGB is justified in claiming that 'the BST draws substantially on the principle of marginal cost'. However, it has also to help recover the CEGB's financial target, and for this the CEGB reported to MMC (1981) that it used the ideas of Ramsey pricing described in Chapter 3. In other words it scaled up to the greatest degree those parts of the BST which applied to what the CEGB, in 1981, assumed were the least elastic demands: the basic capacity charge and the standard daytime energy charge.

However Rees (1983) has pointed out that the CEGB sells all its output onto the public sector itself—the twelve area boards and British Rail. It should be regarded, therefore, as part of a vertically integrated industry with transfer prices being set equal to marginal costs. The use of financial targets would then apply only to the area boards who could impose a Ramsey price structure on their retail tariffs to final consumers. Such a vertically integrated structure was recommended by the Plowden Committee (1975), but has never been seriously considered in practice.

Retail tariffs of area electricity boards

For area boards in England and Wales, the CEGB's BST accounts for about 80 per cent of total costs, the remainder being attributable to the distribution system, customer related costs of metering and billing and overhead expenses.

Suppose the BST consisted entirely of a set of tou prices based on (6.10)–(6.12). The total cost function of the area board is then:

$$C^B = \sum_j MC_j q_j + D(q^*) + CRC \qquad (6.29)$$

where q_j is the mean expected load taken in BST tariff period j, q^* is the distribution system's peak load capacity, and CRC represent customer-related costs. Distribution costs are assumed to be entirely determined by peak load capacity. If the area board adopted tariff periods identical to those in the BST, and minimised (6.29) subject to two types of constraint:

(i) $q_j \geqslant x_j, j = 1 \ldots J$ \qquad (6.30)

(ii) $q_j \leqslant q^*, j = 1 \ldots J$ \qquad (6.31)

where x_j is forecast board demand in period j, then retail tou marginal costs are:

$$\frac{\delta C^B}{\delta q_j} = MC_j \text{ for } j = 2 \ldots J, \text{ i.e. all non peak loads} \qquad (6.32)$$

$$\frac{\delta CB}{\delta q_1} = MC_1 + \frac{d\,D(q^*)}{dq_1} \text{ for the peak load, } q_1 \qquad (6.33)$$

i.e. a set of tou rates that pass on the MC rates in the BST while recovering marginal distribution system costs from mean expected peak load. CRC, invariant to load levels, are then recovered by customer-related standing charges if the board has to break even, and if the $\delta C^B/\delta q_j$ charges do not recover total cost.

However, area boards cannot meter their millions of individual

159

consumers in the way that the CEGB meters its few consumers, so that retail tariffs will always have, at most, two or three tariff periods. We already know from second-best theory that in combining the MC terms for several tariff periods (commodities) into a single rate, the weights required to minimise the welfare losses depend on the relative demand responses, e.g.:

$$MC_D = \frac{\Sigma(\delta q_i/\delta p_i)MC_i}{\Sigma(\delta q_i/\delta p_i)} \tag{6.34}$$

where MC_D is the single daytime rate to be charged by an area board, and MC_i, $i = 1 \ldots I$, are the BST period rates making up the area board's 'day'.

Equations (6.32) and (6.34) give an oversimplified picture of the optimal retail tariff structure, but are useful for comparison with actual practice. The Monopolies and Mergers Commission has produced a detailed study of the retail tariffs of the Yorkshire Electricity Board (YEB) which can serve as a guide.

YEB, like most utilities, has different tariffs for different consumer classes, e.g. domestic and industrial. The benefits of metering by tou differ according to the load taken by consumers, so most domestic consumers did not use a tou structure in 1981–82. Industrial consumers are often given a maximum demand tariff, and where they can take load at high voltage they can reduce the Board's need for additional transformer capacity, so meriting a different tariff.

Consider first the uniform energy charge for domestic consumers not on the tou structure (the large majority), and responsible for roughly 25 per cent of YEB's total kWh sales. YEB claimed to pursue LRMC pricing and so calculated a LRMC based charge: the unrestricted domestic LRMC, illustrated in Table 6.3.

85 per cent of this charge is based on the BST costs which are given a series of special weights. In 1982–83, the illustrative year, the CEGB's BST contained only four energy charges: standard, shoulder, night and peak, with the latter set out as a surcharge of 2.1 p/kWh on the standard rate of 2.70 p/kWh. The demand charges were peaking capacity = £21/kW, and basic = £25/kW, and there was a service charge for bulk supply transmission, as well as a fuel adjustment clause to take account of changing coal and oil prices.

How is this LRMC rationalised? The dominant items are the

160

Table 6.3: YEB's LRMC calculation of the domestic unrestricted energy charge, 1982–83

1. *Bulk supply costs*	*Weight*		*p/kWh*
energy charges:			
standard (2.70p/kWh)	0.861 ⎫		2.325
shoulder (2.27p/kWh)	0.035 ⎬ 1.00		0.079
night (1.37p/kWh)	0.104 ⎭		0.142
	0.098		
peak surcharge (2.11p/kWh)			0.027
fuel adjustment clause			0.130
demand charges:			
peaking capacity (£21/kW)	0.882/3214		0.576
basic capacity (£25/kW)	0.621/3214		0.483
Service charge			0.095
total			4.037
Total times 1.085 for electrical losses			4.377
2. *Distribution costs*			
mains reinforcement and electrical losses			0.579
rates and other expenses			0.180
3. *LRMC*			5.136
4. *Adjust LRMC to meet financial target*			5.10

Source: Adapted from MMC (1983), p. 158, Table 12.1.

weighted BST elements. The weights on the energy charges are the proportionate kWh units consumed in different BST periods ($q_jh_j/\Sigma q_ih_i$) rather than the correct second-best weights given by (6.34). However, the real problem is with the BST's demand charges. The MMC study (1983) reports that national load research had indicated:

1. At times of CEGB system maximum demand domestic unrestricted demand was 88.2 per cent of its own class peak. This is the 'coincidence factor'.

2. Each kW of domestic peak demand was associated with 3214 kWh of annual consumption. This fixes the class load factor at

$$\frac{3214}{(1 \times 8760)} \times 100 = 37 \text{ per cent}$$

161

Hence a weight of (0.882/3214) is used to convert the peak kW demand charge to a kWh energy charge. But although this is a convenient piece of arithmetic, it clearly is not the second-best welfare weight that preserves LRMC pricing principles. Even more oddly, the basic capacity charge is converted to a kWh rate using the same implied load factor, though a different coincidence factor, even though the BST signals the fact that needle peak and broad winter peak are not at the same load level.

The YEB also offered a night–day differential, the 'Economy 7' tariff, for all domestic users of electricity. The night energy charge simply left out most of the demand charge elements and some of the distribution cost element, with the day rate being approximately equal to the domestic unrestricted rate given by Table 6.3. The essence of the day, night and unrestricted calculations is therefore to weight the BST energy charges and demand charges respectively by historically-determined consumption and load factor data (rather than the weights in (6.34)). But to use these historically-determined weights amounts to assuming that they are independent of the price signals in the retail tariffs, i.e. that demand is unresponsive to the price signals being sent. In which case, LRMC pricing offers no welfare benefits. Finally, note that in order to meet its financial target exactly, the YEB sets price fractionally below its own estimate of LRMC, therefore aiming at a third-best price when the first-best is readily available! It can be seen therefore that LRMC pricing principles are not well implemented by such domestic tariffs.

Turning to YEB's industrial tariff, it again seems to be typical of many area board tariffs (see Table 6.4). There is a day–night differential, presumably based on several consumption-weighted BST energy charges, and a demand charge in £/kVa (not kW in order to allow for power factor differences), of the consumer's maximum demand, with a difference in the charges for December to February, compared with November and March. Here the YEB is aware that it is those December to February demands that are most likely to cause YEB to incur the CEGB's basic and peaking capacity demand charges. Note that, as with all maximum demand charges, there is no allowance for the fact that a particular customer's own peak demand may not coincide with the system peak. However, industrial consumers who are able to move their maximum demands away from system peaks may contract with the area board to become load management consumers. For this, the

Table 6.4: YEB maximum demand tariff, 1982–83

Service charge per kVA per month	
first 500 kVA	£0.60
remaining kVA	£0.50
Monthly demand charge per kVA	
Dec./Jan./Feb.	£4.05
Nov./Mar.	£0.90
Unit charge per kWh	
day	3.65p
night	1.60p

Source: Adapted from MMC (1983), p. 161, Table 12.2.

area board will receive from CEGB rebates on either peaking or basic capacity charges or peak energy charges for load that is switched off at short notice. The area board can then negotiate its own rebates and incentives with the industrial consumers who agree to take part in the load management contracts. In this way, industrial consumers across all area boards in England and Wales have in recent years switched off up to 1500 mW at short notice, accounting for a reduction of roughly 3 per cent in what would have been CEGB system maximum demand.

Gas prices

Research and debate on British Gas Corporation (BGC) policies has been less extensive than on electricity supply, but two main issues have been important:

1. the determination of LRMC, and
2. the optimal mix between storage and base load North Sea (NS) supplies to meet peak loads and the corresponding price signals in retail tariffs.

Ignoring peak load aspects for the moment, consider the LRMC of annual gas consumption. BGC itself makes a lot of the distinction between premium and non-premium markets. The former consists of those consumers (chiefly domestic and some industrial such as glass and chemical manufacture), for whom natural gas is particularly desirable because of its chemical properties, its cleanliness and controlability, and who might be prepared to pay a premium

163

for its use over other consumers. Remaining industrial consumers who are indifferent amongst alternative heat sources are classified non-premium. BGC has gradually found the premium market coming to dominate, as in Figure 6.7.

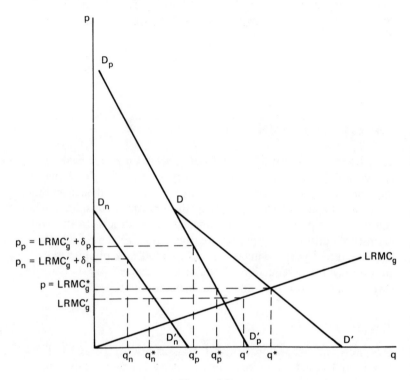

Figure 6.7

In this diagram, $D_pD'_p$ and $D_nD'_n$ are the premium and non-premium demand schedules while the total demand for gas is their horizontal summation D_pDD'. Optimal supply of NS gas is q^* where its long-run marginal cost, $LRMC_g$, intersects the market demand schedule. At the common price $= LRMC_g$, premium and non-premium sales are q^*_p and q^*_n.

Marginal distribution costs are important, and therefore imagine that these differ between premium and non-premium markets, δ_p and δ_n respectively (in practice the differences arise between residential and industrial markets). LRMC pricing yields final prices:

164

$$p_p = LRMC_g + \delta_p \tag{6.35}$$

$$p_n = LRMC_g + \delta_n \tag{6.36}$$

but the prices net of distribution costs: $(p_p - \delta_p)$ and $(p_n - \delta_n)$ must be equal in both markets to $LRMC_g$. Then if the demand schedules are $q_p = D_p (p_p)$ and $q_n = D_n(p_n)$, total sales will be given by the equation:

$$(q'_p + q'_n) = D_p(LRMC'_g + \delta_p) + D_n(LRMC'_g + \delta_n) \tag{6.37}$$

Note here that because of the positive distribution costs, total sales are less than they would be in the absence of distribution costs, and corresponding $LRMC'_g$ is lower down the upward sloping $LRMC_g$ curve, as shown in Figure 6.7.

Again in practice, BGC has three price structures. Consumers taking less than 100,000 therms per year (BGC is only obliged to supply consumers taking less than 25,000), which is all domestic and some industrial consumers pay according to a published tariff. Larger industrial consumers in premium markets can negotiate contracts for firm supply, while large industrial consumers in the non-premium market may negotiate interruptible contracts. In return for a lower average price per therm, these allow BGC to cease supply at short notice at peak times, with the customer switching to an alternative energy source such as heavy fuel oil. By 1982, interruptible contracts did not account for more than 10 per cent of BGC sales.

Two ways of measuring $LRMC_g$ have been used:
  (a) $LRMC_g$ = competitive world price of a substitute fuel,
  (b) $LRMC_g$ = price paid for new NS supplies.
Both versions reflect the fact that for an internationally traded commodity like natural gas, the competitive world price measures marginal cost. Under (a), the appropriate substitute fuel is heavy fuel oil in non-premium markets. Taking the price of heavy fuel oil in the UK as $LRMC_g$, gas prices net of distribution costs in the domestic sector particularly were very substantially below LRMC in the latter half of the 1970s and early 1980s (see Rees, 1983).

Catherine Price (1980) suggests that using the UK price of heavy fuel oil under (a) as a measure of $LRMC_g$ is tricky because BGC can no longer be regarded as a price-taker in UK industrial fuel markets, having captured a 30 per cent market share by 1982.

Method (b) measures directly the LRMC of additional NS supplies. BGC has actively pursued the search for new supply sources, and from 1979 onwards, was buying additional gas from the Norwegian sector of the NS northern basin. Since Norway exports its gas, the price paid by BGC in competition with other purchasers for marginal supplies from the Norwegian fields ought to reflect international market forces that include both the prices of alternative fuels and allowance for the user cost of the finite reserves of this exhaustible commodity. The 1979 Report of the UK Price Commission (PC, 1979) suggested as an estimate of $LRMC_g$, the beachhead price of gas from the Norwegian Frigg field (13.5p/therm in 1979 prices). Using this, PC (1979) found that in all market sectors gas prices net of distribution costs lay below $LRMC_g$, with the largest discrepancy, 36 per cent, being

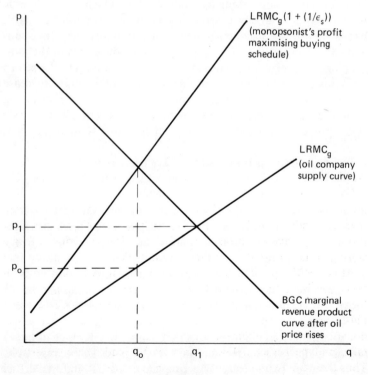

Figure 6.8

in the domestic sector. It was on this basis that the substantial price rises of the early 1980s (10 per cent in real terms each year for three years) were permitted. By 1984 LRMC pricing had been virtually established in the domestic sector, but following a freeze on industrial gas prices, there was still a shortfall for industrial consumers.

Given the upward sloping $LRMC_g$ schedule of Figure 6.7, LRMC pricing must lead to substantial profits for BGC, since the lower long-run average cost curve reflects the relatively low, historically-determined prices in existing NS contracts, many of which date from before the oil price rises of the 1970s. These large profits allowed BGC to repay national loan fund debt and be self-financing in its investment programme. Such profits partly reflect the quasi-rents associated with a competitively priced exhaustible resource, and could enable BGC, in time, to replace its exhausted gas supplies. However, they also partly reflect the economic rent from rising world oil prices. Until the Oil and Gas Enterprise Act 1983, BGC was the sole buyer of gas from the NS oil companies exploiting it. Figure 6.8 shows the textbook monopsonist's decision-making, with the curve labelled $LRMC_g$ $(1 + \frac{1}{\varepsilon_s})$ drawn marginal to the $LRMC_g$ schedule.

In Figure 6.8, BGC could have acted as a profit-maximising monopsonist buying q_0 at p_0 along $LRMC_g$ $(1 + \frac{1}{\varepsilon_s})$, where ε_s is the elasticity of supply. However, existing NS contracts appear to have searched for a pseudo-competitive equilibrium at (q_1p_1) as Rees (1983) suggests. This allows BGC to collect the extra economic rent, represented by the 1974 rightward shift of the marginal revenue product curve, on behalf of the taxpayer. Of course, these profits may have encouraged BGC to subsidise the domestic gas consumer as appeared to be the case until 1984.

After LRMC pricing, the other important issue in BGC's operations has been the optimal mix of gas supplies in meeting peak loads. This is illustrated in Figure 6.9. The load curve of demand illustrates the substantial winter peak associated particularly with domestic sales. NS contracts usually stipulate a maximum daily take, and hence set a lower limit to the load factor of supply. Thus there are two mismatches of supply and demand:

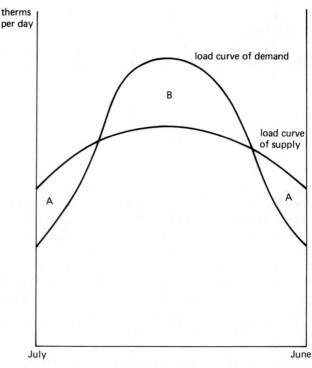

therms per day

load curve of demand

B

load curve of supply

A   A

July   June

Figure 6.9

A: when contracted summer supplies exceed summer demand, and

B: when winter peak demand exceeds contracted winter supply.

The resulting load factors are shown in Table 6.3.

Table 6.3: Supply and demand load factors in UK gas sales

Demand		*Supply*	
domestic market:	38%	Southern basin:	60%
commercial market:	40%	Northern basin:	77–87%
industrial market:	55%		

Source: Deloitte, Haskins & Sells (1984), p. 189.

For A the options are:

A.(i)   Interruptible contracts in industrial and commercial markets to dispose of excess gas. These contracts stipulate on

168

average an interruptibility option of 60 days, though usually fewer are used in practice, the 1982 average being 28. Prices are set at the price of UK heavy fuel oil plus distribution costs (about 12 per cent of the final price in 1982).

A.(ii)   'Take or pay' provisions in NS contracts. Although the gas in A must be paid for, BGC can postpone taking it until subsequent years of severe peak.

A.(iii) BGC may take the gas and store it itself for load balancing in the B mismatch of the current year.

For B, seasonal storage is essential, and the options are:

B.(i)   liquefied or synthesised natural gas (LNG or SNG) storage near centres of demand.

B.(ii)   Storage in partly depleted gas fields or salt cavities.

B.(iii) BGC's own low load factor fields developed purely for load balancing (e.g. Morecambe Bay).

B.(iv)   Take or pay gas accumulated from previous years.

B.(v)   Cessation of interruptible supplies.

These are combined in an optimal mix by trading off the high running costs of those at the top of the list against the high capital costs of those further down. For interruptible supplies the marginal benefit is storage cost saved, while, from BGC's point of view, the marginal cost is the revenue forgone at peak times. Deloitte, Haskins & Sells (1984) report that all options were in use in 1983, but B.(v) was being phased out.

One option not in use, but recommended both by PC (1979) and Deloitte Haskins & Sells (1984) is peak load pricing. We already know how tou prices reflecting storage can be developed. PC (1979) recommended either a straightforward winter–summer differential in pence per therm or, alternatively, a demand charge related to the customer's maximum daily take, like the electricity tariff in Table 6.4. The BGC response was cool, arguing that customer contracts already have minimum load factor provisions, and metering costs would be prohibitive. The main cost associated with a summer–winter differential would be more frequent meter-reading, but BGC does not recognise the welfare benefits of tou pricing, and defends its trend towards *less* frequent meter-reading on 'cost-saving' grounds.

Although BGC sets its retail tariffs centrally—usually in the form of a uniform energy charge with a regionally differentiated standing charge for consumer related costs—there does exist a BGC bulk supply tariff with several notable differences from the CEGB's BST. The chief purpose of this BST seems to be to allow the gas regions to indicate which forms of storage are most in demand: those for the needle peak or those for the broad winter demand. The absolutely fundamental difference from the CEGB BST is that the regions nominate in advance the demand they expect to experience so that they are in fact bidding for storage and pipeline gas availability. These bids then give BGC some indication of the way peak demands are developing over time. The BST then discourages overbidding for winter capacity by a system of capacity and commodity charges, related to the costs of meeting peak demand, while a subsidiary system of penalties is applied if, by underbidding, a region finds it needs more gas at certain times than it has been provisionally allocated.

Although the BST is not published, Deloitte Haskins & Sells (1984) suggest that instead of signalling NEC and running costs along the lines of (6.22)–(6.25), it includes a variety of different energy (commodity) and demand (capacity) charges, along the following lines.

There are two (p/therm) energy charges: the first applies to a fixed quantity of gas and is a residual required to meet the industry's financial target. The second reflects $LRMC_g$, and in 1982–83 was set at the beachhead price of Norwegian gas.

For the broad level of winter demand there are two (p/therm) storage charges, one applied to each therm allocated to the region from its advance nominations, and one applied to each therm of storage gas actually used. For the needle peak of winter demand, there are two capacity charges. The region will have nominated how much gas they would require on a cold day such as would occur in only one winter in 20, and they pay one charge for each therm of pipeline gas allocated as a result, and another for each therm allocated from storage.

Although there is not a direct link with time of use, this BST relates capacity costs to forecast system maximum demand. In doing so, it seems to include running and capital costs for all capacity types instead of indicating the optimal NEC and running charges for demand increments at different times. But its most curious aspect is that since the regions cannot relate their BST charges to retail tariffs, their forecast nominations for capacity are determined by prices outside their own control.

Deloitte Haskins & Sells (1984) comment on this, arguing that there ought to be a peak related set of retail tariffs in conjunction with the BST. They suggest tariffs that have uniform energy charges which are higher for those customer classes with lower load factors. However, although these would penalise those with the peakiest demand, they would offer no reward to those individual consumers able to shift demand away from the peak, since they would remain in the class to which their initial load factor and consumption committed them: another example of the incompatibility of simultaneously relating price to marginal cost and assuming that load factor is insensitive to price changes.

7

North Sea oil and the UK economy

Introduction

The advent of North Sea oil came at a critical time for the UK economy. It was developed just as world oil prices were rising very rapidly, and the world economy began its long recession of the mid-1970s and early 1980s. Moreover, these significant changes in the UK's economic environment began to peak at the time (1979–83) when macroeconomic policy changed direction very substantially towards a monetarist approach, and away from the new Keynesian ideas of the 1970s.

All these factors together have made the effects of NS oil difficult to separate from macroeconomic policy in general. Four separate issues need to be considered in this chapter, but it will be apparent that they cannot in practice be treated in isolation even when this is the convenient analytical expedient adopted; as it is here. The first issue concerns the socially optimal depletion of NS oil and whether this can be left to competitive markets. (The actual depletion rate will be affected by the tax gathering schemes applied to NS oil, and these also need consideration.) The second issue relates to the impact of NS oil on the structure of real national output and whether NS oil is responsible for a trend towards 'deindustrialisation'. A third issue, sometimes confused with the second, is whether the monetary effects of NS oil pose special problems for macroeconomic policy management, especially where some markets (e.g. goods and labour markets) are thought to show less price flexibility than, say, foreign exchange and financial markets. The

172

final issue is what proportion of the NS oil income, if any, ought to be invested. For example, should the temporary NS income be converted to overseas assets that produce a permanent flow of foreign currency income?

Depletion economics

Oil, gas and coal are examples of exhaustible resources; fossil fuels that, once exploited, cannot be reproduced in an economically relevant timescale. The dynamic aspects of LRMC pricing are particularly important here, and there is considerable doubt about whether competitive markets will ever achieve a socially optimal depletion profile, and indeed there is controversy about what this means in any case.

Figure 7.1 shows the demand, DD', in one year, t, for a natural resource flow, e.g. oil. Its marginal extraction cost, c, is assumed

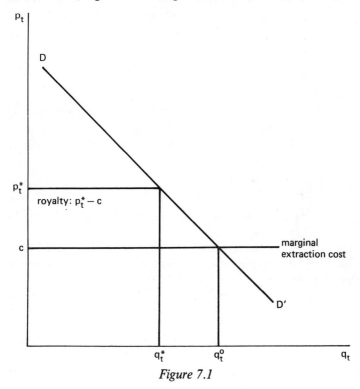

Figure 7.1

constant, and marginal cost pricing at $p_t = c$ would deplete q_t^o units of the finite reserves, R, in year t.

L. C. Gray (1914) seems to have been the first to argue that a competitive market will consume less than q_t^o, because the marginal extraction cost alone ignores the future value of the oil forgone by consuming it this year. Adding this 'user cost', λ_t, to marginal extraction cost, c, sets the competitive price at $p_t^* = c + \lambda_t$, and depletion this year at q_t^*. The conventional name for the user cost associated with not having the oil available in the future is the 'royalty'. Hotelling (1931) gave the classic analysis of royalty and depletion in terms of resource flows, and his ideas can be set out, quite simply, as follows.

Imagine one of many competitive companies depleting an oil-field over two periods: 0 and 1. The initial reserves are R_0 and resource flows during each year from the field are q_0 and q_1. At the end of year 0, reserves remaining are R_1 and this is the maximum amount that can be depleted in the last year, q_1. The resource constraints are therefore:

$$R_0 - R_1 = q_0 \tag{7.1}$$

$$R_1 = q_1 \tag{7.2}$$

so that after year 1 the field is exhausted: $q_0 + q_1 = R_0$.

The objective of the firm is to maximise, as a price-taker, the discounted present value of profits, V, from the field, after taking into account the constant unit extraction cost, c, which we assume is the same for all firms.

$$V = (p_0 - c)q_0 + \frac{(p_1 - c)q_1}{1 + i} \tag{7.3}$$

where i is the company's discount rate, and p_0 and p_1 the market prices of oil prevailing in each year.

The firm will arrange production so that the last barrel of oil in each year makes the same marginal contribution to the present value of profits, i.e.

$$p_0 - c = \frac{p_1 - c}{(1 + i)} \tag{7.4}$$

or, that the *present value* of the royalty is the same in each year:

$$\lambda_0 = \frac{\lambda_1}{1 + i} \tag{7.5}$$

174

These necessary conditions follow from constructing the Lagrangean function for the competitive firm's problem:

$$L = V + \lambda_0(R_0 - R_1 - q_1) + \mu_1(R_1 - q_1) \tag{7.6}$$

and optimising with respect to the three variables under the firm's control, q_0 and q_1 the resource flows, and R_1 the reserves in place after year 0:

$$\frac{\delta L}{\delta q_0} = p_0 - c - \lambda_0 = 0 \tag{7.7}$$

$$\frac{\delta L}{\delta q_1} = \frac{p_1 - c}{1 + i} - \mu_1 = 0 \tag{7.8}$$

$$\frac{\delta L}{\delta R_1} = -\lambda_0 + \mu_1 = 0 \tag{7.9}$$

Together these imply (7.4), and (7.5) follows when the shadow price μ_1 is properly interpreted as a present value $\mu_1 = \lambda_1/(1 + i)$ with λ_1 being the value, *in year 1*, of additional reserves in year 1, i.e. the current value royalty.

In this constant extraction cost case, (7.4) and (7.5) imply that the current value royalty, λ_t, and market price, p_t, are both rising over time when the competitive oil companies are in intertemporal equilibrium. From (7.5) and (7.4):

$$(\lambda_1 - \lambda_0)/\lambda_0 = i \tag{7.10}$$

$$(p_1 - p_0)/p_0 = (\lambda_0/p_0)i \tag{7.11}$$

so that the royalty rises at the market interest rate while the market price rises at a fraction, (λ_0/p_0), of the rate.

Equation (7.10) has been given an interpretation in terms of asset equilibrium by Solow (1974). A resource owner continuing to hold oil reserves under the sea can only gain a return in the form of capital gains from the appreciation of real oil prices over time. This growth of oil prices, net of extraction costs, generates, if it occurs, growing royalties, so that the left-hand side of (7.10) measures the rate of return to the continued holding of oil stocks under the sea. The right-hand side, representing market interest rates, measures the opportunity cost of capital which can only be realised by depleting the oil and accumulating alternative assets. When the two are equal, the current flow of oil ensures asset portfolio equilibrium, and represents the profit-maximising optimal depletion rate.

How do competitive spot markets for oil find the equilibrium royalty and price growth rates? A spot market is one which establishes an equilibrium price only for immediate sales and purchases of the commodity in question, and the answer depends on how expectations are formed.

Resource owners and oil speculators will form a view about the *expected* growth of oil royalties and prices. Suppose this exceeds the critical rate given in (7.11):

$$(p_1^e - p_o)/p_o > (\lambda_o/p_o)i \qquad (7.12)$$

Resource owners then hold oil off the market because of its higher expected capital gains. If they do not, speculators will buy up the oil to hoard. In these circumstances, the current price of oil, p_0, will rise to ration the conserved supply, while the expected future price, p_1^e, will be revised downwards to reflect the fact that suppliers and speculators with rational expectations now know more oil will be available in the future. Hence $(p_1^e - p_0)/p_0$ falls back towards $(\lambda_0/p_0)i$. This argument can be reversed if the inequality in (7.12) runs the other way. This rational expectations model of oil prices therefore predicts that competitive spot markets will re-establish the equilibrium growth rate of prices period after period, providing a sequence of temporary or momentary equilibria.

Such an outcome might be jeopardised if the *elasticity of expectations*, η is not zero.

$$\eta = \frac{dp_1^e}{dp_0} \cdot \frac{p_0}{p_1^e} \qquad (7.13)$$

This measures the effect on the expected price, p_1^e, of a change in the current price, p_0. The rational expecations model assumed market participants used only the model of market equilibrium as the basis of their expectations, so assuming η to be zero. This ensured that their expectations were always self-fulfilling. However if $\eta > 0$, the mere fact of a rise in current prices may be sufficient to raise currently expected prices, independently of the subsequent equilibrating market forces.

Suppose depletion is at an optimum rate as given by (7.11), but that the current price, p_0, now drops as a result of an exogenous shock. The royalty, λ_0, falls in proportion assuming unit extraction cost, c, is constant. If $\eta = 0$, then p_i^e is unchanged, the condition in (7.12) appears and the conservation mechanism of the rational expectations model would come into play. If however $\eta = 1$, p_i^e falls in proportion to the fall in p_0, (7.11) is not disturbed, and depletion continues unchanged. Apart from the once-only drop in p_0, there is no disturbance to the upward path of equilibrium prices. On the other hand, should $\eta > 1$, then the drop in p_0 causes an even larger fall in p_i^e and it becomes apparent that:

$$(p_i^e - p_0)/p_0 < (\lambda_0/p_0)i \tag{7.14}$$

causing suppliers to accelerate current depletion, and therefore further lowering p_0. These effects are illustrated in Figure 7.2.

In equilibrium the oil price is increasing over time at a constant fraction of the discount rate, $(\lambda_0/p_0)i$, as given by (7.11), and represented by the unbroken path (a). At time t_0, we observe the current price p_0. In our example, this drops to p_0' due to an exogenous shock. Under the rational expectations mechanism with $\eta = 0$, price returns almost immediately to the original path along (b)–(a),

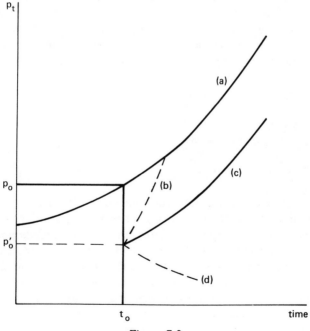

Figure 7.2

177

as markets adjust. This, in fact, would result for any value of η between zero and unity, but the return along (b) to (a) is the more delayed the closer is η to unity.

With η = 1, there are no depletion decision changes, and prices follow path (c) still increasing at the equilibrium rate in parallel to (a), but with the lower displaced starting point p_0'. With η > 1, prices diverge from equilibrium along path (d).

Both Fisher (1981) and Mishan (1981) argue that the assumption of η > 1 is untenable in the long run, since resource owners and speculators will realise that the drop in current oil prices is only exaggerated by their response of increasing current supply, and this will cause them to revise their expectations formation until η tends to unity at most.

The presumption is, therefore, that competitive spot markets in the resource can support a sequence of stable momentary equilibrium positions, characterised by the fact that prices will escalate along one of an infinite number of parallel paths like (a) and (c) in Figure 7.2, all growing at the rate $(\lambda_0/p_0)i$.

In what sense can this sequence be called socially optimal? To begin an answer, consider a conventional utilitarian measure of social welfare that arises by adding up over time the consumer surplus plus total revenue less social cost of oil depletion for each year and discounting this back to the present by a given social discount rate, i. Each year's net benefit is:

$$W_t = CS_t + TR_t - TC_t \qquad (7.15)$$

and the maximand is the present value of this stream of benefits over possibly many generations:

$$B = \sum_{t=0}^{T} W_t(1 + i)^{-t} \qquad (7.16)$$

Now there are many economists who find (7.16) unacceptable as a definition of social welfare, even when later generations are not undervalued by having the discount rate set at zero. On a practical level, Mishan (1981) points out that it hypothesises mechanisms for transferring resources ('potential Pareto improvements') from one generation to another. It assumes that the preferences of unborn generations can be adequately registered today. Aside from the practical difficulties associated with this utilitarian approach, critics such as Rawls (1971) have argued against such arbitrary devices

178

as adding up welfare across generations, or across society. Nevertheless much economic analysis has adopted (7.16) as the social welfare objective and its implications have played an important part in depletion economics.

In (7.16) T is the year in which the oil is finally exhausted, and the maximisation of (7.16) is constrained by the requirement that the total flow of oil over its life should equal the initial reserves:

$$R_0 = \sum_{t=0}^{T} q_t \tag{7.17}$$

Given the welfare criterion based on consumer surplus in (7.15), the optimality conditions include the requirement that the marginal contribution to the present value of social welfare, B, of each barrel of oil, should be the same in each year:

$$p_0 - c = \ldots = \frac{p_t - c}{(1 + i)^t} = \ldots = \frac{p_T - c}{(1 + i)^T} \tag{7.18}$$

where $(p_t - c) = \lambda_t$ can now be interpreted as the marginal social welfare royalty. As with depletion in competitive spot markets, this translates into equilibrium growth rates for both the marginal social welfare royalty and the socially optimal market price:

$$(\lambda_{t+1} - \lambda_t)/\lambda_t = i \tag{7.19}$$

$$(p_{t+1} - p_t)/p_t = (\lambda_t/p_t)i \tag{7.20}$$

This appears to be identical to the competitive spot market solution as long as no externalities are present. However, there is a fundamental difference between this problem and that considered at the beginning. Both solutions contain identical one-period-ahead price relationships, (7.18) and (7.4), but the resource constraint (7.17) is also one of the fundamental optimum conditions for this social welfare maximisation problem. Equation (7.18), which stipulates a series of consecutive price relationships, is called the 'myopic rule' for the socially optimal path. By contrast, equation (7.17), which refers to the whole period of oil depletion, is called the 'global rule'. Now, in the initial problem of the competitive firms each had an arbitrary planning horizon of T = 1 imposed on it. But in solving the problem of socially optimal depletion, an arbitrary T cannot be assumed; it must be solved as part of the problem, and this means that the global rule resource constraint (7.17) has also to be treated as part of the optimum conditions.

179

There may be many price paths fulfilling the myopic rule (7.18), some of which might be discovered by competitive spot markets, but only one path will also exactly fulfill (7.17), the global rule, allowing the oil to be exhausted just at the socially optimal time, T.

There are different ways of finding the solution when T is to be chosen as part of the problem. For some investment decisions evaluated from society's point of view, setting the planning horizon at infinity is clearly the correct procedure. A simple approach is used here by assuming that after a finite T years an alternative fuel source (e.g. the nuclear fast breeder reactor) will become competitive with oil. This alternative fuel is assumed to be renewable rather than exhaustible and can be incorporated in the infinite planning horizon investment programmes beyond T. It is known as the 'backstop technology' (Nordhaus, 1979), and its constant marginal opportunity cost is assumed to be θ per barrel of oil equivalent, as shown in Figure 7.3.

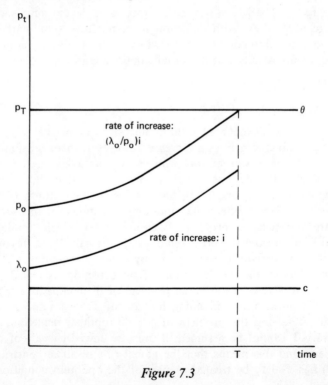

Figure 7.3

In Figure 7.3, oil is clearly preferable as the initial fuel choice, but as time passes its price rises to the level of the marginal opportunity cost of the backstop alternative, and at T, $p_T = \theta$. Beyond T, efficiency dictates use of the backstop so society should aim to deplete oil completely by that year, T, in which p_t has risen to equal θ.

When p_T is known, it can be used in equation (7.18) (the myopic rule) and, together with equation (7.17) (the global rule), the price and depletion profiles that simultaneously maximise the objective (7.16) and just exhaust the oil can be found. Now it is clear that the myopic rule can coincide with the growth path of prices determined by competitive spot markets as long as the market interest rate coincides with the social discount rate (so that (7.11) and (7.20) are identical), but competitive spot markets cannot signal the condition $p_T = \theta$. For this signal, a set of markets is needed that establishes in the present ($t = 0$) the *equilibrium* price for sales and purchases for any date ($t = T$), however far in the future. Such markets are known as complete forward markets, and their existence is a much stronger assumption than the one-period-ahead rational expectations postulate. In fact, their existence can only ever be hypothetical, since it implies that future suppliers and consumers not yet born have their preferences correctly registered by an ancestral agent living in the present, and that each market participant is subject only to a single budget constraint stretching over all the years involved. In the absence of complete forward markets, competitive spot markets, in discovering the myopic rule, will throw up a current expectation for p_{t+1}, but the eventual equilibrium p_T determined in year T's spot market may not coincide with previous expectations, and no forward market is available to signal year T's demands and supplies.

The analysis of the socially optimal path is worth completing nevertheless, assuming perhaps that a social planning authority exercising foresight and setting price signals could in theory replace the absent forward markets, and indicate the future equilibrium p_T.

In this case the myopic and global rules (along with assumed knowledge of the backstop marginal cost, θ, and the market demand curve $p_t(q_t)$ for each year t) together determine the optimal depletion profile q_t, and its exhaustion date T, along with the unique optimal starting price, p_0, that allows p_t to grow to θ by year T.

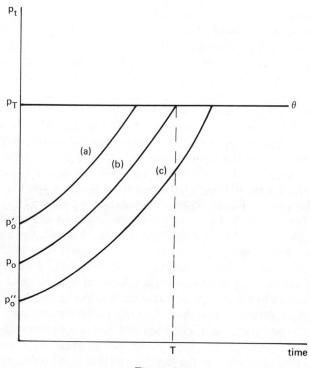

Figure 7.4

Figure 7.4 shows three different possible price paths, each escalating at the myopic rule's required rate of $(\lambda_t/p_t)i$ and, hence, each being compatible with rational expectations behaviour in competitive spot markets. However, only one path, starting at the unique optimal p_0, is the socially optimal path; assume this to be path (b) in Figure 7.4. Along path (a), price is always too high for optimal depletion, starting at $p_0^1 > p_0$. As a result the backstop marginal cost θ is reached in T' ($< T$) years and spot markets will signal a switch to the alternative fuel even though the field's reserves are not depleted owing to a price history lying above the socially optimal path, and inducing too little consumption. The reverse occurs along path (c); price is always too low and demand is encouraged as if reserves were greater than in fact they are. In summary, if (b) is optimal, (a) is inefficient, while (c) is infeasible.

Competitive spot markets are likely to spot both errors eventually. Along path (c), well before p_t has reached θ, suppliers may realise that reserves are almost depleted. In the resulting conservation, price rises towards the higher optimal path, but already many years of excessive depletion will be past. Along path (a) as price reaches θ, suppliers may realise that large reserves are left, and dump these on the market lowering price towards path (a), but again this is only a last-minute alteration to a history of sub-optimal depletion.

So far this analysis of socially optimal depletion has assumed a single oil field with an inexhaustible alternative fuel acting as backstop, but the model is worth extending to include different types of oil field. For example the UK reserves contain both low-cost onshore and coastal fields, and high-cost deepwater fields. In Figure 7.5 the optimal price paths for a low-cost and high-cost field are shown. Field 1 has the low marginal extraction cost, c_1, while field 2 has the higher extraction cost, c_2. Since only one price can prevail for the oil, p_t, it is clear that field 1's initial

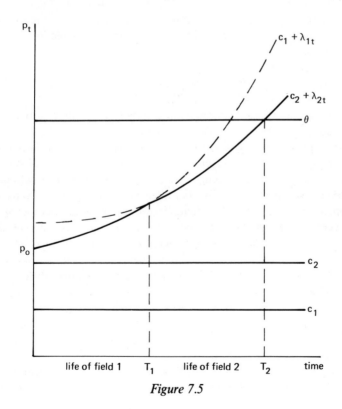

Figure 7.5

183

royalty must exceed that of field 2, and so field 1 will be depleted first, as a straightforward application of the myopic rule, and will be exhausted in year T_1. Field 2 then takes over, being exhausted in year T_2, when p_{T_2} equals the backstop cost, θ. Each field has a shadow price over the years $0-T_1$; that of field 1 is $c_1 + \lambda_{1t}$ while that of field 2 is $c_2 + \lambda_{2t}$, and market price is the lower of the two. Over the years $0-T_1$, this is $c_1 + \lambda_{1t}$ even though $\lambda_{1t} > \lambda_{2t}$, however, by T_1:

$$p_{T_1} = c_1 + \lambda_{1T_1} = c_2 + \lambda_{2T_1} \tag{7.21}$$

and field 2 now acts as the backstop to field 1. Beyond T_1 field 1's shadow price (extraction cost plus royalty) would in theory, were it not exhausted, exceed that of field 2 so that field 1 must be depleted by year T_1. Along both shadow price paths, the growth rate is always $(\lambda_{jt}/p_t)i$ (j = 1 or 2), while the market price growth rate is $(\lambda_{1t}/p_t)i$ to year T_1 and then $(\lambda_{2t}/p_t)i$ from T_1 to T_2. This produces the continuous but not smooth solid line in Figure 7.5 as the market price of oil under socially optimal depletion of the two fields in sequence. It is the low extraction cost of field 1 which favours its initial depletion, but it is the escalating royalty as exhaustion approaches at T_1 that determines the switch to field 2, and optimal exhaustion of field 1 at T_1.

If we could apply this imaginary optimal programme to the UK oil and gas reserves it would ensure that the cheaper coastal fields were depleted first with operations moving into deeper water in sequence as each field farther down the royalty merit order provided a backstop price for the currently exploited field until, eventually, reserves elsewhere in the world or alternative fuels provided a backstop to the last North Sea field. However, with competitive spot markets alone, we cannot expect this sequential discovery of the global rule for socially optimal depletion even when we ignore problems of uncertainty, unstable expectations, random field discovery, and market failure such as oligopolistic behaviour by oil suppliers.

North Sea oil

In the context of the world oil market the UK is a very modest exporter, with its current production contributing a marginal 5 per cent of world oil consumption in 1984. In the same year the

Department of Energy estimated that recoverable reserves lay between 0.5 and 3.5 billion tonnes, compared with proven world reserves of about 90 billion tonnes. The UK therefore cannot be other than a price-taker in world markets, though its support was canvassed by OPEC when the latter restricted production in 1983–84 to prevent the world price of oil slipping far below $30 per barrel in 1983 prices.

In domestic terms, however, oil has been very significant for the UK economy, since its tax revenues have been equal to about 50–100 per cent of the public sector borrowing requirement itself, and it has added considerably to UK wealth with the discounted present value of future NS oil revenues being well in excess of a whole year's GNP in the early 1980s.

The oil itself has largely been developed by consortia of the major oil companies, though public enterprises like the British Gas Corporation and National Coal Board had initial participation along with the later British National Oil Corporation (the latter's production side was subsequently sold to the private sector as Britoil). Although the UK government has, in principle, considerable powers to control depletion, these have not been exercised. From the beginning of North Sea development, government depletion policy has consisted of authorising a series of 'licence rounds' in which blocks of the continental shelf are leased for oil and gas development to companies of acceptable financial and technical competence, with the economic rent being collected not through field auctions, but by taxation. The taxation system itself is not a simple progressive tax on field cash flows as might be advocated by economists (Devereux and Morris, 1983), but has evolved as a set of complex and frequently changing taxes. Following the 1983 budget these were reduced to:

(a) Petroleum revenue tax (PRT)—a percentage of field profits with several allowances to favour development of marginal fields.

(b) Corporation tax—a percentage of the profits accruing to each company operating a field, against which may be set several types of expenses, so long as they occur only in the company's continental shelf activities.

At other times various devices have been used to speed up the advance payment of these taxes, and frequent changes were made to allow for variations in the world oil price. This was especially important since the initial rates and taxes favoured oil exploration significantly. The surge in rents as world oil prices rose was captured in several *ad hoc* adjustments involving advance payment of percentages of revenues, but the 1983 system was designed once more to encourage exploration and reduce the burden of taxation. It appeared to result in new exploration and an upward revaluation of reserves, as methods of secondary recovery of oil and gas were planned, so that production of 1.5 million barrels per day (75 million tonnes per year) until the end of the century seems likely. With consumption running at about 60 million tonnes per year, this would leave UK as a net exporter until the twenty-first century.

Different measures of NS oil impact have been suggested, but most studies use some version of:

(a) GNP contribution: ΔY

value of oil and gas production (V_0)	−	goods and services bought outside NS sector (C_0)	−	interest, profits and dividends remitted abroad (IPD)

i.e. $\Delta Y = V_0 - C_0 - \text{IPD}$; and

(b) the current account balance of payments effect: ΔB:

$\Delta B = V_0 - \text{IPD} - (\text{imported NS materials and services})$

so that (b) differs from (a) in terms of the source of the input services used to produce the oil and gas. The balance of payments effect loomed large in initial studies, but by the 1980s was no longer calculated by the Treasury since a comparison of UK trade without oil was no longer easy. The latter effect, however, clearly did remove much of the difference between the real exchange rate and the shadow price of foreign exchange which dominated much energy policy discussion in the 1960s as the UK was constrained by chronic balance of payments deficits (Posner, 1973).

The range of authoritative calculations is rather large, but typical estimates of the GNP contribution are, for example:

Bank of England (1982): 3–6 per cent of additional permanent GNP per annum available for consumption.

Forsyth and Kay (1980): $5\frac{1}{2}$ per cent of GNP per annum over the 1980s.

The latter estimate amounts to about £10 billion per annum in 1980 prices, and almost all accrues to the economy in general through the government's large (though delayed) tax take. This illustrative figure of £10 billion has been taken as the typical NS impact, the effects of which must be analysed both in real terms and as a macroeconomic management and investment problem.

At the same time, both the possession and the subsequent depletion of the oil, by removing the UK's long-term balance of payments problems and turning it into an oil exporter, strengthened the exchange rate. The critical period was from 1978–79 onwards. Oil began flowing in significant amounts, so that the exchange rate and GNP effects became discernible. At the same time world oil prices rose significantly and stayed firm until 1983. Atkinson, Brooks and Hall (1983) have estimated that about 35 per cent of the actual exchange rate movements over 1979–82 is attributable to the direct impact of NS oil. The two basic direct effects of the oil were therefore:

  (a) a gift of additional GNP in the form of oil, the value determined by world prices and the £–$ exchange rate; and
  (b) an appreciation of the £ *vis-à-vis* other currencies.

The problems posed for the economy as a result were:

  (1) the effect of the new GNP in the form of oil on the existing structure of production;
  (2) the possible need for macroeconomic policy to accommodate the wealth and the exchange rate influences; and
  (3) the division of the permanent income gain between additional consumption and the investment needed to maintain capital intact.

Macroeconomic effects of North Sea oil

The issues described above are now analysed in terms of the different contributions economists have made towards each problem. A set of *ceteris paribus* assumptions is necessary in that even though general equilibrium models are used, only the oil effects are considered so that, for example, upward pressure on the exchange rate was, in the real world, offset by extraneous, non-oil-related events such as the world recession, US budget deficits and rising interest rates over the period 1982–85. Without NS oil, such extraneous events might have had a substantially larger impact on the UK economy than they did have.

The first issue to be considered is the effect of the additional oil-based GNP on the structure of the economy. This concerns the so-called 'deindustrialisation' or 'Dutch disease' effect of NS oil, i.e. the fact that NS oil may supplant the previous leading export sector of the economy, as was said to have happened after natural gas discoveries in the Netherlands, and mineral discoveries in Australia.

The second issue is whether the rising exchange rate and related monetary adjustments will take place without lags or stickiness in price responses so that policy management problems arise. Finally, the proportion of the additional GNP that should be reinvested to maintain capital intact and immortalise the temporary rise in wealth must be determined.

In the analysis that follows it is the first issue, the natural gift of additional GNP, *ceteris paribus*, whose impact must be examined, although clearly there is no doubt that NS oil is a real benefit. The real GNP effect of NS oil can be analysed by models of international trade that allow for technical change, and this is the framework suggested by Corden and Neary (1982), whose model we present here.

Corden and Neary distinguish three commodity types, two of which are traded internationally, 'tradeables', and one of which is not traded:

tradeables: manufactures (M) and energy (E)

nontradeables: services (S)

World market forces determine tradeables' prices, p_M and p_E, which therefore remain exogenous. Since they stay in a fixed relationship with each other, *ceteris paribus*, they can be combined as the single price of a Hicksian composite commodity with given price index p_T. Non-tradeable services, produced and consumed domestically, have an endogenous price, p_S, in the model, and the ratio of the domestically determined price of services to the composite world determined price of tradeables is used as the real exchange rate, RER:

$$RER = p_S/p_T \tag{7.27}$$

In (7.27), as p_S/p_T rises, the real exchange rate appreciates and tradeables become relatively cheaper to domestic consumers.

The version of the Corden–Neary model which seems to underly most commentators' policy discussions has labour mobile among different sectors of the economy so that only one real wage rate

188

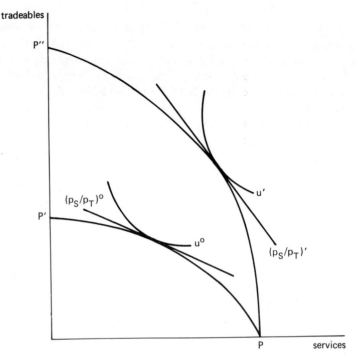

Figure 7.6

can prevail in equilibrium, but has capital specific to each sector so that different rates of return can be expected among sectors.

Begin by assuming that the energy sector uses a negligible labour input so that labour mobility must lie between services and manufacturing. Figure 7.6 shows the economy's international trade position before and after the NS oil discovery.

PP' and PP" are the before and after production possibility frontiers between tradeables and services, and the oil discovery appears as an additional endowment of tradeables in the form of energy, E. This enables the economy to move to the higher community indifference curve, U', from U^0, with higher spending on both types of commodity. Tradeables' prices, p_T, remain fixed and this 'spending effect' leads to an adjustment in services prices, p_S, reflected in the RER appreciation from $(p_S/p_T)^0$ to $(p_S/p_T)'$.

The labour market is illustrated in Figure 7.7, and shows the allocation of a fixed labour endowment between services, L_S, and

189

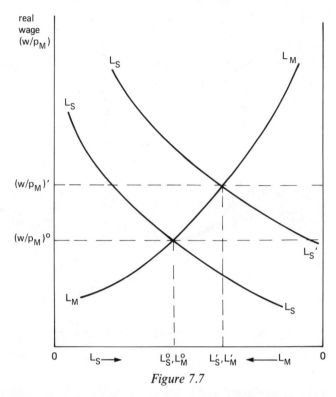

Figure 7.7

manufactures, L_M. The respective labour demand curves are graphed against the real wage rate—measured in the Corden–Neary model as the ratio of the money wage to the exogenous price of manufactures, p_M (the numeraire).

The pre-oil labour market equilibrium is at the real wage of $(W/p_M)^0$ where the labour demand curves $L_S L_S$ and $L_M L_M$ intersect. After the oil discovery and the consequent appreciation of RER by the rising p_s term, the rise in demand for services due to the spending effect can only be supplied domestically by a contraction in domestic production of manufactures. The shift to the right in Figure 7.7 of the labour demand curve in services ($L_S' L_S'$) brings about this shift of labour at the new higher equilibrium real wage $(W/p_M)'$. In the event, those tradeable goods which have not been augmented by discoveries or technical progress—in this case manufactures—must contract. This is the feature known as 'deindustrialisation' or 'Dutch disease'.

The 'spending effect' of NS oil discoveries could be reinforced by a 'resource movement effect' if the energy sector, E, also needed to draw in additional labour supplies. Suppose for the moment that the income elasticity of the demand for services was zero so that there was no rightward shift of L_SL_S in Figure 7.7 as GNP rises. Nevertheless as oil production expands labour must move into the oil sector. Figure 7.8 shows an addition to L_ML_M to represent energy sector labour demand, so that the demand for labour in tradeables is L_TL_T. This has expanded, but L_SL_S has not shifted. Wage rate adjustments then draw labour out of both S and M to a new equilibrium $(W/p_M)''$. Note that this would imply a contraction in the *output* of services, although the assumption of zero income elasticity of demand for services implied no change in *consumption*. This implied excess demand for services is rationed by

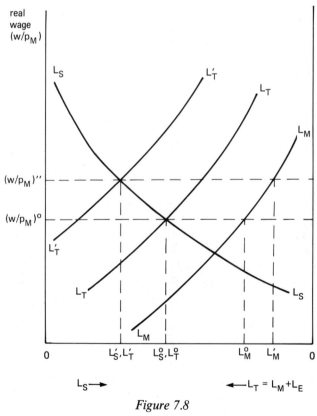

Figure 7.8

rising p_S leading once again to RER appreciation. As before manufactures must contract.

Either, or both, effects of a new endowment of one tradeable commodity—the spending effect and the resource movement effect—have been shown to lead to a contraction in production and labour usage of the other tradeable commodity, accompanied by an appreciation in the real exchange rate as price levels of domestically produced non-tradeable goods rise.

In a well-known paper, Forsyth and Kay (1980) discussed the deindustrialisation phenomenon using numerical examples and bringing out the policy implications. Here we simplify their numerical examples to relate them to the Corden–Neary framework, just discussed. The basic framework is the balance of trade and the structure of GNP. Again, we assume only three commodity types energy, E, manufactures, M, and services, S, the last being non-tradeable. Just prior to the oil finds, UK GNP was about £184 billion in 1980 prices, and Forsyth and Kay's estimate of the North Sea endowment is that it contributes each year about £10 billion to GNP in 1980 prices over the 1980s.

Table 7.2 sets out the basic analysis of these rough figures, with the pre-oil situation illustrated on the left, and the post-oil situation on the right. The bottom line totals represent the output measure of national income and both pre- and post-oil it is assumed that exchange rate adjustments establish a zero balance of trade, so that production of commodities equals the economy's absorption or consumption of commodities (including, therefore, investment expenditure). Exports are subtracted from production and imports added to production to achieve the domestic absorption figure. After NS oil is found, annual national income rises by £10 billion in 1980 prices to £194 billion representing an increase of roughly $5\frac{1}{2}$ per cent. The critical change has occurred in the energy sector and, initially, all of the £10 billion national income increase arises in the form of increased energy (oil) production. It is this fact—that the endowment arises as crude oil which can only be absorbed as other commodities after trading it—which necessitates all the other structural changes. If Forsyth and Kay's assumption that each commodity (E, M and S) has a unitary income elasticity is adopted, then the post-oil half of the table is built up as follows:

1. the NS oil find of £10 billion along with the unit income elasticity produce the unbracketed figures,

2. the bracketed figures follow from the assumption that the RER adjusts to re-establish zero balance on the trade account.

Hence national income rising to £194 billion produces a 5½ per cent increase in the consumption of each commodity type giving the difference between the pre- and post-oil consumption columns. Since energy consumption, even after the rise, is now less than production, £2 billion of oil is available for export, and none needs to be imported. Since services production is non-tradeable, it must rise in line with consumption. Finally, since oil exports have improved the balance of trade, the old position of an 'export drive' in manufactures need no longer be pursued, since zero trade balance now requires an 'import drive' in this remaining tradeables sector. Production of manufactures need only be at £138 billion to meet the new consumption level with imports making up the difference. Hence oil has supplanted manufactures as the critical export sector at the margin (manufacturing still exports 29 per cent of its production even after the change), and manufacturing industry shows the only contraction.

The appreciation in RER will, by making overseas manufactures relatively cheaper than domestic manufactures in UK prices, ensure these changes come about. The Forsyth–Kay conclusion is that 'the contraction of manufacturing output and an increase in domestic absorption of imported manufactures are—whether desirable or not—the only means by which the British economy can benefit from the North Sea.' The changes are only relative however, as Table 7.3 shows.

A further effect now needs to be considered, arising from the altered terms of trade. Relative to UK prices, as represented by p_s, the prices of energy and manufactures' imports have now been reduced, and also energy exports, denominated in dollars rather than pounds, need to be revalued downwards. Table 7.4 shows the post-oil price ratios of each commodity assuming that there has been a 15 per cent real exchange rate appreciation. With the increased weight now given to the relatively cheaper imported manufactures, the net effect is to revalue UK production by 0.99, but to revalue consumption by 0.96, and this is equivalent to a further real income rise of (0.99/0.96), or just over 3 per cent. Hence the terms-of-trade effect will substantially reinforce the initial endowment effect of the NS oil find, both contributing to the struc-

Table 7.2: Pre- and post-oil balance of trade and GNP structure (£ billion, 1980 prices)

	pre-oil				post-oil			
	production	exports (−)	imports (+)	consumption	production	exports (−)	imports (+)	consumption
energy (E)	9	−1	+8	16	19	(−2)	(0)	17
manufacturing (M)	140	−45	+38	133	(138)	(−40)	(+42)	140
services (S)	35	—	—	35	(37)	—	—	37
national income	184	−46	+46	184	194	−42	+42	194

Table 7.3: North Sea oil adjustments in relative terms

	Production change as percentage of pre-oil GNP	Production change as percentage of pre-oil sectoral production	Pre-oil shares in GNP (per cent)	Post-oil shares in GNP (per cent)
energy (E)	+ 5.4	+ 111.1	4.9	9.8
manufactures (M)	− 1.1	− 1.43	76.0	71.1
services (S)	+ 1.1	+ 5.7	19.1	19.1
			100.0	100.0

Table 7.4: Terms of trade effects of 15 per cent RER appreciation

| | | Ratio of post-oil prices to pre-oil prices in each sector | | |
	production	exports	imports	implied price index of consumption
energy (E)	0.85	0.85	0.85	0.85
manufactures				
(M)	1	1	0.85	0.96[1]
services (S)	$\dfrac{1}{0.99}$[2]	—	—	$\dfrac{1}{0.96}$[3]

Notes:
1. Weighted column average: $(138(1) - 40(1) + 42(0.85)) \div 140 = 0.96$.
2. Weighted production row average: $(19(0.85) + 138(1) + 37(1)) \div 194 = 0.99$
3. Weighted consumption row average: $(17(0.85) + 140(0.96) + 37(1) \div 194 = 0.96$.

tural shift in the economy which allows oil exports to supplant manufacturing production at the margin.

So far we have assumed no direct policy response to these structural changes brought about by the mechanism of a real exchange rate appreciation. Clearly, the economy has benefited overall, but equally clearly there have been gainers and losers with the lowest rate of return on capital appearing in manufacturing industry. This has led some commentators to dispute the benefits of North Sea oil, particularly where resistance to downward wage signals in manufacturing has permitted the structural changes to appear as increased unemployment.

This possibility of slowly responding markets has been analysed in a series of models—Eastwood and Venables (1982), Neary and van Wignbergen (1984) and Spencer (1984)—that explicitly concentrate on the macroeconomic policy management of NS oil rather than on the real GNP restructuring issue. For convenience, these models could be called the monetary analysis of NS oil, and their analysis is the second primary issue in the macroeconomic treatment of NS oil effects.

The models assume a small open economy initially at the full employment level of national income, and with zero inflation. To stay at full employment national income, with a given money supply, goods market and money market equilibrium positions are achieved by adjustments to the endogenous level of domestic prices (p), and the endogenous nominal exchange rate (e). The latter expresses the domestic price of imports (i.e. in £). In the goods market a rising domestic price level makes exports less attractive and to leave aggregate demand unchanged, imports must also become less attractive requiring a proportionate rise in the domestic price of imports. These two movements trace out the 'IS_0' curve of Figure 7.9. In the money market, a given money supply leaves income and interest rates unchanged only if the demand for money remains unchanged; this requires a constant weighted average price level for all transactions so that any rises in domestic prices must be accompanied by falling import prices to leave their weighted average unchanged. These adjustments trace out the 'LM_0' curve of Figure 7.9.

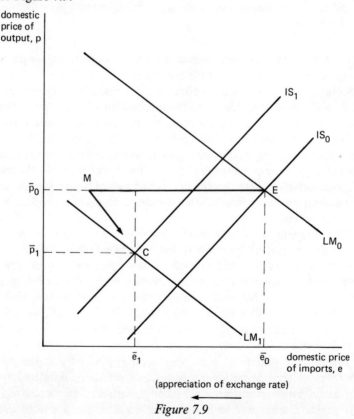

Figure 7.9

Note that the definition of e, the nominal exchange rate as the domestic price of imports, means that a rise in e along the axis is a 'depreciation' and a fall along the axis is an 'appreciation' (and this is the inverse of the earlier treatment of the real exchange rate). Now all the models referred to treat the discovery of oil as a gift of foreign exchange, thereby increasing spending power immediately. (In contrast, the earlier real analysis treated NS oil as an addition to the full employment level of national income.) This increases both aggregate demand in the goods market, and the demand for money. In Figure 7.9, the goods market effect is to shift IS_0 up left to IS_1, as p must rise and e must fall (appreciate) to reduce net export injections and therefore to leave aggregate demand unchanged at the full employment level of national income. In the money market, the increased demand for money needs to be offset by a lower price level of transactions (lower p and lower e) to stay equal to the unchanged stock of money, so that LM_0 shifts down left to LM_1. The initial equilibrium combination $(\bar{e}_0\bar{p}_0)$ becomes $(\bar{e}_1\bar{p}_1)$, which at C must either be above and left of E, or below and left of E; the latter is illustrated in the figure.

If both goods and money market participants responded immediately to such shocks and, with rational expectations, perceived the new equilibrium positions directly, then the exchange rate would jump from $\bar{e}_0$ to $\bar{e}_1$, and the price level simultaneously would jump from $\bar{p}_0$ to $\bar{p}_1$, and in the words of Minford (1977), NS oil 'does not pose special problems of macroeconomic management'. However, the models examined here all reject these neoclassical assumptions, and assume a hierarchy of efficient markets such that some respond more quickly to shocks than others. In particular, they assume that money and foreign exchange markets react according to the neoclassical assumptions, but that the goods market does not. Rather, these models assume that the domestic price level moves sluggishly and continuously with the level of aggregate demand along a simple Phillips curve, and does not jump to its new equilibrium level immediately. This has important consequences for the short-run dynamic path along which the economy moves from E to C in Figure 7.9.

Suppose the exchange rate does jump immediately towards $\bar{e}_1$, but prices remain at $\bar{p}_0$. Following the oil discovery, the economy might be out of long-run equilibrium at a point like M. Indeed, the dynamics of these models suggest that such an 'overshoot' in the exchange rate adjustment is quite plausible. From M the economy converges slowly on C. However, to achieve this slow adjustment to C the price level will only fall along the Phillips curve if the economy is temporarily in recession, so that NS oil might after all have caused a macroeconomic policy problem of temporary unemployment. The cause of this recession is the need for the domestic price level to fall to offset the direct increase in the demand for money arising from the NS oil wealth effect. The recession is deepened by the extent of any overshoot in the exchange rate appreciation. The policy dilemma is then whether to accommodate the increased demand for money by monetary expansion or, if anit-inflation policy predominates, to let a temporary NS oil-generated recession support the fixed monetary target in reducing prices. No such policy dilemma exists, of course, if goods market prices are assumed to adjust instantaneously to the new equilibrium, or if the new equilibrium C lies above left of E. Spencer (1984) simulated a further oil discovery on the UK Treasury model (which he argued reflected the sluggish price level assumptions rather than the neoclassical assumptions), and found that the model predicted a short-run recession as part of the adjustment process, and that the demand for money effect of NS oil was strong. Introducing plausible lags in the NS spending and money demand effects further complicates the dynamic responses, but enough has already been said to indicate that only the very strong neoclassical assumptions about goods market behaviour can dispose completely of the macroeconomic policy management problem.

We should therefore consider the NS oil impact in the context of different possible policy stances, and to do this we can adopt a broad taxonomy of outcomes. Write the current account balance as the difference between the economy's production (the output measure of national income), and its absorption (expenditure on UK and overseas consumption and investment goods):

$$B \equiv Y - A$$

so that:

$$\Delta B = \Delta Y_0 + \Delta Y_{N0} - \Delta A$$

where Y_0 and Y_{N0} represent oil and non-oil contributions to national income. Now clearly $\Delta Y_0 > 0$, and this can permit:

(i) $\Delta Y_{N0} < 0$ (*ceteris paribus*: $\Delta B = \Delta A = 0$)

(ii) $\Delta A > 0$, (*ceteris paribus*: $\Delta B = \Delta Y_{N0} = 0$)

(iii) $\Delta B > 0$, (*ceteris paribus*: $\Delta Y_{N0} = \Delta A = 0$),

or some combination of the three possibilities.

Outcome (i) is what might be called pure deindustrialisation, with zero balance and unchanged absorption and simple swapping of oil for non-oil output. Given the different labour intensity of production in the oil and non-oil sectors, the gift is taken purely as additional leisure (or unemployment), in the sense that an unchanged level of national income is produced with lower labour input. This outcome might be recommended by those who believed that industry needed a shake-out of surplus labour, that it needed to be opened up to foreign competition, and that the possibility of increased absorption might be inflationary. It clearly requires the tightest possible control of monetary policy.

Outcome (ii) allows the net benefits to be consumed and/or invested immediately, though it may stimulate inflationary pressures in the economy. It clearly requires loose fiscal and monetary policy, with some signal about the split between consumption and investment.

Outcome (iii) means that the balance of trade surplus can permit an outflow of capital. This has the advantage of permitting UK residents (or government) to acquire overseas assets that can replace the oil when it runs out. It requires lax monetary but tight fiscal policy to keep domestic interest rates below those overseas, and requires the abolition of exchange controls.

In practice all three outcomes have played a part in the NS oil impact. Over the first half of the 1980s macroeconomic policy had already adopted an anti-inflationary stance so that the medium-term financial strategy could be interpreted as the sort of restrictive monetary policy that reinforced outcome (i). Hence the comment that NS revenues have simply disappeared as higher unemployment benefit. At the same time, the abolition of exchange controls and the emergence of high real interest rates overseas, particularly in the US, permitted a measure of type (iii) outcome, with capital outflows reaching historically high levels. To the extent that the proceeds of NS oil are received directly by consumers (for example, as the government was able to use NS tax revenues instead of income and other taxes to reduce the public sector borrowing requirement) an increase in absorption was also permitted with the result that despite record unemployment and negative income growth, real consumer spending rose over the period.

There remains the question of reinvesting the NS proceeds. Part of this investment has clearly shifted overseas, but many groups have argued that the NS resources should be used to invest in UK industry itself. There are two separate questions here: how much investment should be done, and where should it go. Forsyth and Kay (1980) argued that the investment level over the finite life of the NS fields should be sufficient to turn the temporary consumption increment into a permanent increment. If i is the UK's social opportunity cost of capital (and social discount rate), and V_0 is the present value of the finite NS reserves, then the maximum permanent increment to consumption that can be achieved is iV_0, and this should be the maximum consumption level we permit ourselves while the oil is depleting; any additional oil income needs to be reinvested to maintain V_0 intact. If $\overline{\Lambda}$ is the peak annual revenue from NS oil, then Forsyth and Kay suggest an investment rate as a proportion of $\overline{\Lambda}$:

$$\frac{\overline{\Lambda} - iV_0}{\overline{\Lambda}}$$

that maintains a constant increment to UK consumption forever. At a discount rate of 3 per cent and an assumed constant \$35/barrel price of oil over the period 1980–2014, they suggested reinvesting at least 50 per cent of NS oil revenues.

Assuming such an investment rate could be determined, which projects should be adopted? One view associated with Cambridge economists like Barker (1981) is that the UK's growth rate has always been constrained by a balance of payments deficit at an overvalued exchange rate, and that when NS oil removed this constraint, the investment should have been poured into UK industry. This is another reflection of the views of those economists who believe that shortage of finance has caused the historically low rate of investment in UK manufacturing industry. Many economists, however, find little evidence for this description of the UK economy in the 1970s and 1980s. Rather, it appears that it is low rates of return that have discouraged the investment, and the impact of NS oil is further to reduce this rate of return as part of the market signal to restructure the economy. Unless one believes that increased investment can cause a rightward shift of the marginal efficiency of capital schedule, such a diversion of NS funds to UK manufacturing is clearly a waste of NS revenues. The only remaining argument in its favour is the belief that the structural changes arising from NS oil result in an incurable and unacceptable level of unemployment, and that maintaining workers in non-competitive jobs has a social rate of return in excess of the opportunity cost of capital.

The alternative view reflects the operation of the competitive market depletion rule (7.10), that converts oil under the sea to alternative investments earning at least the opportunity cost of capital. The two principal candidates in the context of the UK in the 1980s have been the new technologically advanced industries like microelectronics, and those overseas investments earning competitive rates of return. In practice the years 1979–83 have been characterised by a net increase in UK ownership of overseas assets of roughly £20–30 billion in nominal terms compared with NS revenues of about £70 billion over the same period.

How has North Sea oil fitted into the overall development of the UK economy? The long view has been outlined by the Bank of England (1982). Comparing the real price of oil before and after the almost simultaneous OPEC price rises and the NS discoveries, gives in 1980 prices:

1973: £23/tonne
1980: £35/tonne

so that the two simultaneous events leave the UK worse off on balance. Industrialised countries without oil were of course much worse off, and had to further 'industrialise', i.e. develop export drives to pay for their dearer imports.

On this basis, finding NS oil relieved the UK of the need to industrialise in the short run compared with the required adjustment of non-oil industrialised countries like West Germany and Japan. In the long run, as oil is depleted and the UK returns to being an oil importer, then it will need once more to foster an industrialisation and export drive—a response signalled by a declining pound. The Bank of England therefore argued that massive structural changes were not needed as a response to the finding of NS oil since the two effects—rising oil prices plus short-term oil discoveries—essentially cancelled out. Assuming some stability in oil prices and a gradual depletion of NS reserves, the period over which the UK must re-industrialise is likely to be lengthy and the adjustment need only be gradual.

Clearly, many factors have been held on one side by a *ceteris paribus* assumption. At the same time as the events analysed, the world went through a deep recession, oil prices first rose, then weakened considerably, and US interest rates and the US $ rose substantially as a result of large public sector deficits.

The oil premium in the exchange rate accounted for a minor part of the exchange rate changes between 1977 and 1980, and since then the exchange rate movements have been much more the result of changes in international monetary policy than the depletion of North Sea oil which has proceeded steadily. It is essential therefore to see the NS oil impact as only a part of the macroeconomic forces affecting the economy; significant, but of less importance than the general stance of monetary and fiscal policy.

8

Issues in policy-making

Introduction

There remain important areas of energy policy only partially treated by the previous chapters, and some of these are considered now.

In the context of the 1970s and early 1980s, energy conservation came often to be regarded as an end in itself, and policy commentators framed questions about which of two options yielded greater net benefit: investment in supply or investment in conservation. This question is essentially fallacious, but the issue needs to be explored.

There also evolved in the early 1980s a strong government commitment to the introduction of competitive market pressures on the public energy utilities, and this issue of privatisation in fuel supply is the second topic examined in this chapter.

More perennial policy objectives have included the issue of the security of supply of the nation's fuel sources, but the issue itself, let alone any policy implications, is relatively unclear. The third topic considered is therefore the question of whether a security of supply policy is needed to supplement market-determined responses to risk.

Another long-lived issue in both the UK and European energy policy debate has been the rundown of the old deep-mined coal industries. This topic is examined in the context of energy policy as a whole in the last case study in this chapter.

Energy conservation

A variety of coincidental circumstances—the emerging importance of oil imports for the US, and the growth of the OPEC cartel among them—succeeded in convincing many commentators that an energy crisis would characterise the 1980s. As a result the idea of conserving energy (i.e. exhaustible fossil fuels) was suggested as a policy objective in itself. Although this idea has not received explicit attention so far in this book, it can be put into perspective here by reflecting that balancing the supply and demand for fuels has been the essence of every part of the analysis. In this way, we can define conservation to be any absolute or relative decline in the consumption of energy.

Following the world oil price rises of 1973–74 and 1979, energy consumption in many countries declined. The figures for the UK are shown in Table 8.1. As this trend emerged, important studies of the potential for reduced energy consumption in the domestic, industrial, commercial and transport sectors of the economy were carried out, with that of Leach (1977) being the most comprehensive. Leach followed a bottom-up forecasting strategy by examining the energy:economic activity ratios in over 400 different end-use categories of energy consumption. He was able to show that rising national income was compatible with reduced energy consumption, or at least with a less than proportionate rise in energy consumption.

Table 8.1: UK energy consumption 1970–83: Total inland consumption of primary energy (temperature corrected) (Index 1975 = 100)

Year	Index
1972	103.2
1973	108.4
1974	103.4
1975	100.0
1976	101.4
1977	103.5
1978	103.7
1979	106.9
1980	99.9
1981	96.5
1982	95.4
1983	95.9

Source: Department of Energy (1984).

That such a possibility exists is, of course, no surprise to economists used to thinking of output as being produced by different combinations of inputs, and the large amount of econometric evidence on the price elasticity of energy demand is confirmation of Leach's findings. Such studies of the potential for energy conservation are an essential ingredient in the flow of information required by consumers and producers in establishing the competitive equilibrium allocation of resources. As energy prices rise, the production of such information is an expected market response.

The problems for economic policy are whether enough information is being exchanged, and whether market price signals correctly reflect the cost information that consumers require to adopt the optimal amount of energy conservation. Conservation is therefore a market response rather than an end in itself.

Nevertheless, in looking at energy policy, the forecast amount of energy conservation has been a focus of attention and measurement. For example, in its consultative Green Paper *Energy Policy*, Cmnd. 7101 (1978), the Department of Energy stated that its demand forecasts allowed for a reduction of energy demand of about 20 per cent compared with the demand that would have been forecast without conservation effort. In this way it made allowance for both technological progress in improving the efficiency of production and a price-induced substitution away from energy-intensive activities. Clearly the net measure of conservation depends on the interaction of three forces: (1) national income growth pulling energy consumption up, in the absence of counter incentives; (ii) the escalation of relative energy prices; and (iii) the rate of technological progress in reducing energy requirements. These three factors acting together determine overall energy usage.

Compare the following two measures of conservation:

(1) falling energy consumption, in absolute terms, and

(2) a falling energy consumption to national income ratio.

The first suggests conservation has occurred when the absolute level of energy consumption has dropped; the second, that conservation occurs when the level of energy used per £ of real national income produced has fallen. The second definition would exclude much of the conservation that is simply due to an economic recession and therefore appears to embody a stronger requirement. However, under plausible circumstances, conservation of the second type may need lower escalation of energy prices, and is even compatible with falling energy prices.

Consider a simple model of aggregate energy demand:

$$g_e = \eta g_y - \varepsilon g_p - \alpha \qquad (8.1)$$

where g_e, g_y, g_p are growth rates of energy, national income, and relative energy prices, respectively, and:

η = income or output elasticity of demand
ε = price elasticity of demand
α = the rate of technical progress in the generation of national income.

For conservation of type (1), we require $g_e < 0$, which in turn implies:

$$g_p > (\eta g_y - \alpha)/\varepsilon \qquad (8.2)$$

while type (2) conservation requires $(g_e - g_y) < 0$, implying

$$g_p > [(\eta - 1)g_y - \alpha]/\varepsilon \qquad (8.3)$$

In those cases where $\eta < 1$, rising national income may itself generate type (2) conservation with g_e still positive, and falling prices, $g_p < 0$. The empirical evidence cited in Chapter 2 suggests these cases are widely experienced.

In essense, therefore, measured energy conservation is the net change in energy or fuel demand resulting from the shifts along and in the position of the relevant demand curve: it is not a new concept, but the degree of attention paid to its measurement has been altogether greater as the expenditure on fuel consumption as a proportion of national income has risen.

Now consider the proposition that, in addition to the four basic fuels used in the UK (coal, oil, natural gas and electricity) energy conservation should be regarded as a fifth *source of supply*. The House of Commons select committee on energy, for example, has used this proposition as the basis of asking: which yields the greater net benefits—investment in energy conservation, or investment in additional fuel supply?

However, both the basic proposition and the question implied are based on the fallacy that reducing demand is the same as increasing supply and that the net benefits are to be measured identically. The difference between these two fundamental ideas can however be emphasised by Figures 8.1 and 8.2.

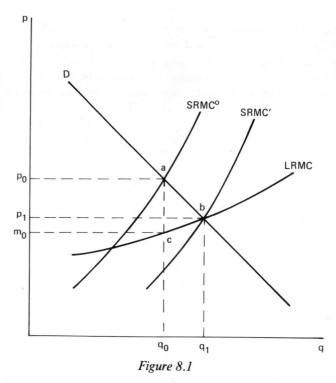

Figure 8.1

Figure 8.1 illustrates the net benefits of a supply increase, i.e. investment in new fuel-producing capacity. For such benefits to be positive, price must currently *exceed* social LRMC, for example at the $(q_0 p_0)$ combination on $SRMC^o$ at a. As we know from earlier analysis, there are net benefits to expanding capacity by shifting to SRMC' further along LRMC, and these are represented by the welfare triangle abc:

$$\Delta W = abc \cong \tfrac{1}{2}(p_0 - m_0)(q_1 - q_0) \qquad (8.4)$$

Consider now the case for energy conservation. Suppose first of all that consumers are made aware of the relevant cost information so that they are at an initial long-run equilibrium in Figure 8.2 at c with combination $(q_0 p_0)$, on demand curve D, and long-run marginal cost curve $LRMC^o$.

If, in this context, the case for energy conservation in the form of lower consumption is to be argued, it can only be on the grounds that price along $LRMC^o$ *falls short* of the long-run marginal social

207

cost of energy use, which should be measured by the higher curve
LRMC'. If this is so, then there are welfare benefits to be gained
by taxing energy production to remove the social loss triangle abc
in Figure 8.2. However, suppose instead mandatory restrictions on
fuel use at all price levels are implemented, for example by restrictions on certain fuel-using activities. Then the effect is to reduce
demand by shifting the demand curve inwards, for example to
D' in Figure 8.2. Now the welfare change is measured by the reduction in social costs abq_0q_1, less the loss of consumer surplus and
total revenue $[Dced' + (p_0cq_00 - p_2eq_10)]$. After the event, price
at p_2 still falls short of long-run marginal social cost along LRMC'.

In either case (i) the tax induced price rise $(p_1 - p_0)$ nor (ii)
the imposed restriction on consumption $(q_0 - q_1)$ are the welfare
changes comparable with those resulting from increased supply
capacity valued at social marginal cost as illustrated in Figure 8.1.

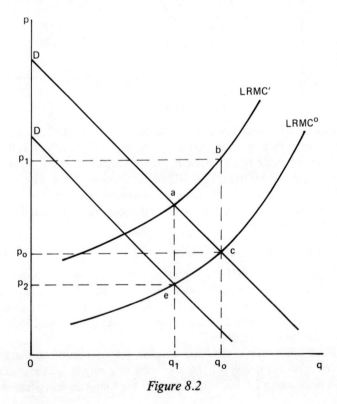

Figure 8.2

This is particularly the case for (ii), where the measured discrepancy between social and private LRMC may play no part in determining the outcome. On this basis, it can be concluded that if consumers are signalled the social marginal cost of energy consumption by setting price along LRMC' in Figure 8.2, then the optimal degree of conservation is already in place, and there are no net benefits to further reductions in energy consumption.

Conservation studies and energy-saving campaigns therefore make sense in so far as they provide consumers with the required information about social marginal costs, or give better informed technical guidance on how to substitute fuels when their relative prices alter.

Such information provision has almost certainly been needed after many years of energy having only a small share in household expenditures with the result that the benefits to the individual consumer of lower energy consumption did not exceed the search costs of fully monitoring conservation possibilities. But those who advocate conservation as an end in itself must provide the additional evidence that markets are not signalling the true social marginal costs of energy consumption, and must then indicate how prices can be set at social marginal cost.

Privatisation in energy supply

Much of the UK analysis of energy economics has been focused on the search for efficiency in the nationalised fuel industries, but several writers have argued that returning such industries in part or whole to the private sector would enable market pressures to eliminate inefficiency. At the same time, government attempts to reduce the public sector borrowing requirement in the 1979–84 period included sales of shares in state-owned corporations to the private sector. The three ideas (1) the search for market pressures, (2) the reduction in public sector borrowing by sales of assets, and (3) the principle that government itself is a drag on efficiency, have come to be known as 'privatisation'. Strictly speaking, privatisation means formation of a public company as defined in the UK Companies Act, and subsequent sale of at least 50 per cent of the shares to private shareholders (Beesley and Littlechild, 1983), but in this context, privatisation is taken as describing the search for market pressures on nationalised industries. An analogous idea in the US is the principle of deregulation of previously regulated public utilities. This has gone furthest in transport, but the deregulation idea has been prominent in both electricity and natural gas supply as well.

When considering the role of market pressures on a public utility, the underlying economic idea is that of 'natural monopoly'. However, it has to be borne in mind that the notion of natural monopoly was only one, and not necessarily the most important, of the reasons for the nationalisation of the electricity, gas and coal industries in the UK. Equally, if not more, important were reasons of political control over strategic industries, improvement of labour relations, wages and working conditions, and cross-subsidisation of deserving consumers in their consumption of essential energy. Nevertheless, it is the policy towards natural monopoly which has dominated the economic debate on privatisation.

Monopoly power can result from several different factors: sole control of an essential mineral input for example, or from possession of patents or statutory government authority, but natural monopoly is the monopoly power that results from market forces when the production level corresponding to lowest unit cost of the firm is sufficient to meet all market demand when priced at unit cost. Such natural monopoly is said to characterise the traditional public utilities: electricity, gas, water, sewage, telephone and perhaps, transport services. Figure 8.3 illustrates the average and marginal cost curves of a firm for which unit cost (AC) is falling up to and beyond total market demand, given by the demand schedule DD.

Such average (AC) and marginal (MC) cost curves will arise where there are large fixed or overhead costs of setting up a supply service, but the subsequent marginal cost of supply is constant: electricity and gas distribution to final consumers spring to mind as the classic examples. If supply was in the hands of a monopolist with marginal revenue curve MR, price and output would be at p_0 and q_0, but such monopoly profits might encourage potential competitors to enter the industry. In that event, the monopolist could simultaneously *expand* output along AC and *undercut* competitors (unless they possessed some innovative technology not available to the monopolist). By pricing at AC (perhaps only temporarily), the monopolist can deter any potential entrants and retain

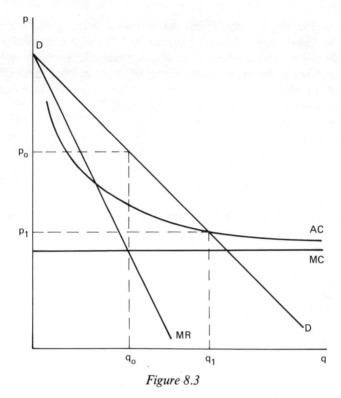

Figure 8.3

100 per cent of the market. In that sense, monopoly is the natural outcome of market forces. Note, however, that if the threat of entry never disappeared (even if the potential entrants came and went), the monopolist might need to go on pricing at AC (i.e. choosing q_1 and p_1) indefinitely. In fact p_1 is the Ramsey optimal price that a public sector monopolist seeking the second-best Pareto-optimal outcome, subject to breaking even, would choose anyway. This idea, that the permanent threat of potential entry may lead to a natural monopolist always pricing at the second-best Ramsey price in order to sustain the monopoly position is, in fact, the basis of recent 'contestability' theories of industrial structure (see below).

The AC and MC curves in Figure 8.3 exhibit economies of scale, but monopoly production may be desirable from society's point of view even when marginal cost is rising. Figure 8.4 illustrates the case where AC is once again falling because of the large overhead costs of setting up supply, but marginal cost is rising in the range of market demand when price is near AC. In this event, monopoly is not the natural outcome since, at q_0 for example, a single supplier cannot simultaneously expand along AC and undercut prices. Indeed, in order to undercut an entrant offering p_0, the monopolist must *contract* output, and lose market share.

Nevertheless, society as a whole might not wish the overhead costs to be incurred more than once (duplication of the distribution system, for example), so that a monopoly structure may be desirable but may never emerge. It is not economies of scale therefore which necessarily make monopoly production efficient, but rather that the total costs of single firm production fall short of the total costs of duplicating multiple firm production (a property known as subadditivity of costs).

However, to return to the main theme, economies of scale in production of a single commodity clearly are sufficient for the emer-

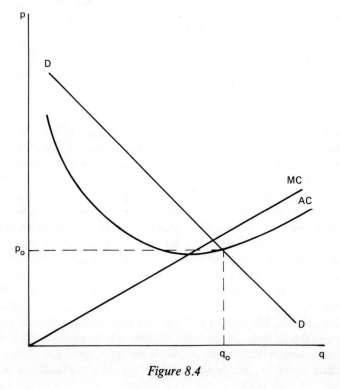

Figure 8.4

212

gence of natural monopoly. The practical questions to consider are therefore these:

(1) Is the economies of scale idea sufficient to describe natural monopoly when firms produce more than one output (e.g. peak and off-peak electricity); and if not, what is the appropriate property?

(2) Are the fuel supply industries, wholly or in part, natural monopolies?

(3) Where a natural monopoly structure exists, what, if anything, needs to be done to restrain the use of monopoly power?

(4) Where a nationalised industry with statutory monopoly power is not a natural monopoly, are there any reasons why it should not be immediately opened up to private sector competition?

Begin with the question of causes of natural monopoly in the multi-product case. It is important to think of electricity and gas supply, for example, as multi-product industries since electricity load (which cannot be stored), and gas load (which can only be stored expensively) vary both by time and place of use. These factors make it inappropriate to model electricity or gas production as a single output variable (e.g. total annual sales). Recent research (e.g. Bailey and Friedlander, 1982) shows that the measure of multi-product scale economies is possible through, for example, the concept of ray average cost (RAC). Figure 8.5 shows a firm producing two outputs, q_1 and q_2 (which might be industrial electricity sales at high voltage, and domestic sales at stepped-down low voltage).

Output must be measured as the vector $(q_1 q_2)'$, for example as a fixed combination of q_1 and q_2 along OR in the $(q_1 q_2)$ plane. Multi-product economies of scale exist if average cost for this output combination, i.e. RAC, is decreasing as both outputs expand in proportion along OR. One possible source of multi-product economies of scale is known as economies of scope. These arise when the total cost of producing both outputs together is less than the sum of the costs involved in individual production. Consider the above example of the supply of domestic electricity at low voltage and industrial sales at high voltage. There may be economies of scale and operational coordination from producing and supplying in both markets, even though concentration on one or other market is feasible.

213

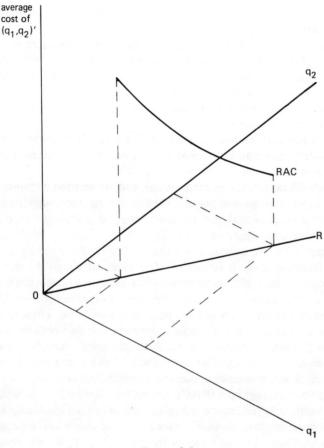

average cost of $(q_1, q_2)'$

q_2

RAC

R

0

q_1

Figure 8.5

A further source of multi-product economies of scale, and hence of natural monopoly, arises from vertical and horizontal integration. For example, it is possible to separate transmission from production (generation) in gas and electricity supply, but it is often the case that generation from distant low marginal cost plant along with transmission can undercut generation in place at a particular load centre. On integrated systems, this is summed up by setting the marginal cost of meeting load at each demand centre equal to a common system value (*system lambda*) to minimise the cost of interconnected supply:

214

$$MC_i = \frac{MC_j}{1 - \alpha_j} = \ldots = \lambda \tag{8.5}$$

where MC_i is marginal generating cost at the demand centre i, MC_j is the same for demand centre j, and α_j is the marginal losses of electricity in transmission from j to i (see Turvey, 1968). Wherever adjacent generating systems are not integrated in one firm, power pools and brokerage systems emerge to duplicate a central load scheduling and despatch system. Joskow and Schmalensee (1983) provide considerable evidence on the nature of these sources of multi-product scale economies in the US.

Additional sources of scale, scope and integration economies in electricity and gas supply arise when the risks of supply failure are considered. For example, to meet specified reliability standards, like those described in Chapter 5 above, it may only be necessary to expand capacity less than proportionately with the *number* of *customers* so that integrating adjacent generation and transmission systems reduces the capacity planning margin per customer.

There are numerous sources of scale economies of this nature in energy supply through distribution networks, with the ability of transmission from distant generating units to substitute for proximate generation among the most notable. Although it is possible to see generation and transmission as separate activities, Joskow and Schmalensee (1983) argue that if there are multi-product scale economies in distribution, together with economies of vertical integration between the generation and transmission stages, then generation may itself be treated as a natural monopoly, even if economies of scale appear to be absent at that stage alone. For these reasons, Joskow and Schmalensee agree with Turvey's long-standing argument that econometric studies that appear to reveal that the minimum efficient scale of generation is relatively low (say, below 4 gW in electricity supply) cannot be accepted at face value. Such studies use accounting data, ignore issues of reliability and load scheduling through central dispatch, and treat individual utilities as isolated firms producing a single commodity: annual fuel sales. They ignore the overwhelming weight of industry and engineering belief and practice which suggest strong natural monopoly tendencies in integrated gas and electricity supply.

Given that economies of scale certainly characterise transmission and distribution, and possibly also generation through economies of vertical and horizontal integration, it must be considered what policies if any are appropriate for dealing with the consequent natural monopoly.

The history of this debate is a long one, and it has recently been revived by the idea of contestability applied to multi-product natural monopolies. However, the case of electricity and gas natural monopoly depends more heavily on some earlier analyses. Traditionally, three solutions have been offered to the 'problem' of natural monopoly, i.e. the possibility that a market with monopoly *structure* may exhibit monopoly *power*. These are:

(a) leave the monopoly unrestricted in private hands, i.e. do nothing;

(b) take the natural monopoly into *public ownership*, and restrict entry to the market, i.e. confirm the statutory monopoly;

(c) *regulate* the monopoly as a permanent franchise that is free from entry: the typical US regulated public utility.

Solutions (b) and (c) are both taken to represent the idea of government control, and economists who simply believe government is bad (e.g. Friedman, 1962) prefer solution (a). Before returning to this, consider how (b) and (c), solutions which legally confirm the natural monopoly *structure* by restricting entry (e.g. the British Gas Corporation's monopoly in gas sales) tackle the problem of monopoly power.

One of the most celebrated solutions is that of Hotelling (1938) who argued that regulated public utilities should charge prices based on marginal cost, and that the resulting losses should be made up out of general taxation. (He advocated a tax on income, but this was criticised as interfering with the conditions for Pareto optimality; and other non-distortionary taxes need to be considered). Although Hotelling's suggestion has never been effectively adopted in the US, it clearly underlies the whole approach to public enterprise pricing in the UK, at least until the late 1970s.

The preferred solution in the US was 'fair rate of return' pricing, i.e. prices were based on a reasonable mark-up over allowable average costs. Such debatable terms as fair, reasonable and allowable have made this approach a regulatory lawyer's paradise and it has largely been treated with scorn by US economists.

A third solution is Ramsey pricing (as discussed in Chapter 3 above). This is the second-best approach, and reduces to average cost pricing in the single product case. There is some suggestion

216

that it is practised by the CEGB (see Chapter 6), but like all the solutions under (b) and (c) there remains the problem of agreement between regulators and regulated, or government and nationalised industry, about what constitutes marginal and average cost. Such disagreement was aired in the case of UK domestic electricity prices in the UK in 1983–84 (SCE, 1984) when the Treasury wished to raise prices while the industry did not.

Given these problems, is there anything to be said for solution (a)? The so-called Chicago school economists certainly argued so, and their position is best represented by Demsetz (1968). In asking: why regulate utilities? Demsetz laid the foundations for the subsequent ideas of contestability of natural monopoly markets. Demsetz argued that a large number of potential suppliers at minimum efficient scale were excluded from offering any pressure on the incumbent monopolist by the regulatory proscribing of free entry. He suggested institutionalising the threat posed by potential rivals by replacing the prevalent system of regulated franchise monopoly (RFM) by periodic franchise bidding (FB). Under FB schemes, the contract to supply a public utility market would be awarded after an auction tender from each supplier. To capture the monopoly, each bidder would have to offer the highest lump-sum or make a commitment to charge the lowest unit price. In this way the FB scheme would cause potential suppliers to bid away their monopoly profits, so that monopoly structure was divested of monopoly power. The Chicago school position was that 'competition *for* the field' could achieve the same outcome as 'competition *in* the field'. It is important to note that the criterion of success was that price is reduced to average cost by the competitive tender. The issue of marginal cost pricing was not raised at all.

The strongest reply came from Williamson (1976). Without being against FB in theory, Williamson argued that properly monitored FB schemes would, in practice, be indistinguishable from RFM. Williamson's critique of FB consists of a detailed analysis of the consequences of designing an FB scheme in practice. He points out that awarding the franchise on the basis of highest lump-sum bids causes rivals to offer their capitalised monopoly profit. The successful bidder *must* then use full monopoly power (output and price determined by marginal cost = marginal revenue) in order to break even. Bidding on the basis of lowest unit price is therefore preferable, and in principle the FB scheme awards temporary mono-

217

poly power to the supplier prepared to undercut right down to the level at which price equals average cost.

In this event it is essential, Williamson argues, to examine the nature of the proposed franchise contract. Long-term contracts (e.g. of 25 years) might be proposed to encourage the monopolist to accumulate the long-lived investment in equipment that permit lowest unit cost to be achieved. In that case, Williamson suggests that uncertainty will be a problem. Contracts covering every possible contingency are impossible, so that renegotiation and escape clauses become an important part of the FB scheme. The bids need then to specify particular price and and quality of service packages. How is the awarding body to choose, for example, between low-price, low-reliability supply packages, and high-price, high-reliability packages? Williamson accepts that solutions are possible, but notes that the initial negotiation, bid, renegotiation as circumstances alter, and monitoring procedures implied do not offer credible cost savings compared with RFM or public ownership.

Much of the uncertainty associated with technology, reliability and investment expectations might be removed by short-term contracts (e.g. 5 years), but in this case, the franchise will expire well before the end of the economic life of much of the plant and equipment. The successful bidder may simply not invest in the appropriate maintenance of the capital stock, unless compelled to do so in order to meet his commitment to price at lowest unit cost. But in that event, the incumbent monopolist will have the advantage at the contract renewal stage of a partially amortised capital stock, whereas all rivals must cover the full costs of the new equipment in their bid. Williamson suggests in this event that parity could be achieved once more between incumbent and rivals by requiring the incumbent, if displaced, to sell his plant at the successor's option to the successor at its partially amortised value. But the negotiating costs of this are once again likely to be substantial: the incumbent has the incentive to manipulate the declared cost of his equipment, while the successor may only offer a value based on its alternative non-franchised use. If the equipment is specific to the franchise, e.g. facilities in place related to a distribution network, the alternative use value is zero.

Where the assets of the incumbent monopolist are *not* specific to the particular market, these problems with FB schemes may be diminished. If the displaced monopolist can easily remove his equipment and leave to compete for some other natural monopoly market, then FB schemes may be able to separate monopoly structure from monopoly power. It is precisely these circumstances (i.e. both entry and exit from a market are easy) and the sunk costs of supply are negligible (i.e. asset specificity is not a problem), that led to an extension of the Demsetz idea, *viz.* contestability. This notion (Baumol 1982) implies that the threat of potential rivals entering a market is alone sufficient to compel an incumbent natural monopolist to behave in a socially desirable way by average cost or Ramsey pricing. Regulation and public ownership, by restricting freedom of entry (and exit—i.e. the scrapping of uneconomic services) actually hinder the second-best outcome. Contestability theory has been mentioned in the context of UK privatisation, but its requirement that asset specificity is not important renders it inapplicable to the natural monopoly characteristics of energy supply.

Among the suggested privatisation proposals for the UK nationalised fuel industries, those of Beesley and Littlechild (1983) and Minford (1984) have attracted most attention. Minford argued that UK nationalised industries operate as fully exploitative profit-maximising monopolists, restricting output to half the level that would be achieved under competition and consequently generating welfare losses as a proportion of turnover equal to half of the inverse of price elasticity η:

$$\frac{\Delta W}{pq} = \frac{1}{2\eta} \tag{8.6}$$

He offers no evidence for this prediction about the behaviour of the nationalised industries, and indeed ignores both the fact that they are instructed to price at LRMC, and the fact that several are price-taking competitors in world markets. All three authors suggest:

(a) Separating the isolated natural monopoly parts of fuel supply (distribution and transmission) from the rest (generation, or production).

(b) Privatising the generation areas by formation of public companies out of the CEGB and BGC, and NCB.

(c) Maintaining public ownership of the transmission and distribution system, by putting its operation and maintenance out to franchise tender (replacing the area electricity boards and the British Gas regions).

Clearly, these ideas reflect a reliance on the assumption that generation or production can be treated as separable single product activities with low minimum efficient scale of output. As we know already, the ability to test this proposition econometrically is limited, and attempts so far in the US have been of questionable success. These ideas also accept the basic Demsetz framework for the natural monopoly problem. However, they do not at all attempt to answer any of Williamson's critiques of that idea, nor do they specify the nature of the proposed contracts, nor do they offer any evidence that the negotiating and transaction costs would be less than those already internalised in the present nationalised industry structure. The proposals for energy supply privatisation therefore remain largely based on the simple application of Demsetz's principles, rather than the fundamental empirical work which Williamson and Joskow and Schmalensee argue is a necessary prerequisite of privatisation and deregulation proposals.

Security of supply

Ensuring the secure supplies of fuels appears to be the stated objective of virtually all national governments, and international bodies such as the European Community. The implication of this objective might seem to be that the government must have a security of supply policy, and as a result all sorts of tax and subsidy instruments are immediately suggested. However, a 'policy' as such is only warranted if the appropriate markets are unable to allocate resources efficiently, and then the nature of the inefficiencies needs to be examined. It is quite clear that supplies of some commodities are more variable than others, yet everyday market behaviour is quite capable of dealing with such variability, and so a security of supply 'policy' is not a necessary implication of the fact that people might prefer less to more variable supplies.

Security of supply is usually mentioned in the context of imported fuels, but can equally be relevant to reliability of electricity distribution, or to the supply of indigenous resources. However, consider the objective in the context of some imported commodity such as crude oil or coal. The analysis to be examined first is that of Tolley and Wilman (1977) who imagined a commodity which might

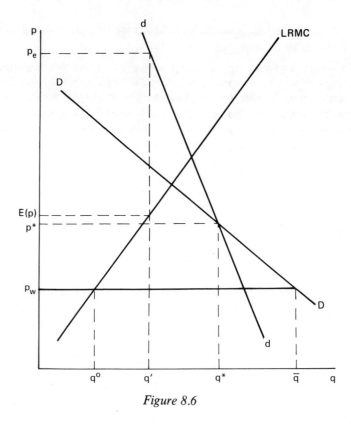

Figure 8.6

periodically be subject to supply disruption or embargo (Figure 8.6).

The UK demand schedule is labelled DD, and the indigenous supply schedule is LRMC. The world price of the good, say oil, is p_w, and this would determine the indigenous price level and marginal cost of home production if no embargo threat ever existed. The level of indigenous production would be q^0, the level of total consumption would be $\bar{q}$, and imports would be $(\bar{q} - q^0)$. This is just the usual outcome for a traded commodity.

Suppose now that supply has been disrupted with a frequency of 1 in $\frac{1}{\pi}$ years, so that for the next period π is taken to be the probability that no imports will be available. In this event, users and domestic producers will calculate the expected price and mar-

221

ginal cost under uncertainty, and the competitive market outcome will maximise the expected level of welfare:

$$E(W) = (1 - \pi)W_N + \pi(W_N - L_E) \qquad (8.7)$$

where W_N is the sum of consumer surplus and total revenue less total cost when no embargo is in place, and L_E is the welfare loss arising from an embargo. By considering the price, marginal cost combinations that produce no more marginal increases in $E(W)$, this welfare-maximising allocation that would arise in competitive markets can be found.

In responding to the uncertainty, domestic producers will expand production beyond q^0 to q', until LRMC equals their expectation of the long-run price when embargo is a possibility:

$$\begin{aligned} \text{LRMC} &= E(p) \\ &= (1 - \pi)p_w + \pi p_e \end{aligned} \qquad (8.8)$$

Now p_e is the price that clears the market when imports are not available, and is found along the demand schedule, dd. This steeper dd schedule represents the short-run demand curve which must prevail in the event of a sudden disruption to supply, since it cannot be assumed that users can move along their fully adjusted long-run demand schedule, DD. If dd is given, p_e and q' are determined simultaneously by equation (8.8) and the shape and position of the LRMC curve. The vertical line above q' and through LRMC up to p_e then represents the SRMC of domestic production. Clearly q' exceeds q^0 which was determined by setting $\text{LRMC} = p_w$.

Similarly, consumers will contract consumption below $\bar{q}$, by also taking account of the expected price, $E(p)$. However, Tolley and Wilman suggest an additional consideration which causes consumers' marginal valuation of consumption, p^*, to lie slightly below $E(p)$. Consumers' marginal valuation measures their value of the first unit embargoed, since it is the value of the last unit consumed. By setting p^* lower than $E(p)$ they attach a lower marginal valuation to this initial unit of consumption from which the embargo starts. This small offset to the welfare loss on each additional unit that is embargoed is called the α adjustment, and leads consumers to determine their marginal valuation under uncertainty as:

$$\begin{aligned} p^* &= (1 - \pi)p_w + \pi(p_e - \alpha) \\ &= E(p) - \pi\alpha \end{aligned} \qquad (8.9)$$

222

i.e. a little lower than E(p). The net result is a long-run reduction in consumption to q* below the no-risk level of $\overline{q}$. It is therefore above q* and at p* that dd must intersect DD. Now it can be seen that α allows for the small reduction in the area left of dd that would arise from dd intersecting DD higher up at E(p) (if α = 0, p* = E(p) = LRMC). Thus when an embargo threat exists, both consumption and imports are reduced (to q* and (q* − q′), respectively), while domestic production is expanded. By assuming consumers and producers respond to the threat of embargo on imports by forming mathematical expectations of the relevant market clearing prices, it is clear that a competitive market adequately handles the possibility of variable import supply.

Now it can be confirmed from Figure 8.6 that the expansion in domestic production arises from the price signal represented by:

$$E(p) - p_w = \pi(p_e - p_w) \tag{8.10}$$

so that $\pi(p_e - p_w)$, the expected jump in embargo price over the long run, can be taken to be the security of supply premium on domestic production determined by the competitive market.

The analysis so far indicates that market participants reach an efficient solution by expanding domestic production and reducing both imports and total consumption, as compared with the no embargo threat position. Would they also build storage to see them through an embargo? The role of storage is to limit the jump in price when demand expands above supply (analogously with the role of storage in peak load pricing). If storage is built, its marginal cost sets an upper limit to the jump from the marginal valuation of oil when embargo is absent to its marginal value when embargoed:

$$MC(\text{storage}) = (p_e - p_w) \tag{8.11}$$

and private storage will be built as long as MC(storage) < $(p_e - p_w)$.

It appears, therefore, that markets can cope with supply disruption and the actions of indigenous producers and users in determining an equilibrium expected price will maximise expected welfare. On this basis, the security of supply problem does not warrant a security of supply policy.

However, a policy or government intervention may be warranted if market behaviour fails to take account of important externalities in the market outcome, and several potential externalities have been described in the literature. The most fundamental arises from consideration of the probability of embargo itself, π. The model above assumed π was exogenous to the market outcome, but it is arguable (e.g. Nordhaus, 1974) that the threat of embargo itself only arises because of the volume of imports determined by the indigenous oil market. In other words, those countries most likely to be embargoed are those who have shown themselves to be most dependent on oil imports. This makes π depend on the total volume of imports itself:

$$\pi = \varphi(q^* - q') \qquad (8.12)$$

and this dependence is an external effect that individual producers and consumers are unlikely to take into account in their market actions.

This idea should be a testable proposition, and clearly makes very sweeping assumptions about the political behaviour patterns in international relations. Little or no evidence has ever been offered to support it, but if it were true, it provides a case for government intervention to reduce import dependence in order to reduce π. Since it is the additional imports $(q^* - q')$ that give rise to the externality, the efficient result would appear to be a tax on imports of the commodity, oil, that is subject to embargo probability. Nevertheless, calculation of the tax is difficult, if not impossible, in practice without first measuring the determinants of embargo probability.

A second form of externality that has been mentioned arises from the macroeconomic consequences of sudden oil disruptions. These may include unemployment and/or inflation, and it is clear that both resulted from the combination of oil price rises and supply disruptions that characterised the winter of 1973–74. Nevertheless, Folkerts-Landau (1984) argues persuasively that such effects are labour and goods market outcomes of the change in oil price, and hence cannot be called external effects proper, they arise because markets are slow to adjust, and as such do not warrant government intervention on efficiency grounds. In fact governments often try to mitigate the unemployment or inflation consequences of supply-side effects for political or equity reasons.

A more persuasive externality might arise from the observation that most people are naturally averse to taking risks: they will always prefer an outcome that is certain to a set of outcomes with the same mathematical expectation of wealth but which in practice may yield either a higher or lower level of wealth. Such consumers will still calculate expected prices as in the model of Figure 8.6, but will additionally seek insurance contracts that provide them with a guaranteed wealth level whatever the event. They will then be willing to pay insurance premia larger than πp_e to guarantee supply in an embargo, implying larger domestic production or storage than result from (8.10) and (8.11). This is not a problem unless such insurance possibilities are not provided by the market mechanism. Nevertheless, this form of market failure is extremely likely since it is difficult to see how a competitive market in insurance against oil supply disruption could emerge. For one thing, oil suppliers could themselves covertly take out embargo insurance prior to disrupting the market (Folkerts-Landau, 1984). This is just one example of the familiar phenomenon of adverse selection and moral hazard that prevents the evolution of the insurance possibilities that risk-averse consumers would pay for. The appropriate policy in this event could arguably be a tax on oil imports, but much more obviously would be government provision of additional storage and strategic stockpiling.

Emergency and storage schemes do exist for the UK as a member of both the European Community and the International Energy Agency. These schemes involve member countries committing themselves to holding in stock a fixed number of days (e.g. 90) of normal consumption. However, the schemes allow members to count as part of their strategic stockpiles the declared stocks of private oil companies. There are fixed rules for establishing when and how stocks should be allocated, though these rules, which are based on predetermined voting strength, have never been tested in practice. The only significant embargo of recent times, following the Yom Kippur war of 1973–74 was in fact completely managed by the private allocation of their own stocks by the major oil companies.

In summary, it is apparent that the market mechanism can accommodate supply variability under uncertainty. The fact that oil, coal and other fuels may be both subject to disruption and have low price elasticities in the short run, do not, as such, necessitate a security of supply policy in the form of import taxes or public sector storage policies. Market participants under uncertainty simply establish the efficient allocation of resources that maximises expected welfare. The justification for a security of supply policy rests on whether there are significant externalities in fuel supply and demand not reflected by expected market prices and marginal costs. Two have been mentioned in the literature: (i) the possibility that the risk of embargo is itself determined by the normal level of total consumption, in which case a tax on imports may be warranted; and (ii) the possibility that risk-averse consumers are unable to find insurance contracts that provide the hedge they are prepared to pay for, in which case a public sector storage programme may be warranted. In either case the determination of the optimum policy is extremely problematical, and there have been no attempts to establish empirically whether these possible externalities are large in practice.

Sectoral guidance policy and the supply of coal

Along with providing instructions and guidelines to nationalised industries, several UK governments have produced documents on energy policy; Bates and Fraser (1974), therefore, draw the distinction between price-setting policy—the whole body of pricing and investment appraisal guidelines as set out, for example, in the White Papers Cmnd. 3437 and Cmnd. 7131—and what they call sectoral guidance policy. The latter refers to planning the overall supply and demand of the whole energy sector covering both nationalised industries and private sector producers. Recent documents include *Fuel Policy* (1967), Cmnd. 3438, and *Energy Policy—a consultative document* (1978), Cmnd. 7101.

Generally speaking these energy policy documents have only a tenuous relationship with the trends that subsequently developed, and contain a mixture of reasoned predictions, optimistic targets and simple assumptions. Government itself in the 1979–84 period largely ignored them as contrary to the more *laissez-faire* attitudes that were then evolving. Each document however does have a significant role in setting out the value judgements adopted by the sponsoring department and the Treasury in designing price policy and forecasting. Both the 1967 and 1978 documents are, therefore, primary sources for ascertaining which, if any, divergences of social cost from private cost the government of the day was prepared

226

to regard as important. In both cases, the role of the National Coal Board was pivotal in these social cost assumptions, and it is the particular focus of attention here.

Each energy policy document begins with a statement of objectives, e.g. that 'there should be adequate and secure energy supplies', that 'they should be efficiently used', and that both objectives 'should be achieved at the lowest practicable cost to the nation' (Cmnd. 7101 (1978), p. 3). Following such statements, the 1978 document is typical of its predecessors in having several main themes.

First is an attempt to forecast energy demand taking separate fuel markets into account. Such forecasts usually enshrine particular assumptions about income and prices; in the case of Cmnd. 7101 these were:

(1) 2–3 per cent annual growth of national income to the year 2000;

(2) a doubling of world oil prices (taken as the marginal cost of energy) by the year 2000;

(3) an overall reduction of 23 per cent in heat supplied by the year 2000 compared with the previous trend levels of demand (i.e. presumably those characterising the late 1960s and early 1970s before the impact of higher energy prices) (Ibid., p. 85).

Following such assumptions, individual growth or decline forecasts are made for particular industries. These may then be qualified by expressing the social costs involved if the rate of expansion or contraction were left entirely to market forces. As an example, Cmnd. 7101 notes that pit closures may have a high social cost, so that accounting principles alone provide inadequate assessments about the need to retain high financial cost capacity.

Finally, a view is generally taken on the need to expand or contract supply to meet the central demand forecast, with some comment on the policy instruments to be used. In the case of the latter, we have examined public enterprise prices, the cost of capital signal embodied in RRR, the use of external financing limits, and financial targets. However, there are usually implicit assumptions made that the government may directly intervene in decisions, e.g. as when the CEGB was instructed to increase its use of coal-fired generation following the 1967 fuel policy document, Cmnd. 3437. Cmnd. 7101 (1978), in fact, sidestepped the instrument question by stating that its demand forecasts and supply targets left a so-called 'import gap'. Such a gap cannot appear in real world markets since some form of demand rationing will evolve, but as Robinson and Marshall (1981) argue, the statement of an 'import gap' not only left the policy response unformulated, but implicitly adopted a further objective of import-minimisation.

The difficulty with energy policy documents is that their enshrined assumptions are quickly overtaken by events and market shocks, and they have to be vague about policy stances in order that policy itself can be flexible. There is every reason therefore to be very sceptical about what statements on energy policy can really achieve. The robust elements in 'policy' appear to be:

(a) the need to provide up-to-date forecasting of market trends, as frequently as possible, and

(b) the explicit statement of social costs,

while the general framework of price signalling policy will then be used to cope with supply and demand balance.

The centre of attention in the social costs of energy developments both in Europe as a whole and in the UK has been the long-term decline of the deep-mined coal industry, and this is taken as a final case study here.

Despite years of continuously optimistic forecasts, sales of the National Coal Board (NCB) have declined steadily. Even though Cmnd. 7101 (1978) was prepared to forecast demand for 178 million tonnes by 2000, production dropped steadily to about 120 million tonnes by 1982. In the process pits have closed, with miners being redeployed or offered early retirement, and government underwriting the financial costs of the schemes involved. Nevertheless, a long tail of high-cost capacity remains and the Monopolies and Mergers Commission report on the National Coal Board (Cmnd. 8920, 1983) showed that more than 50 per cent of coal output was produced at pits with the operating cost per tonne above the NCB's net selling price. The most marginal pits had a unit cost up to 300–400 per cent in excess of current prices in 1982. Even so, it appears that NCB prices in the UK have been higher than those it could obtain on coal exports, for example, to continental power stations. Although the world market in traded coal is still only developing (in 1983 it was about the size of total NCB output), Cmnd. 8920 (1983) does suggest that in 1983 NCB prices were some 30 per cent in excess of world prices.

With its high-cost pits and declining demand, the NCB has suffered huge financial losses, and in addition to the social cost grants for redundancies, the government has provided straightforward deficit grants to cover these, amounting in 1981–82 to about £0.5 billion, or 13 per cent of turnover. The clear message of the statistics is: the world price of coal lies below the UK prices, set by the NCB; the NCB makes financial losses; and some pits are cheaper to operate than others. These ideas can be put together in the usual diagram of an internationally traded commodity, as in Figure 8.7. The curve labelled MC ranks the NCB pits in ascending order of their marginal operating plus capital costs, and AC is the NCB's average cost curve. Both are rising steeply reflecting the structure of a long-established, mature extractive industry. DD is the UK demand curve, and a single grade of coal is assumed for convenience. The world price is given exogenously at p_w, which pro-

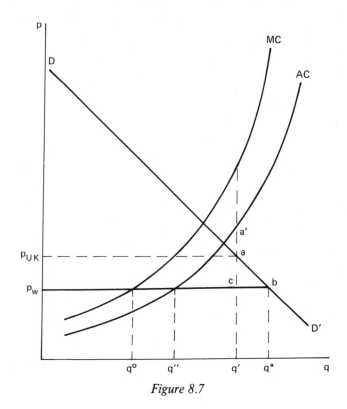

Figure 8.7

229

duces total welfare-maximising UK consumption of q^*:

$$q^* = q^0 + (q^* - q^0) \tag{8.13}$$

i.e. the sum of domestic production from pits with marginal cost less than or equal to p_w, along with imports of $(q^* - q^0)$.

MMC (1981) and Cmnd. 8920 (1983) both indicate that the NCB sets its price level above world prices, although it is often assumed that the NCB practises average cost pricing. However, this assumption is incompatible with the observed chronic financial losses, and it must be assumed that the NCB's price level is set at some other point. Assume that AC in Figure 8.7 does not include the deficit grant, and that NCB price is set at the point where some existing or target level of output could supply all of the home market (p_{UK} in Figure 8.7) at which total UK consumption is q'. Imports are effectively disallowed to enforce the NCB's price, p_{UK}, so that more UK pits are working ($q' > q^0$) than if imports were permitted at the world price. In this case, welfare losses to coal consumers are the triangle abc, while financial losses per tonne of coal produced are aa'. From the general point of view, only the ($p_{UK} - p_w$) distortion needs to be removed, by lowering p_{UK} to p_w and permitting ($q^* - q'$) of imports. The financial losses ca' per tonne are borne by the NCB (i.e. the taxpayer), and there is a transfer of resources from taxpayers to coal consumers including the CEGB and private industry.

If p_w were to prevail, the NCB could break even with capacity of q'', but while no welfare losses are observed from pricing and output, the NCB is still not making the profits attainable from its rising MC structure, and available on capacity of q^0, so there would remain some transfer of resources to consumers from taxpayers and loss of real (factor) income.

What then is an uneconomic pit? The question cannot be answered until the level of UK coal prices is set at the level of world prices, $p_{UK} = p_w$ in Figure 8.7. When this is done, all capacity for which the marginal cost exceeds the world price might be called uneconomic, i.e. all capacity beyond q^0 in Figure 8.7. Nevertheless, society might as a whole elect to maintain any greater level of capacity but still sell the output at the world price, p_w. Some of this extra capacity will make financial losses (i.e. all above q''), while some will still be in profit. It is perfectly reasonable for society to elect to maintain uneconomic capacity by transferring resources

230

from the taxpayer to the consumer and workforce. The efficiency argument relates partly to whether $p_{UK} > p_w$. For example, NCB output could be maintained at q' with no pit closures, and the apparent welfare losses will be zero as long as consumption is allowed to expand through imports to q^*. Income, however, is redistributed away from taxpayer to the NCB and is reduced because inputs earn below their opportunity cost.

One justification for maintaining q' units of capacity could be that the social costs of coalmining are not reflected in the MC curve, because a pit closure programme involving the loss of $(q' - q^0)$ tonnes of coal could leave many miners permanently unemployed. If this were true, then the opportunity cost of much mining labour is zero, since these workers would have no contribution to make to national output outside the NCB. In that event the social marginal cost curve must shift downwards. It then becomes a matter of empirical research to discover whether q' is the level of NCB capacity at which p_w = social marginal cost.

A second possible justification arises from the largely irreversible nature of the decision to close down a pit. In the event of a future rise in p_w, much more capacity might be rendered economic if it had not already been closed down. As in the security of supply argument, the efficient allocation results from the market coming to a conclusion about the future expected world price of coal. Should this coincide with p_{UK}, then once again a pit closure programme would not be justified on expected welfare-maximisation grounds. Both of these arguments—that social marginal cost is nearer p_w than the MC observed with present capacity, and that the expected world price will rise to or above p_{UK}—have been widely current in discussions of UK energy policy. The social costs argument was used in the Fuel Policy White Paper, Cmnd. 3438 (1967) to slow down the contraction of the NCB, particularly by requiring the CEGB to maintain a longer coal burn than cost-minimisation warranted. The expectation of continuing high world energy prices following the 1973–74 oil price rises led the government, NCB and unions to agree on a *Plan for Coal* (1974) (see also the subsequent *Coal for the Future*, 1977) that looked forward to an extended investment in total capacity, about half of which was to replace exhausted capacity. In the event, demand for coal has continued to decline steadily, and stocks have risen up to the 1984 coal strike against the pit closure programme.

231

Although the factors mentioned above (social costs and energy price uncertainty) can be used to justify a level of capacity that includes uneconomic pits, it is not at all clear what the magnitude of the adjustment should be.

Robinson and Marshall (1981) have rejected the use of these arguments to maintain coal capacity. By restricting imports, the NCB would, it is argued, be able to avoid the signal to set p_{UK} = p_w, and in any case the social objectives of supporting displaced miners and rundown communities might be better met by using the social security payments system. Again, this is partly an ethical and partly an empirical question. It is ethical because unemployment benefit and social security payments may not be capable of replacing the earnings from lost jobs either financially or psychologically, and it is empirical because the possibility of making the NCB charge world prices (assuming these can be determined) remains untested.

The analysis of Figure 8.7 is conducted wholly in static terms in order to determine a definition of economic or uneconomic capacity. In policy terms it poses a stark contrast between what Rees (1983) refers to as the absolute free trade and the absolute protectionist lobbies. The former advocates the immediate rundown and replacement by imports of all UK coal capacity for which the marginal cost per tonne exceeds the expected world price, while the latter proposes the continued transfer of wealth from taxpayers to the NCB to subsidise the uneconomic pits being kept open.

Consider for a moment the consequences of the proposed contraction of the free trade advocates. Apart from the drop in UK coal production, wage rates in UK coal mining will be depressed, and miners will leave the industry. Now if it is the case that coal mining is more labour-intensive than manufacturing or services production generally, real wage rates everywhere must fall (perhaps only slightly) in order to absorb the additional pool of unemployed labour on the market.

Suppose now that wage rates in coal mining are particularly sticky and also general wage rates are less than completely flexible. Then the pressure on wage rates simply appears as additional unemployment. This unemployment could be said to have two implications:

(a) GNP is below what it otherwise should be, both in the short run, and the very long run when capital has left the mining industry; and

(b)   as long as it persists the unemployment acts as a source
      of downward pressure on the slowly adjusting wage rates
      outside the NCB.

Rees (1983) and also Forster and Rees (1983) suggest that, in a
sense, (a) and (b) can be thought of as respectively a cost and
a benefit to be traded off. Strictly this analysis requires a dynamic
general equilibrium framework, for which the static partial equilibrium framework of Figure 8.7 is no substitute. However, it is
possible to follow out the argument in simple verbal terms.

Under immediate free trade adjustment, the loss of output under
(a) is potentially greatest, while the beneficial pressure on sticky
wage rates to adjust under (b) is also greatest. On the other hand,
under protectionism the loss of output under (a) is least, but the
movement towards the long-run efficient outcome resulting from
(b) is also least. Rees, therefore, is prepared to argue that there
may be a preferable intermediate rate of contraction of UK coalmining towards the long-run efficient allocation. He suggests a
policy measure that measures the difference between the maximum
level of GNP represented by the efficient outcome (including q^0
domestic production in Figure 8.7), $\hat{V}$, and the lower actual level
of production associated with a continuing inefficient level of UK
coal production, V. In both cases, coal production would be valued
at world prices, p_w. The object then is to choose a dynamic adjustment path to the efficient allocation that minimises the present
value of the differences between $\hat{V}$ and V over the adjustment period.
Attainment of this objective is constrained by the rate at which
the sticky wage rates outside the NCB are in fact depressed by
the migration of workers out of the NCB into the rest of the economy:

minimise PV $(\hat{V}_t - V_t)$
subject to:
$$\frac{dw}{dt} = \lambda \text{ (excess supply of labour)}$$

where w is the general level of wage rates, and λ is the parameter
that measures the rate at which unemployment depresses these sticky
wage rates.

The appropriate policy instrument is a subsidy to coal production
to reflect the discrepancy between Figure 8.7's $LRMC^0$ schedule
corresponding to actual wage rates, w, and the LRMC schedule

233

that would exist further down to the right in Figure 8.7, if the low or zero shadow factor cost of mining labour is used instead of w. This shadow factor cost is gradually allowed to approach wage rates outside the NCB as the dynamic adjustment approaches (slowly, relative to absolute free trade adjustment), the finally economic level of coal capacity. Forster and Rees (1983) suggest that this dynamic adjustment 'can be thought of as trading off the lost output arising from unemployment against the value of unemployment in generating the required resource allocations in a decentralised economy'. It is an improvement, in the sense of contributing lower GNP loss, over the instantaneous adjustment to the free trade allocation at q^o in Figure 8.7, when wage rates are known to be sticky in general.

Clearly, other models could be developed of this process of decline, but this description gives a general flavour of the sort of negotiated rundown that might effectively be a compromise between the free trade and the protectionist positions.

References

Atkinson, A.B. and Stiglitz, J. (1980) *Lectures in Public Economics*, Maidenhead, McGraw Hill.

Atkinson, F.J., Brooks, S. and Hall, S. (1983) 'The Economic Effects of North Sea Oil', *National Institute Economic Review*, 104 (May), pp.38–44.

Atkinson, S.E. (1979) 'Responsiveness to Time-of-Day Electricity Pricing', *Journal of Econometrics* (suppl.), 9, pp.79–95.

Bailey, E.E. and Friedlander, A. (1982), 'Market Structure and Multiproduct Industries', *Journal of Economic Literature*, 20, pp.1024–48.

Balestra, P. (1967) *The Demand for Natural Gas in the United States*, Amsterdam, North Holland.

Bank of England (1982) 'North Sea Oil and Gas: Costs and Benefits', *Bank of England Quarterly Bulletin*, 22 (March), pp.56–73.

Barker, T. (1981) Evidence to Select Committee on the Department of Energy Report, *North Sea Oil Depletion*, session 1981–82, HCP 337, London HMSO.

Bates, R. and Fraser, N. (1974) *Investment Decisions in the Nationalised Fuel Industries*, Cambridge, Cambridge University Press.

Baumol, W.J. (1982) 'Contestable Markets: An Uprising in the Theory of Industry Structure', *American Economic Review*, 72, pp. 1–15.

Baumol, W.J. and Bradford, D.F. (1970) 'Optimal Departures from Marginal Cost Pricing', *American Economic Review*, 60, pp.265–83.

Beesley, M. and Littlechild, S.C. (1983) 'Privatisation: Principles, Problems and Priorities', *Lloyds Bank Review*, July, pp.1–20.

Berrie, T.W. (1968) 'The Economics of System Planning in Bulk Electricity Supply', in R. Turvey (ed.), *Public Enterprise*, Harmondsworth, Penguin.

Boiteux, M. (1956) 'Sur la gestion des monopoles publics astreints à l'equilibre budgetaire', *Econometrica*, 24, pp.22–40, translated as 'On the Management of Public Monopolies Subject to Budgetary Constraints', *Journal of Economic Theory*, 3, pp.219–40.

Central Electricity Generating Board (CEGB) (1979–80) *Annual Report*, London, CEGB.

Central Electricity Generating Board (CEGB) (1980) Memorandum of evidence (M17) to the Select Committee on the Department of Energy Report, *The Government Statement on the New Nuclear Power Programme*, session 1980–81, HCP 114, London, HMSO.

Cmnd. 3437 (1967) *Nationalised Industries: A Review of Economic and Financial Objectives*, London, HMSO.

Cmnd. 3438 (1967) *Fuel Policy*, London, HMSO.

Cmnd. 6388 (1976) *The Structure of the Electricity Supply Industry in England and Wales* (Plowden Committee of Inquiry), London, HMSO.

Cmnd. 7101 (1978) *Energy Policy: A Consultative Document*, London, HMSO.

Cmnd. 7131 (1978) *The Nationalised Industries*, London, HMSO.

Cmnd. 8920 (1983) Monopolies and Mergers Commission Report on *The National Coal Board*, London, HMSO.

Cmnd. 9014 (1983) Monopolies and Mergers Commission Report on *The Yorkshire Electricity Board*, London, HMSO.

Corden, W.M. and Neary, P. (1982) 'Booming Sector and De-

Cmnd. 9014 (1983) Monopolies and Mergers Commission Report on *The Yorkshire Electricity Board*, London, HMSO.

Corden, W.M. and Newry, P. (1982) 'Booming Sector and De-Industrialisation in a Small Open Economy', *Economic Journal*, 92, pp.825–48.

Crew, M. and Kleindorfer, P. (1979) *Public Utility Economics*, London, Macmillan.

Deloitte, Haskins & Sells (1984) *British Gas Efficiency Study for the British Gas Corporation and the Department of Energy*, London, British Gas Corporation.

Demsetz, H. (1968) 'Why Regulate Utilities?', *Journal of Law and Economics*, 11, p.55–65.

236

Department of Energy (1978) *Energy Forecasting Methodology*, Energy Paper 19, London, HMSO.

(1979) *Energy Projections 1979*, memorandum of evidence (M16) to the Select Committee on the Department of Energy Report, *The Government Statement on the New Nuclear Power Programme*, session 1980–81, HCP 114, London, HMSO.

(1983) 'Methods for Projecting UK Energy Demands Used in the Department of Energy', by K. Wigley and K. Vernon, in P. Tempest (ed.), *Energy Economics in Britain*, London, Graham & Trotman.

(1984) *Digest of United Kingdom Energy Statics*, London, HMSO.

(1984) *Report by Coopers and Lybrand Associates on the Electricity Bulk Supply Tariff*, London, Department of Energy.

Devereux, M. and Morris, C. (1983) *North Sea Oil Taxation*, IFS Report Series no. 6, London, Institute for Fiscal Studies.

Diamond, P. and Mirrlees, J. (1971) 'Optimal Taxation and Public Production I: production efficiency, and II: tax rules', *American Economic Review*, 61, pp.8–27, 261–78.

Eastwood, R. and Venables, A. (1982) 'The Macroeconomic Implications of a Resource Discovery in an Open Economy', *Economic Journal*, 92, pp.285–99.

Electricity Council (1974) *Domestic Tariffs Experiment*, Load and Market Research Report no. 121, London, The Electricity Council.

Feldstein, M. (1972) 'Distributional Equity and the Optimal Structure of Public Prices', *American Economic Review*, 62, pp.32–6.

Fisher, A. (1981) *Resource and Environmental Economics*, Cambridge, Cambridge University Press.

Folkerts-Landau, E. (1984) 'The Social Cost of Imported Oil', *The Energy Journal*, 5, pp.41–58.

Forster, B. and Rees, R. (1983) 'The Optimal Rate of Decline of an Inefficient Industry', *Journal of Public Economics*, 22, pp.227–42.

Forsyth, P. and Kay, J. (1980) 'The Economic Implications of North Sea Oil Revenues', *Fiscal Studies*, 1, pp.1–28.

Friedman, M. (1962) *Capitalism and Freedom*, Chicago, University of Chicago Press.

de Graaf, J. V. (1957) *Theoretical Welfare Economics*, London, Cambridge University Press.

Gravelle, H. (1976) 'The Peak Load Problem with Feasible Storage', *Economic Journal*, 86, pp.256–79.

Gray, L.C. (1914) 'Rent Under the Assumption of Exhaustibility', *Quarterly Journal of Economics*, 28, pp.466–89.

Green, H.A.J. (1961) 'The Social Optimum in the Presence of Monopoly and Taxation', *Review of Economic Studies*, 29, pp.66–78.

Green, H.A.J. (1975) 'Two Models of Optimal Pricing and Taxation', *Oxford Economic Papers*, 27, pp.352–82.

Heald, D. and Steel, D. (1981) 'Nationalised Industries: the search for control', *Public Money*, 1 (June), pp.13–19.

Henderson, J.S. (1983) 'The Economics of Electricity Demand Charges', *The Energy Journal*, Special Electricity Issue, 4, pp.127–40.

Hirschleifer, J. (1958) 'Peak Loads and Efficient Pricing: Comment', *Quarterly Journal of Economics*, 72, pp.451–62.

Hotelling, H. (1925) 'A General Mathematical Theory of Depreciation', *Journal of the American Statistical Association*.

Hotelling, H. (1931) 'The Economics of Exhaustible Resources', *Journal of Political Economy*, 39, pp.137–75.

Hotelling, H. (1938) 'The General Welfare in Relation to Problems of Taxation and of Railway and Utility Rates', *Econometrica*, 6, pp.242–69.

Houthakker (1951) 'Electricity Tariffs in Theory and Practice', *Economic Journal*, 61, pp.1–25.

Joskow, P.L. and Schmalensee, R. (1983) *Markets for Power: An Analysis of Electrical Utility Deregulation*, Cambridge, Mass., MIT Press.

Lawrence, A. and Braithwait, S. (1979) 'The Residential Demand for Electricity with Time of Day Pricing', *Journal of Econometrics* (suppl.), 9, pp.59–77.

Leach, G. (1977) *A Low Energy Strategy for the United Kingdom*, London, The International Institute for Environment and Development.

Lewis, W.A. (1941) 'The Two-Part Tariff', *Economica*, 8, pp.249–70.

Lipsey, R.G. and Lancaster, K. (1956) 'The General Theory of Second-Best', *Review of Economic Studies*, 24, pp.11–32.

Littlechild, S.C. (1970) 'Marginal Cost Pricing with Joint Costs', *Economic Journal*, 80, pp.323–35.

238

Marshall, A. (1920) *Principles of Economics*, 8th edn, London, Macmillan.

Millward, R. (1971) *Public Expenditure Economics*, Maidenhead, McGraw Hill.

Millward, R. (1976) 'Price Restraint, Anti-Inflation Policy, and Public and Private Industry in the United Kingdom 1949–1973', *Economic Journal*, 86, pp.226–42.

Minford, P. (1977) 'North Sea Oil and the British Economy', *The Banker* (December).

Minford, P. (1984) 'State Expenditure: a study in waste', *Economic Affairs* (suppl.) April–June.

Mishan, E. (1981) *Introduction to Normative Economics*, Oxford, Oxford University Press.

Mitchell, B., Manning W. and Acton, J.P. (1978) *Peak Load Pricing: European Lessons for US Energy Policy*, Cambridge, Mass., Ballinger.

Mohring, H. (1970) 'The Peak Load Problem with Increasing Returns and Pricing Constraints', *American Economics Review*, 60, pp.693–705.

Monopolies and Mergers Commission (MMC) (1981) *Report on the Central Electricity Generating Board*, session 1980–81, HCP 315, London, HMSO.

Monopolies and Mergers Commission (MMC) (1983) see Cmnd. 8920 (1983).

Munasinghe, M. (1979) *The Economics of Power System Reliability and Planning*, Baltimore, Johns Hopkins Press for the World Bank.

National Coal Board (1974) *Plan for Coal*, London, National Coal Board.

National Coal Board (1977) *Coal for the Future: Progress with 'Plan for Coal' and Prospects to the Year 2000*, London, Department of Energy.

National Economic Development Office (NEDO) (1976) *A Study of UK Nationalised Industries*, London, HMSO.

Neary, P. and van Wignbergen, S. (1984) 'Can an Oil Discovery Lead to a Recession?: Comment on Eastwood and Venables', *Economic Journal*, 94, pp.390–95.

Nordhaus, W. (1974) 'The 1974 Report of the President's Council of Economic Advisers: Energy in the Economic Report', *American Economic Review*, 64, pp. 558–65.

Nordhaus, W. (1977) 'The Demand for Energy: an international perspective', in W. Nordhaus (ed.), *International Studies of the Demand for Energy*, Amsterdam, North Holland.

Nordhaus, W. (1979) *The Efficient Use of Energy Resources*, New Haven, Yale University Press.

Pearce, D.W.P. (1979) 'Social Cost-Benefit Analysis and Nuclear Futures', *Energy Economics*, 1 (April).

Pearce, D.W.P. (1980) 'Energy Conservation and the Official Energy Forecasts for the United Kingdom', *Energy Policy*, pp.245–48.

Peterson, W. (1979) 'Fuel Use in the UK: A study of substitution responses', in A. Strub (ed.), *Energy Models for the European Community*, IPC Science and Technology Press Ltd for the Commission of the European Communities.

Pindyck, R. (1979) *The Structure of World Energy Demand*, Cambridge, Mass., MIT Press.

Plowden Committee (1976) *see* Cmnd 6388 (1976).

Posner, M. (1973) *Fuel Policy*, London, Macmillan.

Price, C.M. (1980) 'Gas Price Increases', Public Sector Economics Research Centre papers no. 80/81, University of Leicester.

Price Commission (1979) *Report on British Gas Corporation—Gas Prices and Allied Charges*, session 1978–79, HCP 165, London HMSO.

Ramsey, F.P. (1927) 'A Contribution to the Theory of Taxation', *Economic Journal*, 37, pp.47–61.

Rawls, J. (1971) *A Theory of Justice*, Cambridge, Mass., Harvard University Press.

Rees, R. (1968) 'Second-Best Rules for Public Enterprise Pricing', *Economica*, 35, pp.260–73.

Rees, R. (1983) 'Energy Pricing: 8 proposals for a better fuel market', *Public Money*, 2 (March), pp.13–17.

Rees, R. (1984) 'Energy Prices and Economic Pricing', *Public Money*, 4 (September), p.12.

Robbins, L. (1935) *An Essay on the Nature and Significance of Economic Theory*, London, Macmillan.

Robbins, L. (1980) 'Economics and Political Economy', *American Economic Review*, 71, pp.1–10.

Robinson, C. and Marshall, E. (1981) *What Future for British Coal?*, Hobart Paper 89, London, Institute of Economic Affairs.

Ruffell, R. (1977) *The Household Demand for Electricity*,

Edinburgh, Scottish Academic Press.

Samuelson, P.A. (1956) 'Social Indifference Curves', *Quarterly Journal of Economics*, 70, pp.1–22.

Select Committee on the Department of Energy (SCE) (1980) *The Government Statement on the New Nuclear Power Programme*, session 1980–81, HCP 114, London, HMSO.

(1981) *North Sea Oil Depletion*, session 1981–82, HCP 337, London, HMSO.

(1984) *Electricity and Gas Prices*, session 1983–84, HCP 276, London, HMSO.

Slater, M. and Yarrow, G. (1983) 'Distortions in Electricity Pricing in the UK', *Oxford Bulletin of Economics and Statistics*, 45, pp.317–38.

Solow, R. (1974) 'The Economics of Resources, and the Resources of Economics', *American Economic Review*, 64, pp.1–14.

Spann, R. and Beauvais, E. (1979) 'Econometric Estimation of Peak Electricity Demands', *Journal of Econometrics* (suppl.), 9, pp.119–36.

Spencer, P.D. (1984) 'The Effect of Oil Discoveries on the British Economy—Theoretical Ambiguities and the Consistent Expectations Simulation Approach', *Economic Journal*, 94, pp.633–44.

Steiner, P. (1956) 'Peak Loads and Efficient Pricing', *Quarterly Journal of Economics*, 71pp.

Taylor, L.D. (1975) 'The Demand for Electricity: a survey', *Bell Journal of Economics*, 6, pp.74–110.

Taylor, L.D. (1977) 'The Demand for Energy: A survey of price and income elasticities', in W. Nordhaus (ed.), *International Studies of the Demand for Energy*, Amsterdam, North Holland.

Taylor, L.D. (1979) 'On Modelling the Residential Demand for Electricity by Time of Day', *Journal of Econometrics*, (suppl.), 9, pp.97–115.

Tolley, G. and Wilman, J. (1977) 'The Foreign Dependence Question', *Journal of Political Economy*, 85, pp.323–47.

Treasury (UK) (1979) 'The Test Discount Rate and the Required Rate of Return', Government Economic Service Working Paper 22, London, UK Treasury.

Turvey, R. (1964) 'Marginal Cost Pricing in Practice', *Economica*, pp.429–34.

Turvey, R. (1968) *Optimal Pricing and Investment in Electricity*

Supply, London, Allen & Unwin.

Turvey, R. (1969) 'Marginal Cost', *Economic Journal*, 79, pp.282–99.

Turvey, R. and Anderson, D. (1977) *Electricity Economics*, Baltimore, Johns Hopkins Press for the World Bank.

Webb, M.G. (1977) 'The Determination of Reserve Generating Capacity Criteria in Electricity Supply Systems', *Applied Economics*, 9, pp.19–31.

Webb, M.G. (1980) 'A Critical Appriasal of United Kingdom Policy for the Nationalised Industries', in B.M. Mitchell and P.R. Kleindorfer (eds), *Regulated Industries and Public Enterprises*, Lexington, Mass., Lexington Books.

Wenders, J.T. (1976) 'Peak Load Pricing in the Electric Utility Industry', *Bell Journal of Economics*, 7, pp.232–41.

Wenders, J.T. and Taylor, L.D. (1976) 'Experiments in Seasonal Time of Day Pricing of Electricity to Residential Users', *Bell Journal of Economics*, 7, pp.531–51.

Williamson, O.E. (1966), 'Peak Load Pricing and Optimal Capacity under Indivisibility Constraints', *American Economic Review*, 56, pp.810–27.

Williamson, O.E. (1976) 'Franchise Bidding for Natural Monopolies—in general and with respect to CATV', *Bell Journal of Economics*, 7, pp.73–104.

Wright, F.K. (1968) 'Measuring Asset Services: a linear programming approach', *Journal of Accounting Research*, 6, pp.222–36.

Name Index

Subject Index